THE
MOTHER
CODE

THE
MOTHER
CODE

My Story of Love, Loss, and
the Myths That Shape Us

RUTHIE ACKERMAN

RANDOM HOUSE
NEW YORK

Random House
An imprint and division of Penguin Random House LLC
1745 Broadway, New York, NY 10019
randomhousebooks.com
penguinrandomhouse.com

Copyright © 2025 by Ruthie Ackerman

Illustrated poem on pp 7: "There Was a Young Woman Who Swallowed a Lie"
by Meredith Tax, Atlanta Lesbian Feminist Alliance (ALFA) Archives,
circa 1972-1994, Women's Liberation Movement Print Culture,
David M. Rubenstein Rare Book & Manuscript Library, Duke University
(https://repository.duke.edu/dc/wlmpc/wlmms01010).

Library of Congress Cataloging-in-Publication Data
Names: Ackerman, Ruthie, author.
Title: The mother code / Ruthie Ackerman.
Description: First edition. | New York, NY : Random House, [2025] |
Includes bibliographical references.
Identifiers: LCCN 2024047813 (print) | LCCN 2024047814 (ebook) |
ISBN 9780593730119 (hardcover) | ISBN 9780593730133 (ebook)
Subjects: LCSH: Ackerman, Ruthie. | Motherhood. | Childlessness. |
Human reproductive technology.
Classification: LCC HQ759 .A194 2025 (print) | LCC HQ759 (ebook) |
DDC 306.874/3—dc23/eng/20241121
LC record available at https://lccn.loc.gov/2024047813
LC ebook record available at https://lccn.loc.gov/202

Printed in the United States of America on acid-free paper

2 4 6 8 9 7 5 3 1

First Edition

BOOK TEAM: Production editor: Cassie Gitkin • Managing editor:
Rebecca Berlant • Production manager: Jenn Backe • Copy editors:
Faren Bachelis, Megha Jain • Proofreaders: Russell Powers, Taylor
Teague, Rachel Twersky, Emily Zebrowski

Book design by Jo Anne Metsch

This book is for anyone who needs to hear it: there is more than one way to have a good life. Going after the same things on the same timeline as everyone else might be the capitalist dream, but that's how we get robots, not humans.

And for Rob and Clementine, my inner circle, my loves.
I finally found home and it's with you.

There was a young woman who swallowed a rule

"Live to serve others," she learned it in school

She swallowed the rule to hold up the lie

We all know why she swallowed that lie

Perhaps she'll die

—MEREDITH TAX

This is a work of nonfiction and all the stories within are reconstructed from my memory. Much of this book centers around the very real and very private lives of my family and others. I tried my best to write with the utmost care, respect, and compassion, but the nature of memoir is that people are translated for the page and as such remain static. Because of that, some names and identifying details have been changed.

These pages are my attempt to engage with the concept and conversation around motherhood as it continues to evolve, with the ultimate goal of breaking free from the patriarchy's framing of what mothering means and expanding our imagination about how we talk, and think, about motherhood.

My hope is that after you read the book you feel more connected to your own story, no matter who you are and where you are.

THE
MOTHER
CODE

1

My Ancestors, Myself

I come from a long line of women who abandoned their children. Or at least that's what I'd been told.

For as long as I can remember, I've heard about how my great-grandmother Kitty and my grandmother Ruth ditched their kids because of men or money or mental problems—or all of the above. As the story goes, Kitty left her son and daughter with her in-laws so she could gallivant around Europe, "man hunting," as my mom calls it on a good day. On a bad day, my mom will let it all hang out. "Kitty was a gold digger," she told me recently when I called to let her know that I'd been researching the women in our family.

We were on video so I could see my mom's face. The way her lips curled in disgust when I mentioned Kitty's name. "What you don't understand is that all Kitty cared about was money," she said. She'd marry one rich man only to leave him when she met another man who was even richer.

As I listened to my mom, what I heard was the conviction in her voice. She was certain that her take on Kitty was "true." There couldn't be any other explanation for my great-grandmother's behavior. Kitty was cruel to her children and her grandchildren and money was the culprit. End of story.

"She was married twenty-five times," my mom said. "I know it sounds crazy"—here's where she rotated her finger several times next to her ear, the universal symbol for cuckoo—"but she was."

I shook my head. Twenty-five times sounded ludicrous. Impossible. Yet, despite all the hyperbole and hysteria about Kitty, the stories about the men she loved and left as quickly as a mouse can snatch a piece of cheese from a trap, I later learned that there was some truth to the family legends. Over the years, I interviewed an aunt, an uncle, and a cousin. I even spent a weekend in Baltimore with Kitty's son before he died. "Kitty didn't want to be a mother," he told me unequivocally, which is something I'd never heard anyone admit out loud about a woman. Especially one who became a wife for the first time in 1917, when women were meant to worship their husbands and children.

Much later, I searched through census records, old newspapers, marriage and divorce decrees, and immigration files. I learned Kitty went by at least five first names: Kitty, Kune, Katie, Kate, and Katherine.

Eventually, I could decipher facts from fables. I dug up documentation for fourteen of Kitty's marriages. Her shortest was only ten days. She married my great-grandfather Irving twice, the first time at just seventeen.

My grandmother Ruth followed in her mother's footsteps, abandoning her first child, Beth, to marry my grandfather.

The truth is this: I'd always secretly rooted for Kitty and Ruth, though I never told anyone in my family. I assumed that everyone denigrated them because they roamed around for their own pleasure, as if there was anything wrong with that. But I understood that of course there was. A woman living her life for herself has never been allowed.

Women at that time didn't choose whether or not to be mothers. What would choice have even meant for my great-grandmother and grandmother when the system—their family, their community, their religion, the culture they were steeped in—only showed them images of women as mothers? Mothering was natural. It was normal. There was no question of desire. Or a path for opting out. They could only choose to mother as much as a fish chooses to live in water. It's what they had to do. It's what women did.

We now have a language, a lexicon, for maternal ambivalence, but back then, back in the early to mid 1900s, women were mothers, and that was that. Yet Kitty and Ruth always scoffed at the rules, which is what I admired about them.

The problem with public records is that the emotional tenor of the past is erased. I have no idea if Kitty loved any of her husbands (or if Ruth loved hers). I have no idea why Kitty left them, or if, perhaps, they left her. I have no idea if she was looking for money from them or some other type of security. I have my guesses, though. Citizenship was a priority for a Jewish girl who spoke only Yiddish and never went to school after arriving at Ellis Island in 1906 at the age of just six.

It may be true, as my family tells me, that Kitty married a Chicago gangster then divorced him because Chicago was too cold. Or that she married the owner of a jewelry store empire in South Florida and left him when his business went kaput.

And then finally in her nineties, living out the last of her days in a nursing home, she married the man, several decades her junior, whom she called "what's his name."

Everything I know about Kitty and Ruth has been passed down to me through a web of grief and sorrow. It's like the Indian parable of the blind men and the elephant. In the parable, none of the blind men had encountered an elephant before, and they could only imagine what one looked like by touching it. But each man felt a different part of the elephant's body. One man felt the side and determined that an elephant is smooth and solid like a wall. The next man felt the trunk and thought the elephant was like a giant snake. The third man felt the pointy tusk and decided the elephant was deadly like a spear. The fourth man felt the tail and figured the elephant was like an old rope. The lesson of the story is that each man could only see the world through his own personal experience, and yet we all use our partial point of view as the whole truth.

2

A Leap of Faith

It was a cold winter day when I ran into my ex-husband, Evan, at my local indie bookstore, where a friend of mine was giving a reading for her new book. I was already late, so I barely looked up as I pushed open the glass door and quietly maneuvered my way through the obstacle course of people huddled together with plastic cups of cheap wine. All I could think about was whether I could locate my friend in this roomful of strangers, give her a quick hug of congratulations, and dash to find a seat before the event started.

It wasn't until I was halfway into the room that I even saw Evan. By the time I noticed him, there was no way to run for dear life, and there certainly wasn't time to pray for the floor to open below me and swallow me whole. I felt like I was under the ocean and everything was slow and garbled. I didn't know if I should go with the current, moving with the crowd in front of me. Or stand frozen exactly where I was. I was in fight-

or-flight mode, but I was only fighting or fleeing from myself. Evan was facing the other way. He didn't know about the tug-of-war happening inside my body.

Evan and I hadn't laid eyes on each other in over four years, and my first thought was: *Why are you in Brooklyn?* Okay, it was a little more complicated than that. I'd tracked him across social media and knew that he and his girlfriend, the one he started dating mere months after our separation, had moved not only to Brooklyn, but to the neighborhood that was a fifteen-minute walk from where I now lived. This was after years of him swearing that he'd never, ever live in Brooklyn whenever I pushed for us to move there. After our divorce, I'd gone to a breathwork practitioner/acupuncturist who told me to write down all of the reasons I was angry at him on pieces of paper and burn them in a pyre. I only had a candle, so I figured that was good enough, but instead of feeling relief or closure after sending my fantasies of our long life together up in smoke, the next day I ran into Evan's girlfriend walking down the street in our neighborhood. When I told a friend this story, she said, "How did you know it was her?"

How was that even a question?

"Um, because I stalked them both incessantly on Instagram," was my answer. That's also how I found out they were living in the same zip code as me.

All my friend could say was that I'd *conjured* Evan's girlfriend. That my witchy, fiery attempt at a goodbye to my marriage created some sort of rupture in the space-time continuum and brought us together on that street corner.

So that night in the bookstore, I knew why Evan was in Brooklyn: he lived here now. My next feeling was anger. *How dare you step foot into our neighborhood bookstore when you know writing and books are my thing.* Of course, he'd read books when we were together, too, but not intellectual books, newsworthy books, books written by *my* friends. He read sci-fi, fantasy, things I'd always looked down on for being something other than literature. I can still see his ragged copy of Ray Kurzweil's *The Singularity Is Near* on our bookshelf. And now he was standing in this bookstore holding Pablo Neruda's *Love Poems,* a book we once owned together and displayed prominently in our apartment.

At that moment, I was forty-two years old and twelve weeks pregnant. All the same, as soon as I saw Evan, all I could think about were the seven years we spent together, almost three of them married, arguing over whether we'd break up once and for all because he didn't want under any circumstances to have children. When we first met I agreed on the baby thing. My family hadn't exactly made motherhood look like a good option. And looking around me—at TV shows and movies and, well, everywhere—having kids seemed like a scam. Let's be honest: moms look like they're having no fun at all. I didn't want to be selfless, sacrificing, saccharine. Not to mention when I met Evan I was thirty-one and had finally created the life I wanted for myself. An entry-level reporter job at *Forbes.* A steady paycheck. A studio apartment on a tree-lined street in Park Slope with a much-dreamed-about brick wall. I'd made it. Now I'd give it all up? For what?

But as time marched forward I wobbled in my certainty. What started as a small flicker grew and grew until I was thirty-five and I'd softened to the idea of having a baby. Even though it was clear we wanted different things, Evan and I got married, anyway, and I fantasized that maybe he would change his mind, too. Together, we'd dive into our fears and decide to start a family together. In the end, love would conquer all.

·   ·   ·

THAT'S NOT WHAT happened.

Instead, Evan and I had gotten divorced. And he was now in the same bookstore as me, having moved with someone else to Brooklyn. Did that mean he was now willing to give the whole baby thing a shot, too? My mind latched on to this possibility with ferocious speed, certain that in the future, I'd be forced to run into Evan on the street carrying a BabyBjörn and a diaper bag, wearing a T-shirt that read *I've Evolved.*

My next thought was that if he changed his mind and decided to have a baby with his new partner, did that mean there *was* something wrong with me? Did that mean that he didn't think I'd make a good mother and that's why he didn't want a baby? That his decision not to have kids was about *me* specifically?

Even though I'd made up this whole fantasy, it was so clear to me. I saw myself ducking by him on the sidewalk, the woman he *didn't* want to have a baby with. And then I pictured our friends—the ones we'd had at our house for dinner—gossiping about it, feeling sorry for me, and all the "fertile years" I'd wasted thinking Evan might come around.

I stood there huffing and puffing, fuming and raging, all the while staring at the back of Evan's head wondering why he'd let his hair get scraggly and his clothes get frumpy. And then suddenly he turned around and looked right at me, and I saw a faint trace of recognition on his face. For a second, I wondered if we'd both spontaneously combust. But instead he turned back around as if I wasn't even there. I looked to see if there was another way to grab a seat at the front of the room like I'd hoped, but there wasn't. I'd have to push past Evan, which I wasn't willing to do because I feared that would entail speaking to him. I had no choice but to stare at his shoulders, cold and bony in their silence.

Defeated, I ensconced myself in a corner, peering through an opening in the wall, half listening to my friend speaking radiantly about her new work all the while wondering if Evan could tell that I was pregnant. You see, the truth was that while one part of me was mad at him, the other part wanted closure. I needed validation that getting divorced was the right decision. I deeply needed him to be happy for me. To tell me that he always believed I'd make a good mother and that we were right to end our marriage so I could pursue that option. I desperately clung to the story that this man whom I'd once vowed to spend the rest of my life with would hug me and say: *I'm so proud of you. I always knew you'd become a mom. You're doing it. Can't you see? You've. Got. This.*

Let's leave aside the fact that at that point no one could tell from the outside that I was pregnant, not even me. For weeks I'd been taking photos of my "bump" and sending them to my family to show them how my body was growing and changing. But there was no protrusion to speak of. Mostly I just looked like I had gained a bit of weight.

No matter. The voice in my head still told me that in the 1.3 seconds he'd looked in my direction Evan had somehow magically perceived that there was a baby growing inside me, and was in his quiet way thrilled for me.

But for now at least, he was doing a marvelous job of pretending I wasn't even standing there. When I think about it, he was just doing what he'd always done—he was not seeing me. He was choosing to turn the other way when parts of me didn't line up with his vision for his life. I told myself he *wanted* to speak to me; he just didn't know how. I told myself I was the stronger one and that I should make the first move to acknowledge him. And as I watched him, wondering what to do, my body flooded with grief. My limbs felt heavy, my breathing ragged. We'd blown up our marriage so I could have a baby, and here I was with one inside me, and still I yearned for Evan, or anyone really, to tell me I was on the right path.

When I look back at this scene, with me in that bookstore, it hits me: I didn't believe I was actually carrying a baby. A baby seemed far fetched. A baby would require a leap of faith I couldn't muster. A baby would mean I was going to be a mother. And a mother was something I could never imagine for myself.

All of this was running through my mind as I stood in that bookstore staring at Evan, numb, in shock, uncertain of what to do. Until I felt a wet stickiness between my legs. *My baby,* I thought. *My baby.* And I ran to the bathroom and saw blood.

3

The Default

The light in the bookstore bathroom was dim. Even so, I could see the blood on the toilet paper. I wiped some more to make sure I wasn't just seeing things, and then stood, grabbing on to the porcelain sink so I wouldn't fall. Suddenly, I understood. I wanted to be this baby's mother more than anything I'd ever wanted in the world. I would do anything in my power to keep it alive. The trouble: there wasn't much I could do.

A few more minutes passed, and then I slowly made my way out of the store and onto the street, no longer worried whether Evan was still there. Once I was on the sidewalk, I closed my eyes. Nightmare scenarios pushed out all rational thought. I had recently read a book on how to control your mind when it's like a runaway train. The first step is to name five things you can see in front of you.

There was a parked car, a tree, the subway station, the bookstore, and a garbage can.

Now breathe.

The second step, the book outlined, was to realize that in the present moment, nothing you've anticipated has come true.

I looked around. The ground was still firm beneath my feet. I could feel my breath coming into my nose. I wasn't in pain. I could inhale and exhale.

I'm going to be a mother, I told myself. *I'm going to be a mother.*

That's when I texted Rob and told him about the blood. "Come home," he wrote back quickly.

ONCE I WAS safely in our apartment, I immediately dove into the bathroom and wiped again between my legs. More blood. I came out, my underwear still down around my thighs, and called to Rob.

"Blood. Blood," I said, pointing, hoping he would verify whether there was in fact blood in my underwear.

He tried to calm me. "Everything is okay," he said, stepping forward and holding my cheeks gently between his palms.

"Look." I pointed again. He nodded.

"I see it," he said, trying to reassure me. "Why don't you call the doctor?"

So I did. I no longer could think for myself. I was a robot. Following directions. It was nine at night and the doctors weren't in the office. I called the answering service and told the woman on the other end what was wrong. I heard her typing and I thought: *Can't you just get the doctor?*

The woman's voice sounded unfazed. Like she was just trying to get through her shift.

"The doctor will call you back," she finally said.

"Call me back?" It came out like a shriek. Rob's hand was

on my back. "When? How long? Don't you understand? I don't want my baby to die."

THE NEXT THING I remember, the doctor was on the phone, calmly asking me questions. *How much blood is there? What color is it? Does the blood fill one pad per hour?*

"I don't know, I don't know," I said. Then, inanely, "I'm sure it's nothing." I'm still not sure why I said this. My mind was chattering so hard words were just coming out of my mouth.

"It's fine, this is my job." His voice was kind. "Blood is normal. Twenty percent of women experience spotting in the first trimester. Put on a pad, and if you fill it up within an hour then call me back. Do not hesitate. In the meantime, try and get some rest," he said.

After I hung up, I cried into Rob's shoulder. I was sure our baby would die and it would be all my fault. The machine of my body would fail. The batteries would corrode. The on/off switch would get stuck. The engine would rupture. My irrational thoughts kept churning. As a woman, biologically speaking, I was a vessel with one job: to reproduce, and I couldn't even get that right.

It's not like I didn't know how I'd gotten here. A year and a half after Evan's and my marriage dissolved, I met Rob. Both of us were still fragile from our divorces. So fragile in fact that when we first got together we called our exes "ghosts" because of the way they haunted our relationship. The other thing that haunted our relationship? My sudden certainty that I wanted a baby. Now.

Rob was on board, but his timeline was different from

mine. As in, he didn't have one. Eventually, though, we figured it out, and I stupidly assumed that once we got on the
same page about when to have a kid it would all be smooth
sailing. Now I was pregnant and having a full-blown panic attack.

I couldn't catch my breath. I couldn't slow down my brain
enough to observe anything in front of me like I knew my
therapist—and all the self-help books I read—would urge me
to do. I couldn't do anything but make guttural sounds and
gush snot all over our pillows. It wasn't just that I was certain
we'd lose this baby. I was certain our child's death would be
my punishment: for aborting the baby I got pregnant with
when I was seventeen, for marrying someone who didn't want
kids to prove to myself and the world that I was lovable, for
traveling and pursuing my career and having adventures and
believing I could be anything I wanted to be on my own timeline.

NOT LONG AFTER my wedding to Evan, I sat across from
my therapist and said the truest thing I knew at that moment,
"This whole baby question is driving me nuts."

"Well," she said. "On a scale of one to a hundred, how badly
do you want a baby?"

I thought about it for a few seconds—letting my breath fill
my body and then relaxing as the air pushed its way out of my
nose.

"The honest answer is fifty-five percent."

Apparently I wanted a baby a teensy-weensy bit more than
I didn't want a baby. No amount of analyzing or contempla-
tion, books or talks with friends, moved the needle signifi-

cantly on that 55 percent. I'd made pros and cons lists and my conclusion was that there were lots of good reasons to have a baby and lots of good reasons not to. The best I could muster was that I wanted a baby slightly more than I didn't.

"There you go," she said, smiling, as if that's all I needed to know.

I had no idea back then that maternal ambivalence is the norm. In fact, Dr. Veerle Bergink, the director of Women's Mental Health Center and professor at the Department of Psychiatry at Mount Sinai hospital, says maternal ambivalence is "the default." I *was* normal, and yet I believed everyone else was.

Whenever I disclosed to friends or acquaintances that I wasn't sure how I felt about having kids, I was told some version of: Look inside yourself. Forget about what society tells you or what other people want for you. What do *you* really want? Which was profoundly unhelpful on so many levels. My whole life I'd been told by my family and the world around me to self-silence. There was no memo that outlined this expectation, but it was clear from the ways I was rewarded by society that self-abnegation was the key to survival. Now I was supposed to try and figure out my purest desires untrampled by what the world wanted from me? "As if there is some core truth resting deep inside of us and if we only had a few hours of quiet time, we'd find it," writes the author Jill Filipovic.

So I waited for a sign, an aha, or as Filipovic writes so beautifully, a "magical moment when I will *know:* when my heart will wobble with tentative yearning at the sight of a big-headed infant, or when my brain will firmly settle into a clear *no, ma'am* as I help a harried mother drag her stroller up the subway steps."

And when that magical moment never came, I was left feeling like a failure. That I'd failed at the most essential, *natural,* of human decisions.

I'm white, well educated, privileged in every way, and I understood that I was making this all-important decision about whether to become a mother from my perch as a financially independent woman with a full and fulfilling life. Still, that *choice* meant that I understood what I was giving up when I picked one life over another. And I hesitated extra-long before choosing motherhood because, let's be real, I was told that a mother's life happens in a distant galaxy from a life without kids—one where I would be overwhelmed, exhausted, depressed, and likely resentful of my partner if I was lucky enough to find one. I was warned that I would no longer recognize my carefree, pre-baby self. I was told that those two sides of myself, warring in my heart—the one who wants children and the one who doesn't— had to duke it out till death. And one must win out forevermore.

Did I really *want* a child, or did I just not know what to do with myself if I didn't have one?

It's Lydia Davis's one-sentence story "A Double Negative" that put into words what I'd been feeling for so long. *At a certain point in her life, she realizes it is not so much that she wants to have a child as that she does not want to not have a child, or not to have had a child.* That was exactly it. I had FOMO for the life I thought I was supposed to be living. And yet I didn't know how to pursue the life I wanted either. Or at what cost that desire would come.

If I loved my life, the message I'd absorbed about motherhood was: *get ready to lose it.* But what if I didn't want to?

If I was in my thirties today and ambivalent about motherhood, I would be obsessed with the viral TikTok meme "I think I love this little life," a parody of the British singer-songwriter Cordelia's song, posted over videos of women's enviable childfree lives. These #richaunties, as some of them call themselves, are often affluent Black women, and the comments section of their videos are a master class in IDGAF—I don't give a fuck—about society's rigid rules. From "It will be your biggest regret" followed by the face with tears of joy emoji to "We all die alone no matter if we have kids or don't," these videos show women taking the reins of their own lives.

At the time I was deciding whether to become a mother, though, there weren't Reddit threads and viral TikTok videos addressing those of us who were on the fence. "Some people might say you should *really* want a baby if you're going to have one," I told my therapist that day.

"Who are those people?" she replied.

I shrugged. I didn't know anymore. Parenting just seemed like something I should be all-in about if I was to have a kid. Maybe I should adopt a dog or get better at keeping my plants alive first. Maybe I should offer to babysit for my friends' kid for a weekend. The truth is: What should the parent-curious do? How can we try out parenthood to see if we like it? In the end, babysitting isn't the same—you always know you'll be giving the child back at the end of the day. With parenting there are no returns, no guarantees that you'll be good at it. So I waited, hoping my body or my doctor would tell me what to do. I fretted over the "ghost ship," as Cheryl Strayed calls it, wondering about the path not taken.

Before I left my therapist's office that day, I tried saying the words out loud. *I want a baby. I want a baby. I want a baby.* A part of me figured that once I named it, it would be true. All of the female empowerment rhetoric I'd been digesting for decades made it seem that easy: "name it to claim it."

The deep ambivalence I felt was colored by the fact that I wanted to be a writer and I feared that having a child would make that impossible. When I think back to that time, the words of the author Louise Erdrich wash over me. "Every female writer starts out with a list of other female writers in her head. Mine includes, quite pointedly, a mother list . . . Jane Austen—no children, no marriage. Mary Wollstonecraft—died in childbirth."

Erdrich's list goes on for more than half a page.

Children.

No children.

No marriage.

Marriage.

As I stare at her words, my confusion and pain returns. Back then, I wanted so badly for someone else to tell me how to live. For someone else to define what a "good life" meant to me. But I didn't know what to make of the puzzle pieces of other women's lives. What could I tell about my own life from examining theirs? What answers did their hopes and dreams hold? What paths had they carved out for me? Or as Erdrich writes, what "toughness of spirit" do these women have to help me deal with mine?

It didn't help that I'd spent my whole life hearing everyone else's tales about my great-grandmother Kitty and my grandmother Ruth. And through those shards of misinformation and conjecture, I started to piece together a narrative of who in turn I thought I would be. I told myself I should be ashamed of the women in my family. I believed their minds were messed up in one way or another. So, I ran far away, seeking out foreign places and stories, to avoid the contagion I was certain I'd catch if I got too close. I blamed their trajectories on trauma, bad luck, poor decision making, and their dependence on men for money and power. And later, when I'd gone to college and had just enough knowledge under my belt to be dangerous, I gave them diagnoses even though they were dead.

I convinced myself that what I inherited from the women in my family was a glitch in my genetic code. A mutation that would destine me to abandon my children, too. The only way to avoid what I came to think of as the curse was to not have offspring at all.

That was my plan throughout my twenties and early thirties. And then in my mid-thirties, as I felt the pull to decide once and for all whether to have a child or not, I began to wonder about the stories I'd been fed my whole life. What if the women in my family hadn't abandoned their children? What if they weren't bad moms, but good *enough* moms or at the very least decent moms? If that was possible, then maybe I could be a good enough mom, too. Maybe I wouldn't abandon my kids.

I no longer wanted to wander through the world feeling broken. I didn't want my future to have been written before I was even born. I wanted to understand whether DNA was really a *blueprint* for my life, or if I could decide my own future. I wanted to know whether motherhood was off-limits to me— or whether I could carve out a different path.

Maybe I *could* have the agency and ability to do things differently than my own mother and her mother and her mother before her. Maybe I could create the life I wanted for myself and my child.

What I wanted was a story I could live with—free of regret, free of expectation, and free of everyone else's ideas of who and what I should be. Around that time I opened my eyes with a vision—a waking dream, really—of walking down the street holding a little girl's hand. When I sat up in bed I knew her name: Olive Ackerman.

Even after years of convincing Evan, and myself, that I shouldn't have a baby, I was suddenly overcome with an all-consuming certainty that I deeply wanted one. I tried to push away the thought, but images of Olive intruded on my day. I'd see her as I drank my morning coffee. I'd hear her as I commuted to work. When it became impossible to ignore, I floated variations of how this child might fit into the childless life Evan and I had agreed to. "What if I had a baby alone?" I asked Evan as we were washing up for bed. "We could stay married and live next door to each other, and we could still have dinner together every night."

It made perfect sense—to me. I mentioned this idea to my friend Sara to test the waters and was surprised to learn about a friend of hers who made it work. Sara's friend now lived a mile away from her partner who didn't want kids. Once the baby was born, though, he agreed to co-parent. Now they lived happily, apart. There was even a name for this phenomenon—LAT, or living apart together—and an article about it in *Elle*.

Evan wasn't interested. So I asked if he might consider adoption. But that was a hard no, too.

I even went so far as to fantasize about scenarios where I could raise a baby in community with other mothers, a "mommune" of sorts, before I'd ever read about the concept in *The New York Times*.

I had plenty of reasons to opt out of motherhood, and yet there was something inside of me that kept pulling me toward wanting a child.

NOW FIVE YEARS later, I lay in Rob's arms as he whispered, "Remember what the doctor said?" I shook my head. "You just need to rest." But his words didn't sink in. My body heaved. Snot covered my face. I wondered if we could buy an ultrasound machine for our living room so I could see that our baby was swimming around peacefully in my amniotic fluid. *Or maybe I could go to sleep and wake up when the baby is born in six months.* All my thoughts felt crazy. Rob's answer was to curl his body around me from behind and whisper that everything was going to be okay.

That's how we fell asleep, warm and scared and pressed against each other.

4

Figs

When Rob and I woke up the next morning, I ran to the bathroom to look for blood. But there wasn't any. When I told him, he smiled. I wasn't ready to let go of my hypervigilance, though. I needed some kind of proof that everything was okay. Yet certainty was the one thing no one could promise me.

At the clinic later that morning, I lay in a darkened room, listening to the crinkle of my paper gown as I waited to hear our baby's heartbeat. The ultrasound technician with the vaguely Russian-sounding name cleared her throat as she moved the wand over my belly. When she was done the doctor examined me.

"I see dried brown blood," he said. "It looks like you have a subchorionic hematoma. We'll keep watching it." He paused when he saw my face. "It's just a small pocket of blood, and sometimes it moves and a little blood spills out. It's nothing to worry about. Your baby seems fine."

The truth was that I was happy he found *something*. I'd convinced myself that maybe there wasn't any blood at all. I'd worried everyone for nothing. I was being a drama queen. Making a bigger deal out of this than necessary.

"You just have to believe that your body is doing its job," the doctor said, and I knew he meant this advice to be reassuring. But Rob and I had undergone years of failed fertility treatments, and his words sounded ridiculous. *Believe my body would do its job?* If my body did what it was supposed to do, I wouldn't have needed to shoot myself up with boatloads of hormones and surgically remove my eggs in the hopes that my doctor could create a baby in his lab, which he'd then insert back into my body to grow.

Since I didn't know how to have faith in my body, that night I googled stethoscopes. My plan, if you can call it that, was to order a stethoscope so I could press it against my belly whenever I felt anxious and listen to our baby's heartbeat. I typed "stethoscope" and "baby's heartbeat" into Google, and before I opened any of the links, I took a sip of my tea. Beside me, Rob was asleep, and I could hear the long, slow draw of his breathing. He had been calmed by the doctor's visit in a way that I hadn't been.

I hovered over Stethoscopes.com. Who knew there were so many kinds of stethoscopes in so many different colors? I placed a red stethoscope in my cart, and even though he was asleep beside me, I heard Rob's voice asking, *How is this helpful?*

I don't know, but somehow it is, I answered imaginary Rob. I wondered what else women bought besides stethoscopes to feel in control of their bodies, of their minds. I wondered why I needed a guarantee that my pregnancy was progressing normally. When she was pregnant with me, my mother heard my heartbeat in utero, but she didn't see me moving around inside her on an ultrasound screen. How did she know everything was okay? And even if I *could* hear my baby's heartbeat from the warmth of my own apartment, what did I think that meant? That nothing bad could happen? That I'd have some high level of mastery over fear and fate?

My mother didn't know if I was the size of a lentil or a blueberry or a kidney bean. These baby-fruit size comparisons weren't invented until 1997 when BabyCenter staffers noticed that parents called their fetuses "little peanut" or "little bean" and thought it would be a cute marketing concept. My mother didn't compare the size of her bump to strangers' bumps on social media. Quite the opposite. Maternity clothes back then, she told me, were designed to cover your stomach. And there obviously wasn't Instagram to show her all the ways motherhood looked in other people's homes.

The stethoscope was my talisman. It became my desperate, anxious way of proving to myself that I was doing motherhood "right." If my baby was still alive, I was doing a good job. If my baby had died, I wasn't.

The stethoscope would help me monitor and study this growing life. It would help me understand this creature that was simultaneously of me and wholly its own, feeding off of my body to nourish and sustain itself.

WHEN I WAS in college in the mid-nineties, my best friend, Laura, and I would sit in cafés drinking coffee, talking about the older women we knew (women who, looking back, were likely in their early to mid-thirties) who didn't have children.

In our view, these women were better dressed, edgier, more fun. They had lives of freedom, travel, and adventure. They weren't tied down by men or babies. They'd figured something out.

The women we'd met who had kids looked grayer, sadder, and more beaten down. They'd clearly bought into the *institution* of motherhood, as the poet Adrienne Rich aptly described it—filled with self-sacrifice and never-enoughness—and I looked down on them for it. If these moms were trying to sell us on how great their lives were, they were doing a terrible job. I had no desire to be *that* kind of woman. I wanted very much to live for myself.

I believed that other young women, the ones who sat beside me in my classes at Boston University and lived on my floor in the dorm, had an insatiable drive to become mothers. These women struck me as strategic in the choices they made after college—and the idea of being strategic rankled me. Having a strategy when it came to love felt cold, mercenary, capitalistic in a way that grossed me out. Call me old-fashioned, but I believed in romance, the idea that around the next corner I'd find love if only I focused on fulfilling *my* dreams and finding *my* purpose.

In my mind, the women who got married were the ones sitting near the men's bathroom entrance at the Harvard Law Library, which is something my father had implored me to do. He was being practical: he figured that men who studied law would someday earn a lot of money, making them a good bet as a provider. It was the same type of thinking that went along with one of his favorite sayings: "It's just as easy to fall in love with a rich man."

My mother's expectations could be just as insidious. She emphasized my looks above all else. She entered me in beauty pageants. She seemed to believe that if I smiled and waved like I did on those stages in suburban shopping malls, my prince was going to show up, and even if he didn't have a horse, he'd have a safety net. After all, that's what had happened to her. Once she divorced my dad she met and married my stepfather in six weeks. He had a gold credit card and a job running his parents' business. He could take care of her.

I hated the system that made women believe they had to give up their dreams of self-actualization to become mothers. But it was easier to turn my rage toward the women I was surrounded by who I believed were throwing away their own lives so their someday husbands and babies could live theirs.

I told myself I was different. Special. I wouldn't narrow down the paths in front of me to appease a man. The men I hoped to find, when I was thinking about men at all, were explorers, seekers, artists, who wanted to create meaning and mastery together.

And yet when my roommate my junior year of college told me that she believed pregnancy was like being seeded by an alien, like a potentially hostile force was invading your body, my reaction to it, which surprised even me, was to push back, to tell her she was being too extreme. *No,* I thought, as strong and automatic as a gag reflex, *She's wrong.* But I couldn't explain why the idea that there was something gross or foreign about having children didn't sit right with me.

I hadn't yet read the work of Shulamith Firestone, who wrote that "pregnancy is barbaric" and childbirth is "like shitting a pumpkin." Firestone argues that for true equality to exist we have to disconnect pregnancy and childbirth from the female body. Some of today's scientific advancements—artificial wombs, in vitro fertilization—would have been right up Firestone's alley. Only when women are freed from societal expectations of childbirth and mothering, she wrote, can we have a chance at self-actualization.

Later that same year, another friend announced over Indian food that having children was "natural," by which he meant that humans were born to breed, our bodies designed to procreate. This was in its way as bad as the idea that pregnancy was like being taken over by an alien. My instinctive reaction was to swing wildly in the other direction. I was offended. Sure, giving birth was natural, as in, it was something a woman's body *could* do. But what I very much understood, but didn't have the words for at the time, was that *not* having children also felt natural. This was also something our bodies could do.

Meanwhile, I found it hard to even picture myself as a mother. A blankness appeared in my mind whenever I tried to think about it. *Would I be a single mom? Would I be married? Would I have two kids or three?* It was a black box with nothing inside. Looking back, maybe the black box was actually resignation. Maybe it had to do with my complicated relationship with my own complicated mother. Or maybe it was a lack of imagination—I assumed that like most women before me I'd also become a mother without thinking through how I'd get there.

Yet the biggest change since my parents' generation was that I had a *choice* whether or not to become a mother. Motherhood wasn't a foregone conclusion like it had been for my great-grandmother, grandmother, and mother. My lower-middle-class Jewish parents, who were both the first in their families to graduate from high school, actually lived down the street from each other in North Miami Beach, but didn't meet until their first year of college when they recognized each other on campus at the University of Florida. They'd barely thought twice about whether they wanted a child when my mom got pregnant with me at twenty-one. It wasn't just that the wave of feminism I was born into told me that having a child was my choice, but the availability of birth control and abortion access created the *concept* of choice. My generation had something the women before us never had: the freedom to choose how and when and even *if* we would mother. And there was no way given how hard I knew my feminist foremothers had fought for these choices that I was going to go gently into motherhood. In a post-Dobbs world the concept of choice is under threat. But in 2024, at least, young women can still get emergency contraception over the counter at CVS. They still grew up in a country where they understand motherhood as something they can choose to do—or not.

When I graduated from college in 1999, I looked down on my peers who wanted to get married and start families as sell-outs, Stepford Wives. I fancied myself like the poet Dylan Thomas. I would not "go gentle into that good night," the good night, of course, being motherhood and marriage. I'd "Rage, rage against the dying of the light," the light being my youth and potential.

After college, the messages ramped up. I was told to lean into my career, focus on my own personal growth. I was told the world was my oyster. My playground. "I was the captain of my own ship—the boss," writes the author Jo Piazza. And that's how I thought of myself, too. "I spent fifteen years taking care of one person—me. I was good at it. I reveled in my solitude and independence."

In my mind, settling down in a relationship before I'd figured out my own life would have been considered shameful. Embarrassing. Retrograde. As if I'd let down the feminist movement.

Throughout my twenties, the messages being pounded into

me didn't change. I was told: *Be whoever you want to be. The sky's the limit. Don't let anyone or anything hold you back.* And I listened. My career was like a jungle gym, and I climbed from this rung to that one, trying on diverse identities as I ascended: the social justice warrior, the artist, the scholar. And then I embraced a new identity, that of a carefree, world-traveling woman, not bound to a person, place, or traditional conventions so I could travel without a timeline when I decided that bureaucracies and hierarchies weren't for me. My sex life was no different, a cornucopia of possibility. Sometimes I had sex with strangers. Sometimes I had sex with men I thought I had a future with. I played in the sandbox of my life, studying ceramics, painting. And then I returned to Corporate America, bumping my head against glass ceilings. I got wasted because time was mine to waste.

Until suddenly I was closing in on my early thirties and the tone of all the messages I was bombarded with shifted drastically. All I heard now was *quick, find a husband, have a baby, settle down.* Yet I wasn't sure how to put the brakes on my previous life, which had been about me and my identity building to the exclusion of all else. How was I to instantaneously become a person who dropped everything to find a man and start a family? How was I to shift from a freewheeling, untethered woman to someone's wife?

Wait, why was the world suddenly not my oyster anymore?

I'D KNOWN I wanted to be a writer ever since I won a writing contest in middle school, so I decided I'd look to other writer-mothers as role models for the woman I wanted to be. But my research became a self-fulfilling prophecy: Because of the stories I'd heard about the women in my family, I believed mental illness and motherhood went hand in hand, so I sought out women who proved my shaky thesis. Anne Sexton. Sylvia Plath. Did motherhood make one crazy? Or was it that only the crazy became mothers? Or did creativity and caretaking drive women to the brink? I convinced myself I could either be somebody *or* be a mother. I couldn't have it both ways.

Eventually, I found my way to other examples, but they presented a new problem, one I'll call the time-baby conflict. I devoured Alice Walker, who said that in her first year of motherhood she wrote nothing "that didn't sound as though a baby were screaming right through the middle of it." Much later I'd read Claire Dederer, who wrote: "Maybe, as a female writer, you don't kill yourself, or abandon your children. But you abandon *something,* some nurturing part of yourself."

That one hit close to home. I didn't want to abandon my kid. Neither did I want to abandon myself. But I wasn't sure how to keep my identity and devote myself to a child, too.

In my twenties and early thirties, instead of grappling with the confounding decision of motherhood—and wondering why it raised such profoundly ambivalent feelings in me— I ignored the topic of children altogether, handing off the decision to my future self. I figured that Future Ruthie would better know how to make this kind of life-altering decision.

During those years when I turned my back on the question of motherhood, I traveled around the world—wandering aimlessly through Southern Africa, riding the Eurail around Western and Eastern Europe, jetting off to Thailand. I thought I'd figured something out that no one else had realized yet: that the only way to solve the riddle of life was to opt out of the normal milestones altogether. If I took marriage and motherhood off the table, at least for now, I could be anything I wanted to be.

I didn't realize that as I was *choosing* travel and adventure, I was cutting off other paths for myself. Inadvertently, by picking one life, I was shutting the door on another.

I spent the year I turned twenty-six living in a small fishing village on the shores of Lake Malawi. Part of the day I worked at a hostel, feeding hungry backpackers, in exchange for room and board. By the afternoon when the sun was high in the sky and the heat grew unbearable, I walked over to the dusty clinic further into the village and volunteered there. I helped bandage small children and bring them clean water. Sometimes I sat under the baobab tree with groups of women and talked about how they could turn their traditional craft making into small businesses weaving beautiful clothing and beading jewelry.

During that year, I took a trip to Kenya, where I met some British tourists. As I was putting up my tent and unloading my backpack, we began sharing stories about how we'd been crisscrossing Southern and East Africa, running away from, or toward, something or other. Earlier that year I'd packed up my whole life and moved from Boston, where I went to college, to South Africa on a whim. I was offered an internship to work at a printmaking studio in Johannesburg and dropped everything to take it. On a weekend trip to Cape Town I met a Zimbabwean tour guide who I was convinced, despite all evidence to the contrary, was my forever person. When he asked me to be his girlfriend and join him in his itinerant life, I couldn't think of anything I'd rather do. A few months later we were living together on the shores of Lake Malawi. He got a job as a kayak guide and I spent my days volunteering at the clinic. A few more months and he cheated on me with a German tourist. My fantasies of marrying him and traveling the world with just a backpack deflated quickly.

I'm still not sure why I played a lot of Bob Marley and hung around this man incessantly in the hopes of winning him back. He'd shown me who he was, yet I wanted to stick around. But eventually I fled east to Mozambique and on to Tanzania and Kenya once it registered that he was never going to be the kind of man I wanted to spend my life with.

I was sad, out of sorts, certain I'd die alone. When I met the British tourists at a beach with a campsite, they seemed like a life raft. My hope was that over the next few days I'd drink beer with my new friends, snorkel, and have far-flung conversations deep into the night. Somehow these strangers would resuscitate me—something I was unable to do for myself.

"If I knew I'd get married someday, then I'd stop being so anxious and just let myself have fun," I said emphatically to Sharon, a practical-seeming, dark-haired woman a few years older than me, as we cooked pasta on our travel stoves and the sun set over the water. Remembering those words now, I cringe at how stupid they sound. I want to distance myself from that girl. And yet she is a part of me.

I still remember the look on Sharon's face, a mix of seriousness and sadness. "You'll get married someday," she responded without hesitation. And I wondered: *How did she know? How could she be so sure?*

"So just have fun," she added with a shrug.

I barely knew her, but her matter-of-factness had a soothing, prophecy-like quality to it. Like she'd looked into a crystal ball and had seen my future laid out before her. She seemed so certain of my marriageability in a way that I wasn't. So I decided to listen to her, to try to enjoy the moment, to be present, at least for that night, at least until the three of them drove away, leaving me, my backpack, and my overactive mind alone, far away from home.

The truth is that I was certain even back then that I was messing something up. That if I ran too far, too fast, someone would come down from on high and yell at me, forcing me to get back to the life I was supposed to be living.

Nevertheless, as the deadline I set for myself to "figure out my life" and decide whether I was going to stay in Malawi and live there permanently, or go back to the United States, neared, I sat on the sand staring at the lake and asked myself who I wanted to be in the world. Did I want to settle in Malawi permanently and make a life there like so many of my friends had? They got married, had children, built two- and three-story huts out of bamboo. They spent their days kayaking and eating fish and fresh vegetables on the beach. Sure, there were parts that were difficult. Malaria and parasites were very real fears. Friends died early of preventable diseases. A crop wouldn't make it and children would starve. There wasn't enough gas for cars or medicine for illnesses. But that life was also lovely.

Another option was to move back "home," except I no longer knew where home was. I'd grown up in South Florida and my dad and stepmom still lived there, but it never felt solid and safe. My mom was in Boston, and many of my friends from college were still there. But in some ways it felt like a step backward—what would I do there that was any different than what I was doing right after graduating from college?

There was nothing pulling me anywhere. Sitting here now with the distance of twenty years, I want to shake that girl: Move to Stockholm! Tokyo! Berlin! You have time and youth on your side! But that girl would never listen to the "me" of today. She had to figure things out for herself.

There was one other option I contemplated: my half-sister, Alex, dangled a chance to move to New York City in front of me. She'd pay my first month's rent living in Brooklyn with her. She'd give me a chance to settle in, find a job and a new apartment. I'd applied to graduate school for journalism at New York University a few months before on a whim, sending in my application from an internet café in a tiny town that often lost electricity for days at a time. Not long after, I learned I was accepted.

I could see the faint sketches of two lives unfurling in front of me: the one where I stayed in a village in Malawi and the other where I moved to Brooklyn to go to graduate school and become a journalist.

Both lives had their pros and cons. Both lives were good choices. But each would take me on a completely different path. Who's to say which was better? Who's to say which was the "right" option?

Ultimately I picked New York City. And yet I told myself as soon as I saved the money and got a job as a foreign correspondent for *The New York Times* (my younger self had no idea how these things worked) I would move back to Malawi and build a life there.

I didn't see my decision to move to Brooklyn and go to NYU as cutting off my chance at living in Malawi. Just as I never saw my decision to move to Malawi in the first place as sending me down a path that I couldn't turn back from. In my mind, all roads were open to me—and always would be. No choice stood in the way of any other. There were no losses. No sense of scarcity. Just an abundance: of time, energy, options, lives.

In Sylvia Plath's novel *The Bell Jar*, Esther Greenwood is nineteen when she lands in New York City from Massachusetts for a summer internship at *Ladies' Day* magazine. She is hungry for food, for sex, for a life that is hers alone. The world is open to her. "I am I am I am," she repeats over and over.

But later in the book she compares her life to a fig tree. Choosing one fig means allowing the others to rot. "One fig was a husband and a happy home and children, and another fig was a famous poet and another fig was a brilliant professor . . . and another fig was Europe and Africa and South America, and another fig was Constantin and Socrates and Attila and a pack of other lovers with queer names and offbeat professions."

Each fig was tempting, a parallel life with its own beauty and pain. But as Esther tried to figure out which fig to choose, "the figs began to wrinkle and go black, and, one by one, they plopped to the ground at my feet." Inertia, Esther realized in that moment, was a choice. Stagnancy didn't mean that all her options remained open. In fact, it was just the opposite. The figs grew rotten.

As I sat in that village in Malawi, wondering which version of myself to be, I didn't understand the fragility of the figs. I didn't understand that travel and adventures *were* like figs on a tree. It wasn't the choice many of my friends had made—to find a stable relationship and climb the career ladder and set up their lives to bring a baby into the world—but it was a choice nonetheless. A choice to explore the world and not answer to anybody or anything. It was a choice to prioritize spontaneity and autonomy. It was a choice to live in a different country and try on a different life. And as I made those choices, the other figs began to shrivel. I didn't mean for that to happen. I didn't mean to close the door on any of my options. I didn't understand the equation. I didn't even know that there were doors that would close. All I could see was a vast expanse of time in front of me—time that was mine to play with in whatever way I saw fit.

What I didn't know was that the freedom to not make any choices yet *was* a choice—and it came with a price.

5

Freezing Time

Only nine months after Evan and I tied the knot, when I was on the verge of turning thirty-six, I sat across from a German doctor at one of the top fertility clinics in Manhattan talking to him about freezing my eggs. I couldn't appreciate the absurdity at the time—that I was here because I was in a marriage where my husband and I wanted different things. I wasn't trying to freeze eggs; I was trying to freeze time. And in my mind the procedure would give me the breathing room to figure out whether I should remain in my marriage or try to have a child.

What I didn't understand as I sat across from the doctor was that "fertility preservation"—which is what many doctors ironically call egg freezing—has only a 2 to 4 percent success rate per thawed egg, according to the fine print on the agreement I signed with my clinic. This meant that more likely than not my eggs would fail me. At the time, though, none of this was discussed with me by my doctor—nor did I ask. I had faith that the doctor would tell me anything I needed to know. I had faith that I could have a baby if I wanted to when the time came.

By then Evan and I had become expert avoiders. We were brushing our teeth before bed when I told him I'd met with a doctor about egg freezing. I said it matter-of-factly, as if there was no room for discussion, as if freezing my eggs wouldn't have any impact on his life whatsoever. He looked at me as I spoke and I could see my words—one by one—sinking into his brain.

And then he went back to flossing.

When he'd finished and put his toothbrush away, he walked over to where I was standing, kissed me on the forehead, and said, "I'm proud of you," before walking past me into our bedroom. I didn't know what he meant—and I didn't ask. But I reassured myself that what he was trying to say was: *Look at you, worrying about what you need for once and not what everyone else wants for you.*

I went to my next doctor's appointment solo and planned all the logistics independently, which was symptomatic of what wasn't working between me and Evan. And yet I didn't notice it then. I didn't notice how alone and isolated I felt in my marriage. My therapist called it "parallel play." Like children on a playground our lives unfolded alongside each other yet they rarely overlapped. I laughed when she said those words, amused that she pegged us so clearly. But I also felt winded by the gut punch of it all. My whole life, I'd learned to bury my own needs. Not to hear my desires whispering beneath the surface. So I picked a man who kept me at a distance, who refused to notice that I wanted a different life, which conveniently let me do the same.

My family and my friends advised me not to worry about what Evan wanted. My friend Emma made my decision sound so simple. We were drinking fancy cocktails at a bar in Brooklyn when she said, "You have to decide who *you* want to be in the world." I balked. As a philosopher, she saw the decision of whether I should become a mother as an existential one. "Do you want to be a person who has kids or a person who doesn't?" she asked, holding her hands up on either side of her body so I could see just how large the gap between those two options truly was.

As I got into bed that night next to Evan I repeated, *Who do you want to be in the world?* over and over until I fell asleep. I already knew what my life with Evan looked like: it had an orange glow to it, warm and safe. My life without Evan, my life with children, I could only partially picture. I saw Olive, but I also harbored deep anxieties about being a mother. I was still waiting for whatever cosmic reckoning I imagined would come for me.

It wasn't only that I couldn't see myself as a mother. I felt grateful for what I did have. Some people never found love. I had a man who adored me. And I wanted *more*? Why couldn't I just be happy with what I was given?

The longer I contorted myself to fit into my marriage, the more I couldn't hear what my own voice was telling me. Instead of seriously talking to my husband and telling him what I needed, I decided it was easier to politely go to a doctor and pay ten thousand dollars to have my eggs frozen.

At the time, I thought my acquiescence was a personal flaw. But now I wonder if a society that bombards women with so many images of who and what we're expected to be keeps us from recognizing who we actually are.

Coincidentally, Evan was away for my first week of hormone injections, the ones I needed to prepare my body for the surgery to remove my eggs so the doctor could freeze them. I had wanted him to be home, but he couldn't get out of a work trip. His absence left me free to sit at our dining room table for as long as I needed, mixing the bottles of medicines, trying to get the measurements just right. I turned our home into a science lab; a big red tub for all my discarded needles sat within arm's reach. Empty glass bottles were strewn everywhere. The plastic that kept the needles sterilized was scattered haphazardly on the countertop nearby. Another week passed, and I was commuting thirty minutes to the fertility clinic at 7:30 every morning so a team of nurses could prick me with more needles and monitor my hormone levels.

On the final day of the cycle, my nurse Shakira warned me about the "trigger" shot that I had to twist around and inject into my back thirty-six hours before my egg retrieval surgery, preparing my body to release the eggs at just the right moment. I asked Shakira if I could come back to the clinic to have her give me the shot, but she told me what I in fact already knew: that their office would be closed by then. "You can do it," Shakira said reassuringly.

But I didn't believe her. By then Evan had returned, and when he came home that night he immediately knew something was wrong. "You can tell me," he said, and something in his eyes made me believe him.

"My last shot is a really big one and I'm kind of scared. I called the walk-in clinic and they said the doctor could give it to me."

There was a long silence, and just as I was about to turn around he surprised me. "Maybe a piece of chocolate cake would make you feel better?"

How did he know that chocolate was exactly what I needed

at that moment? Maybe he'd always understood my feelings better than I gave him credit for. I walked over and gave him a hug. "I'd love that," I said.

Evan walked me to the clinic so the doctor could give me the shot, and afterward we ate the fudgiest, darkest chocolate cake, as if we were celebrating a new job or an engagement, not a batch of frozen eggs that left a big question mark over our future.

Two days later, I had fourteen eggs safely ensconced in downtown Manhattan somewhere, an insurance policy against my waning fertility, but not against my wavering marriage.

WHAT I DIDN'T know when I walked into my fertility clinic in 2013 to freeze my eggs was that it was only the year before, in 2012, that the American Society for Reproductive Medicine (ASRM) had announced that egg freezing was no longer considered experimental. I also didn't know that the ASRM ethics committee had issued an opinion warning that egg freezing "may give women and couples false security about their ability to have children in the future."

There'd only been five hundred births from frozen eggs worldwide by the time I sat in my clinic's waiting room, not enough data to guarantee that my eggs would produce a baby in the future. With so few women returning to use their frozen eggs, the pool wasn't large enough to determine the chances of a baby being born from my almost-thirty-six-year-old eggs.

Only once my friends in their early to mid-forties began seeking out assisted reproductive technologies to start their families did I really pay attention to my fertility at all. I naïvely believed that if down the road I decided I wanted a baby, I could just do a round of in vitro fertilization, and it would be all but guaranteed. What I didn't know was how many women had tried fertility treatments only to be disappointed. Those women weren't sharing photos of their babies on Facebook and Instagram. Those women weren't gushing about their fertility doctors.

I didn't know that I had Dr. Debra Gook to thank for the fact that I could freeze my eggs at all. While sperm was first seen in 1677, the egg was not seen for another 150 years even though it's the largest cell in the body and can be seen without a microscope. At least part of the reason for the century-and-a-half delay was that sperm could be extracted without surgery, while eggs couldn't be removed without cutting a woman open. C-sections didn't really start until the early 1800s, and early experimental C-sections were terrible (as is easy to imagine) and sometimes done without anesthesia.

But another reason it took so long for eggs to be studied, and for scientists to ultimately figure out how to freeze them, came down to one thing: as long as women were having children young, there wasn't a real urgency to think about researching, or freezing, eggs. If you were a woman before the late 1980s and you wanted to try to have a child later in life, you were out of luck. If you didn't have a devastating disease, the understanding was you'd either be having kids—or trying to. And that's what most women did. In 1970, the average age was 21.4 years for a first birth. By 1980, the average age was 22.7.

Yet Dr. Gook, who was working at an IVF clinic in Australia when a friend of hers was diagnosed with cancer, had an idea. At the time there was only one thing a woman who underwent chemotherapy and radiology could do to try to salvage her chance at having a baby: freeze her *embryos* in advance, which meant she needed to have a partner or someone whose sperm she could use. No one had ever tried to freeze eggs before. When Dr. Gook asked her boss if she could study egg freezing to expand fertility options for women, he nixed the idea, saying that eggs were too fragile to be frozen (the prevailing thinking was that eggs would never survive the freeze-thaw process). Eventually, Dr. Gook convinced him to let her try, and she found the golden ticket: an antifreeze that wasn't toxic to the egg and prevented ice from forming. Now women who had cancer or other serious diseases would have a way to preserve their fertility. By 1994, Dr. Gook opened the world's first egg bank in Australia.

Not only was the world watching, but Dr. Eleonora Porcu, a researcher in Bologna, Italy, decided to take Dr. Gook's work one step further. Dr. Porcu wanted to use Dr. Gook's freezing technique to help *all* infertile women, not just those with cancer or other serious diseases. She ran trials at her IVF clinic for three years, and in 1997 one of her patients gave birth to the first baby from a frozen egg.

By the fall of 2014, egg freezing was catapulted into the spotlight when Facebook and Apple announced that they'd begin covering the procedure for their employees. Hailed as a progressive move, the media wrote breathless stories about the decision. Tech companies messaged the move as women getting to choose the timing of their families. Executives scrambled to portray egg freezing as a medical procedure everyone should have access to—and something more employers should offer. But some critics called the companies out for what they saw as the corporate self-interest in play: if women delay motherhood, the companies could keep them chained to their desks, working. Or as Claire Cain Miller of *The New York Times* wrote, "workplaces could be seen as paying women to put off childbearing."

But I knew from my own decision to freeze my eggs, and

talking to others who'd frozen theirs, too, that for most of us who chose elective egg freezing, the decision was much more complicated than just wanting to focus on our careers. Some women hadn't found the right partner with whom to have children. Some, like me, were partnered with people who didn't want kids and needed more time to decide what to do. Still others didn't know if they wanted children at all and were using egg freezing to kick the can of indecision down the road, hoping they'd be better equipped to make that choice in time.

Around the same time I was freezing my eggs, Doree Shafrir, author of the memoir *Thanks for Waiting*, was considering freezing hers, too. "I didn't tell many people I was planning on freezing my eggs—it was a private thing, the world didn't need to know," she later wrote, describing how she hoped to avoid "the flash of pity in their eyes" when she confided in her few close friends about her plan.

I, too, was terrified of people's pity, of feeling like everyone was looking at me like I had a terminal disease. I wanted to scream, "It's biology, not cancer," but then I'd fit the stereotype of the hysterical woman. I was trapped in a cage of my own making. I was filled with so much shame for being a married woman whose husband didn't want to have children with her. Weren't men supposed to want to have kids with their wives? What was wrong with me that Evan didn't want to share in this supposedly life-affirming experience with me? If our friends found out, what would they think?

Eventually, Shafrir decided not to freeze her eggs. "It's the most apt metaphor to say that I realized I was putting all my eggs, literally, in that particular basket, and I had imbued the idea of freezing my eggs with so much meaning that I expected to see all of my anxieties and fears about getting older and being single and dying alone to disappear instantly the second I went through with it." Not freezing her eggs meant facing that such fears wouldn't go away.

When I look back at my own decision to freeze my eggs, I see a similar hope was in play—that with one medical procedure I could, in effect, put all of my inner turmoil on ice. I convinced myself that treading water was an option. I convinced myself that I could freeze my marriage and I could come back to the baby question later. I convinced myself that staying in place was viable. I thought of it as simply postponement—breathing space. What it really was, of course, was a suppression of my own wishes and happiness, a habit that wreaked havoc on my mind and body. Decades earlier, I would later learn, the psychologist Dana Jack had studied female patients and learned that self-silencing, which she defined as "the propensity to engage in compulsive caretaking, pleasing the other, and inhibition of self-expression in relationships in an attempt to achieve intimacy and meet relational needs," increased a woman's chances of developing depression.

In other words, my coping mechanism, which can be summed up in four words—*don't rock the boat*—was actually a health risk. But how was I to know that?

Instead, I woke up the day after freezing my eggs and felt a great relief. One of the few people I told, a male friend, hugged me when he heard the news. He believed I was an empowered woman making an empowered decision. I did, too. But within a few days that elated feeling had disappeared.

A decade later, elective egg freezing no longer carries the same stigma it once did. Now the trend is for women like the journalist and author Liz Plank and others to share their journeys on Instagram and TikTok. Plank, who froze her eggs in 2022, documented her "eggventure" for her hundreds of thousands of followers. Thousands commented on her Instagram posts with their own stories.

Frankly, if Instagram Stories had been around in 2013, I might not have felt I was the only one freezing my eggs. If my peers had been on IG Stories, I would have known I was part of a community of women, a community taking their fertility—and their lives—into their own hands.

But because I wasn't talking with my friends—or for that matter, my husband—about what was happening, doubt and shame multiplied like gremlins in my thoughts. Over the five years we'd been together, I'd evolved, while Evan remained steadfast. Even so, I couldn't help but wonder: *Why did Evan not want to do what humans since the beginning of time have been doing—procreating?* I built up this rationale in my mind that if he really loved me, he'd want to have babies with me, which, unsurprisingly, only made me feel worse.

Why not me? my mind cried. *Why not me?*

TWO YEARS AFTER I'd frozen my eggs, I felt something slipping away between Evan and me. By now it was 2015 and I was manic. Evan had retreated from my constant drumbeat of questioning: *Should we have a baby? How? When?* He was tired of needing to repeat the same answers over and over. No, no, no, no, no. It wasn't registering for me. I was still hoping to change his mind. I pushed harder. Maybe if I shouted, screamed, he would finally hear me?

By then I had stayed with Evan for seven years, the tug of safety overwhelming me. I held tightly on to the hope that someday, somehow, we would have a baby together. And during that entire time, Evan pulled out when he came so he wouldn't accidentally get me pregnant. Not even once, in the throes of passion, did he forget. Even when I was on the pill. Even when we used a condom. He always wanted double assurance that there was no *possibility* that he'd become a dad even by accident.

In this increasingly untenable situation, I became the exact person I didn't want to be: the woman who loses her mind trying to have a baby. The only things I knew for sure were that I finally decided I wanted to be a mother, and that I would have done anything to stay married to Evan. But those things were not compatible, and I was spinning out of control, doing regrettable things, trying to make it so.

I could pretend that I had a long talk with Evan, explaining that we couldn't stay together because it was clear we wanted different things in life. But this is a true story and that didn't happen.

Instead, I bought a syringe and planned to try to use it to impregnate myself with Evan's sperm.

In retrospect, I know how unethical and unhinged this sounds. I wouldn't want to live in a society where women were expected, or worse, forced, to have children. We've seen that world in *The Handmaid's Tale*—where women are put out to pasture when they can no longer conceive, and young women are raped in order to bear children for the commanders' wives— and it looks terrifying. Nor would I want to live in one where men who didn't want children were forced to become fathers.

In the end, I didn't go through with it.

Instead, one night around this time, as we lay next to each other in bed, Evan said the words I never wanted to hear or say: "I think we should get separated." Even as he said it I knew he meant divorce.

We spent the next few weeks disentangling our lives. If I came home before him, I would take a sweater from his bureau and sink my face into the smell. Gradually, we packed up the detritus of our former life, carefully placing our dishes next to our Christmas ornaments in the box I would put in a ten-by-ten storage unit in the Bronx and then not open for half a decade.

As much as I loved the warmth and coziness of inertia, Evan took staying in our marriage off the table. Standing still was no longer tenable. I would be dragged kicking and screaming toward change.

Recently I was speaking to a new friend who didn't know anything about my past, and before I knew it the words, "When I left my husband" had slipped out of my mouth. It wasn't until she said, "That's so brave of you," that I stopped midsentence, a laugh curdling in my throat, and said, "I don't know why I just said that. I didn't leave my husband. He left me."

The sad truth is that even after I knew for certain that I was married to a man whose vision for his life was so different from my own, I wasn't going to do anything about it.

I would have stayed because I thought I was supposed to.

I would have stayed because I thought: *What other choice do I have?*

I wasn't brave. I was anything but.

I wasn't ready to say, *No, this isn't enough.* "To hold the word *no* in my mouth like a gold coin, something valued, something possible," as Louise Erdrich writes. "To celebrate *no* . . . To grasp the word *no* in {my} fist and refuse to give it up."

I wasn't ready to admit that my desires mattered.

6

Triple Whammy

By now I was out of the fragile first trimester, yet every few days I would look down when I was on the toilet and see blood. And just like the first time in the bookstore, my whole body would freeze. Blood felt unnatural. Blood felt wrong. Blood made me think something bad was happening to the baby.

Even though I knew that 80 percent of miscarriages happened before the twelfth week, and we were now safely on the other side, I couldn't stop myself from worrying. I googled the stats each night just to remind myself: only 1 to 5 percent of pregnancies end in miscarriage in the second trimester.

And because I'm a writer, I both observed the worry and analyzed it. Interestingly, the word "worry" comes from the old English "wyrgan," which means "to strangle." All the while I was worrying about whether our baby would make it,

I was choking off my chance at joy. All the while I was worrying, I couldn't be in the present moment.

Years before, I sat in a movie theater anxious about some worst-case scenario or other when a friend said, "You need to make a distinction between what is probable and what is possible." Her words came floating back to me. Was it possible I could miscarry? Yes. Was it probable? No.

For a few minutes, I felt better.

And then my mind started spinning again.

My half-brother Adam was born with a triple whammy of rare disorders that all struck him in the womb: Albright hereditary osteodystrophy, hypo-hyperparathyroidism, and Tourette syndrome. For so long I told myself that I shouldn't have kids. That maybe I'm a carrier for Adam's conditions and I should be careful not to pass my genes onto someone else. Once I even marched into a geneticist's office at New York University with Adam's medical files and begged her to tell me what the chances were that any child of mine would inherit the same genetic mutations as Adam. Back then I told myself that if the doctor determined the chances were 50 percent or higher, I'd forget about motherhood once and for all and put all my energy into making my marriage work.

I explained to the geneticist with her white lab coat and mousy brown ponytail that Adam is my half-brother, the son of my mom and my stepfather, so we only share some genes. By now I knew he had a mutation in the G-protein, alpha-stimulating 1, or GNAS1, gene. But I had no idea what the GNAS1 gene was. Or how likely it was that I could have the same mutation on my gene.

"I wouldn't be able to tell you anything," the geneticist said, staring at the paperwork I handed her. "Unless I mapped both your mom and stepdad's genomes." My mom was on Medicaid, and extensive genetic mapping was way too expensive. Not to mention that her insurance deemed it unnecessary since whether she was a carrier didn't impact *her* health.

What I didn't understand as I sat there in the geneticist's office was how little geneticists actually know about the thirty thousand genes in the human body. My whole life I'd believed that doctors were all-knowing. I believed that because sheep could be cloned, pinpointing whether I was the carrier of a devastating genetic disease would be pretty straightforward. But I left the office that day no closer to knowing whether I should give up on the idea of having a child.

Now I walked over to the red filing cabinet next to our bed and took out Adam's medical files that I'd asked my mom to send me years before. As I opened the big yellow envelope with the words *Brigham and Women's Hospital* typed across the front, I was fifteen weeks pregnant. By the time I got to the last page of the document, my eyes latched on to the words that I hoped my mom never saw, but I knew she had:

"Adam has profoundly limited intellectual capacity and will not be able to achieve occupational success."

"He is emotionally labile and is not safe to be placed in an unsupervised setting."

The words in front of me informed me coldly that Adam's IQ would continue to slide. His body would continue to disintegrate.

I thought of Adam's life. He's hilarious—a natural storyteller, a man who will talk to anybody, with a gentle streak that has both served him well and put him in danger. Thinking about him then I wondered what he'd be like when I saw him next. Each time I'd gone to Boston over the past few years he'd been noticeably worse. His involuntary tics forced his 250-pound frame to suddenly squat down every few minutes. The jerky movements twisted and contorted his body into unnatural shapes. He had trouble taking care of himself. Showering, shaving, brushing his teeth, and taking his medications were all tough for him to remember. The last time I picked him up from the group home he now lived in, he had urinated on himself, had holes in his sneakers so big I could see his toes, and smelled like he had slept on the street. There are staff that are supposed to be watching over him, but since he's an adult there's only so much they can do. After we parted, I watched him stumble through a crowd of people and I teared up, painfully aware all over again how hard his life was, not just here, now, with me standing there, but every single day.

IF I CLOSE my eyes I can still remember the day that Adam and I followed the cobblestone streets of the Freedom Trail to Paul Revere's house in downtown Boston and he pelted me with questions about which phone plan I used while strangers stared at us. I was twenty-eight and he was twenty-one, and as I dropped him off on the platform to wait for his train back to whatever bleak apartment he could afford with Section 8 in whatever grim neighborhood outside of Boston he lived in, my guilt suffocated me. I was going back to my studio in a leafy neighborhood in Brooklyn known for its brownstones and double-wide strollers and family-oriented fun. He was shuffling through the open doors of the train, crouching down quickly while everyone around him darted away, terrified of the hulking man, the man whose pants were falling down and whose shoes were untied. The man who might be having a seizure or be mentally ill or who might suddenly lunge. The man who might need something they couldn't give.

The roll of the dice—his life, and mine.

"Each pair of parents could produce over 70 trillion genetically unique offspring," the psychologist Kathryn Paige Harden writes. My puny brain can't even process the enormity of that number. "Like a specific 6-ball combination in Powerball, the fact that you have your specific DNA sequence, out of all the possible DNA sequences that could have resulted from the union of your father and your mother, is pure luck."

Reading about genetic lotteries, I understood: I was lucky. Adam was not. The baby I was now pregnant with could be lucky. Or not. There was no way to know.

I'd recently read Doris Lessing's novel *The Fifth Child,* a horror story about a happily married couple with four children whose life crumbles when their fifth child, Ben, is born. Harriet, Ben's mother, wonders if he is a "hostile little troll," though eventually she and her husband, David, conclude his otherness is because of a genetic mutation. He can't communicate. He commits acts of violence. The family isn't sure what to do with him, and the idea that permeates the whole book is how quickly the life you built can vanish, how having a baby means inviting the unknown into your home.

"We are being punished, that's all," Harriet told David. When David asked why they'd be punished, she responded: "For presuming. For thinking we could be happy. Happy because we decided we would be."

The Fifth Child played into all of my fears. Of our baby being born with a hodgepodge of genetic anomalies. Of abandoning our child, either because there was something wrong with it, or there was something wrong with me.

.　　.　　.

IT WASN'T UNTIL Adam was just a few months old that I noticed his head was too big for his body. In one photo his head teeters to the side, his body too weak to hold it up. A few years later, I remember running into my mom's room wailing because I saw his thumbs, as if for the first time, and they looked wider, larger than they should have been. I thought he was hurt. Maybe I'd injured him? I was inconsolable.

Now we have names for his trifecta of disorders. But until Adam was nineteen years old—almost two decades of life (I have to repeat this because I still can't believe it)—we had no idea what was wrong with him. Not only that, but for many months the doctors (and my stepfather) reassured my mom that he seemed fine.

Women who worry that there's something wrong with their babies are a dime a dozen. I'm sure there's some inside joke among doctors that goes something like this: *If I had a dollar for every time a woman came into my office thinking her child had a devastating disease, I'd be rich by now.*

Can you hear them all laughing? Har-dee-har-har-har.

But there *was* something wrong. We just didn't know what it was called, and science couldn't tell us yet.

This isn't a story about the years my mom tried to get a diagnosis for Adam and couldn't, though. It's not a story of the gaslighting by his doctors or her ex-husband either. This is the story of how so many of my views on motherhood have been shaped by Adam and observing the ways he's been forced to navigate the world. This is the story of how so many of my views on motherhood have been shaped by my fears of having a baby like my brother.

When kids in my class would whisper, "What's wrong with him?" when they saw Adam, or ask, "Is that your *brother?*"

their words stung. I'd hope Adam didn't hear them, but I knew he had. "I think of how the world saw us," writes the author Joanna Hershon about what it was like to grow up with her brother who was developmentally disabled. "Or, more accurately, I think of how I was always acutely aware of how we were perceived."

Adam was aware of how he was perceived, too. And it broke my heart.

By the time I was fourteen and Adam was seven, things had deteriorated at home. My mom got him into a special program for kids with developmental disabilities, but we still weren't sure what was wrong or how to help. She felt certain that if his doctors tweaked one of his meds or offered him a special skill-building program, he'd be off to a flying start, able to go to college and have the "normal" life every mother dreams of for their child. But taking care of Adam's needs overwhelmed her, and rightfully so. Even though she was a special ed teacher and had worked with differently abled kids for much of her career, Adam was a particularly difficult case. She couldn't get Adam to stop repeating himself. To play with the other kids. To sit still long enough to finish his homework. My stepfather's answer was to hit him. As my mother grew more fragile, she threatened all of us with wooden spoons and "just wait until your father gets home."

Her naps became more frequent. Her fights with my stepfather, more volatile. Her medications, more numerous. I believed if I could be a good daughter, she'd get better. And being a good daughter meant helping Adam, too.

My mom had taken me with her to her classroom where she taught enough times that I thought I knew what to do. When I came home from school I playacted a special-needs teacher, sitting Adam down and asking him to recite lists of words. If he got one wrong, I would make him start over. Hours would pass in this way. He was never able to remember long chains of letters or mathematical formulas. I would be frustrated—at him for not trying hard enough and at myself for my poor teaching skills.

Eventually I became Adam's guardian, overseeing his care, after years of my mother trying to help him. I met with his doctors. I ensured he got funding for services so he could go to school, get a job, spend time with those his own age. Adam would call me—sometimes daily—and ask me for money for food, rent, anything really. After my mom and stepfather got divorced, she would call, too, and beg for cash. Or, one time, toilet paper. They both asked to come live with me in my tiny studio apartment, even though I was in my twenties and barely getting by myself. My whole life my mother bombarded me with stories about a baseball player who had Tourette syndrome and another one about a famous classical musician. *Adam would be somebody, too,* was her message. And I believed her.

Once we had labels for Adam's condition—and for my mom's (she was diagnosed with borderline personality disorder when I was thirty)—I believed we'd find a medicine or a magic cure that would make them better. I also believed that if I took care of them well enough I could fix my mother and brother. But even though I tried with every ounce of energy and love in my body, I was never good enough to work that magical trans-formation. Instead, I had to learn to mother my brother and my own mother at such a young age that when my peers were deciding whether they wanted to become parents I was so ex-hausted I couldn't imagine nurturing another human for one more fucking second.

.   .   .

AND YET, HERE I was, pregnant and hoping I'd finally put enough distance between those days to want to nurture again, all the while waiting for the other shoe to drop. I had no idea where the shoe would come from or what kind of shoe it would be (a high heel? a sneaker?), but I was certain there was a shoe, and it was headed my way. Just three weeks after running into Evan in the bookstore, the shoe fell: the whole world went into lockdown when a global pandemic descended.

On the phone with my therapist that week, I told her I wasn't surprised about Covid-19. "I was waiting for my punishment, and here it is," I said.

I could hear my therapist's skepticism through the phone. "You think your punishment for pushing to have a baby is that a global pandemic erupted all over the world?"

She had a point. When she repeated it back to me it did sound irrational.

This was magical thinking to the max. I not only was the center of *my* world, but I was now the center of the *entire* world, and I believed my decisions around whether to have a child could wreak havoc on the planet, causing horrible death and economic destruction.

I knew I was being ridiculous. "But it still *feels* like Covid is my punishment."

I thought back to the last decade when my friends all started to have babies. As their pregnancies progressed, they seemed largely untroubled. They knew somewhere deep down inside that creating a child was a gamble, but they must have repressed it, or they figured the chances something would go wrong were so miniscule it wasn't worth worrying about.

And they were right. But I couldn't stop obsessing. I wished I was more like them—able to move through the world with calm confidence, oblivious to the potential horrors around me.

Or . . . another thought came to me. Maybe these other women, friends of mine, but also strangers on the internet, were everything I wasn't. They were better equipped to mother. They were able to roll with the punches, able to laugh easily. They were infinitely patient. Their feathers didn't ruffle. They didn't suddenly burst into tears because they broke the yolk of their sunny-side up egg or were overwhelmed by the thought of making the bed. My takeaway was devastating: Aren't those the characteristics that every mother needs to do a good job? Wasn't this further proof that I wouldn't be a good mother? The fact that I couldn't imagine anything but the most rosy version of motherhood made me question my ability to be a mother at all.

I walked over to my computer and clicked open a letter my mom sent me, written from one doctor to another about Adam when he was twenty-four. In it, the doctor writes what must be the cruelest words a mother could ever read about her child:

Zero expectation of improvement.

Guarded optimism of remaining stable.

Every pregnant woman has to wrestle with the crapshoot of uncertainty. Every pregnant woman must accept that there's no way to control whether something goes wrong with her genes. There's no way to control which of the seventy trillion genetically unique outcomes your child will be born with.

Having a baby never felt like a lottery to me, though. It felt like a game of Russian roulette.

By the time I was pregnant there was genetic testing for both Rob and me—and for our embryo—not only before it was implanted but once the fetus was growing in my womb. Rob and I had spent heart-wrenching nights talking about what would happen if one of the myriad genetic tests came back positive. What if our baby had Down syndrome? Or

Turner syndrome? Or Tay-Sachs disease? Or worse. What if the doctors couldn't tell us for sure something was wrong, but could only say there was a 60 percent chance that our baby would be born with some kind of abnormality? And the truth is: we would have aborted.

Here I was, a woman who loved her brother with all her heart, and yet I knew that if I was told my child would turn out like him I wouldn't have wanted to bring them into the world. For our child's sake and mine and ours as a family.

Recently when I video chatted with my mother, she mentioned that her psychiatrist asked her a question. "I couldn't even let the question enter my brain. Like I know it went in my ear and through my brain and out," she said, rotating her finger in loops around her head. "He said: 'Have you, God forbid, ever thought it might've been easier if Adam wasn't around?'"

My breath caught. The same question had been tugging at me for most of my life. There were two facts that felt equally true: I love my brother, *and* his existence pushed my already fragile mother to let go of whatever frayed rope tethered her to the world. I worried it would be the same for me: if anything was wrong with my child, I would lose my footing. I would fall. I would tumble into the darkness, too.

I understood something deep and terrifying then, something I'm only now able to put into words as I sit here and type this: that even without a genetic disorder or accident at birth, my child could walk outside and get hit by a bus. And everyone I love could, too. Or like Jayson Greene's daughter, Greta, whose death he wrote about in *Once More We Saw Stars*, my two-year-old could randomly get struck by a brick one sunny day and I would be left to bear it, howling like a wounded animal.

Jayson knows that. I know that. You know that. I looked at the letter my mom sent me about Adam with a new certainty: that everything is uncertain. At any moment everything and everyone I ever loved could be swept away, and yet the beauty of humanity is that we continue living anyway. We know the enormity of everything that could go wrong and yet we keep getting out of bed.

7

Life, Interrupted

If you believe my father, he'll tell you that my mother's suicide attempts started before I was even born. She scrawled notes that willed all of her belongings to him, and when I arrived, she added me to the list, too: "I leave everything, including Ruthie, to you," she once wrote.

But then there's another story: the car accident I'd heard about my whole life, the one where the green Datsun my mom had been driving crashed headfirst into the median with me, just over a year old, in the backseat. Turns out that accident, the one where my mom swears that she fell asleep because she was exhausted, may have been a botched suicide attempt.

The pendulum in my heart swings wildly between my desire to believe my mother's version of the story and my sense that my dad's version rings true. At first I told myself that my mother wouldn't want to hurt me. *She just hadn't been thinking about me. She was suffering too much to see beyond her own pain.* But after reading about Margaret Garner, who was born enslaved and ultimately killed her two-year-old daughter to avoid relegating her to a life of enslavement, I wondered if my mother's actions could be seen as a sacrifice, as a twisted attempt to free me from the cycle of mental illness and trauma she and her foremothers suffered through.

After reading Margaret's story, something terribly sad clicked inside me, and with it came a piece of new understanding. That for me being normal wasn't just about fitting in. It had taken on another meaning altogether. Normal meant *not* crazy, *not* mentally ill, *not* broken. Normal meant *not* killing myself or my child.

Back when I was married to Evan, I'd cut out an article from *The New York Times* about a forty-four-year-old woman who lived down the street from me in Harlem, a woman who jumped off the roof of her eight-story building with the baby she so desperately wanted strapped to her chest. The baby survived; she did not.

I didn't know this woman, but something about her story haunted me. What switch had flipped in her that sent her over the edge of that building with the baby she'd gone to the ends of the earth to conceive? What switch may have flipped in my mother as her car careened into the median over four decades ago on her way home from work?

I understood my mother was capable of hurting herself—I'd seen that year after year—but what I couldn't imagine was that she would intentionally want to hurt me. This is the woman who cut up my hot dogs until I was a teenager so I wouldn't choke. Who wouldn't let me ride a roller coaster. Who rocked me in her arms and sang me a vaguely Eastern European–sounding lullaby until I was eleven or twelve, and probably even older, too big to fit into the crook of her arm like I did when I was a baby.

But then there was also the version of my mother who could throw daggers with her words.

"You're lucky you have a mother," she would say.

"My mother was dead by the time I was ten," she would add.

"Just wait until I die, and you'll be sorry," she continued.

By the time I left for college, my mother had begun to disintegrate even more. She spent weeks in the hospital. Cycled in and out of group homes. Slept in her car. Underwent countless rounds of electroshock therapy sending short electrical bursts into her brain until her long-term memory was fuzzy. I couldn't get the image of my mother strapped down to a table, convulsing violently, out of my head. The only thing I knew about electroshock therapy was what I'd seen in movies like *One Flew Over the Cuckoo's Nest* and *Girl, Interrupted* when all the life was sucked out of Angelina Jolie's eyes after the "shocks" were administered. Coincidentally, my mother attended group therapy at McLean Hospital in Belmont, Massachusetts, the same hospital that eighteen-year-old Susanna Kaysen, the author of *Girl, Interrupted,* was admitted to after her own suicide attempt. Sylvia Plath spent time there, too.

My mother's illness became its own kind of abandonment. Whatever was happening to her mind meant that I had to take care of her. I kept waiting for her to snap out of it, realize she was my mother and act like how I imagined a mother would act, how I was told a mother *should* act: selfless and nurturing. Instead, because of her mind or the trauma she'd experienced or maybe just because of who she was, she needed me to take care of *her.* When I was invited to give a talk in Boston about my experiences working at the health clinic in Malawi, we planned that she'd attend and I'd spend the night at her house. But the evening before she swallowed a bottle of pills and drank enough brandy to land her on the fourth-floor psych ward at Beth Israel Deaconess Medical Center. I was confused. Angry. *I thought we'd made a plan. Why try to end your life now?*

As I stood at the door of the ward, waiting to be buzzed in, I felt sad. I wanted the day to be like how it had played out in my head the past couple of weeks: I'd give the talk; my mother and I would go out to dinner after; she'd tell me how proud of me she was. Instead, I was here. I felt ashamed that my mother was locked up, and then felt ashamed of my shame because I knew about her parents' dying, about the abuse she suffered. If I couldn't find empathy for her, who could?

A man with a clipboard led me down a long hallway, and suddenly I saw my mother come running out of a nearby room. She gave me a thumbs-up like this was the most normal thing in the world—to meet here in the hospital. And then she started waving at me as if I was far away and she was trying to catch my attention, but I was right there. She looked strange. Out of sorts. A social worker walked over and put his hands on my mother's shoulders to guide her. "Step forward," he said, nodding at me, and just then my mom bounded over to give me a hug and stepped on my foot, causing me to stumble backward. "Mo-om," I said agitated, stretching the word out into two syllables.

"It wasn't my fault," she said quickly with a desperate cry in her voice, and I immediately felt bad because I didn't want to ruin our time together. My second thought was: *She* ruined our time together. *Why are we here in the fucking first place?*

I fluctuated between anger and sadness, anger and disappointment, anger and hurt. The pendulum swung between wanting to run and wishing I could simply disappear.

The social worker mumbled something about the visiting room, and I noticed after my mother sat down that she looked small and vulnerable in the big chair. I hated her vulnerability at that moment. She was weak and I wanted her to be strong. She was wobbly and I wanted her to feel safe. *When could I crumble? Who would take care of me?* But those weren't questions I could ask. It was too dangerous to consider since it wasn't even a possibility. I couldn't be fragile. I couldn't fall apart. But maybe that's what ultimately saved me.

I made sure there was one chair between my mother and me to guard myself against her. I didn't want to look at her or be close to her or even for our arms to touch accidentally. The social worker left the room and I felt like screaming out to him: *No, don't leave me here with her!* And then when he came back a few minutes later he asked me to tell my mother how I was feeling. I just stared blankly ahead.

Was this some kind of joke?

I could have spent the rest of my life creating bullet-pointed lists of all the reasons I was angry at my mother. But now I wonder why the social worker was so focused on my anger and not my sadness. The what-ifs make me weepy. What if my mother's mother, Ruth, hadn't died when she was so young? Or if my mom's family handled the death differently? In that parallel life, instead of not telling my mother that her mom was dead and not letting her attend the funeral or even grieve, what if someone had sat her down and explained everything to her? What if when my mother's father died a year later, my great-grandmother Kitty had kept the children together? Or tried to keep them herself instead of adopting them out to separate families? What if my mother hadn't been abused by her adopted family? What if someone had said early on *The way you're feeling is normal, there is nothing wrong with you?* Would my mom have felt less broken? Less terrified? More able to stand on her own two feet?

If you ask my mother, she'll tell you that she's not mentally ill. Depending on the day, she'll tell you she has complicated grief, which is like being on a roller coaster where you can't get off, immersed in the ups and downs of mourning that keep you from ever truly healing. Or she'll tell you about her complex post-traumatic stress disorder from all of the trauma and abuse she experienced. Or maybe she'll tell you, like she told me over a decade ago, that she has "very bad luck" and "bad stuff just keeps happening" to her.

"It's not me that's sick," she'll try to tell you. "It's the world. What kind of family doesn't let children mourn their parents? What kind of family abandons their children and sends them off to be adopted? What kind of adopted family abuses their kids?"

I had, and still have, no answers to these questions. I now understand that some things can't be comprehended. The author Suzanne Scanlon calls borderline personality disorder, my mom's diagnosis, an "outlaw, ugly diagnosis," "an expansive disease," marked by chronic feelings of emptiness. "Never mind that it [is] too vague to mean anything," she writes.

And that's exactly how I feel.

Whether we want to call what's going on with my mom borderline personality disorder, complicated grief, complex PTSD, bad luck, or mental illness, no longer means much to me. What does mean something is that I lost the woman I'd known as my mother at a young age. I lost the mom who could be my rock. I lost the mom I could call and confide in. I lost the mom who could truly *see* me.

I've spent my life haunted by my mother and half-brother's illnesses—and by the fact that I'm lucky. I still have two parents, as imperfect as they are. I was eventually able to build a community of people who could see me in the ways I needed someone to when I was young.

Even typing the words "mental illness" makes me cringe. But what other words are there? Madness, crazy, nuts, insane. I'd wondered my whole life if I'd somehow caused what happened to my mother, if me being born when she was only twenty-two strained her already fragile mental state. Was I the one who kept her from fulfilling her dream of becoming a nurse? Or traveling to the Galápagos to watch turtles lay eggs on the beach? Or had her genes doomed her from the start, her future written into her DNA?

Or maybe it was something else entirely.

Wouldn't you go crazy, too, if you had her life? I've asked myself more times than I can count.

EVENTUALLY, MY MOM'S suicide attempts gave way to a depression so severe she couldn't leave her bed, which in turn led to a handful of back surgeries, which became a decades-long addiction to Oxycodone. As I write this, I hear my mother's voice in my head saying, "It's not an addiction, it's a dependence." I also hear her saying, "It's not my fault I have a bad back."

Because of the years of lying in bed, my mom's limbs have atrophied. At times she has cut her arms. Starved herself. Slid down to less than 120 pounds, a stark difference from the over 200 she had been when I was a child. It's as if she's a balloon and the universe has sucked all the air out of her. Each time she has swallowed pills or stopped eating feels like an abandonment, like she's saying *you're not worth sticking around for.*

There have been phone calls where she has pleaded with me

to call her doctor, to find out why she's in so much pain. The pain that began in her back now radiates down her legs; "It throbs," she has told me again and again. Surgeries that were supposed to relieve pain only worsened it. Opioids make people feel pain, too. Is the pain real or imagined? Because of the drugs or a botched surgery or from lying in bed for so long? At what point does it stop mattering?

Over the years, whenever I called my mom, she reminded me that, "Raising you kids were the best years of my life." Listening, I would try to remember. For all the hard times, there have been good times, too. We would go on mother-daughter dates at the department store Burdines, where after lunch she'd buy me the cake with the princess on top. I loved those cakes, and how the buttery icing of the princess's skirt was laced with beads of sugar I crunched between my teeth. There were nights we'd cook stuffed peppers and spaghetti sauce, brisket and kasha. She planned elaborate birthday parties with "pass the baton" games and piñatas. Once she had taken me to the elementary school where she taught for Take Your Daughter to Work Day, and I could still remember the pride I felt watching her at the front of the classroom—my beautiful, fun mother.

I used to beg the universe for a diagnosis. Like with Adam, I thought that when we finally had something real we could point to and say, *This is what's wrong,* I could fix them both. But now I wonder what good a diagnosis does without a cure. What good is knowing the name of whatever is happening inside my mother's mind if there's no treatment that works? If there's no care to deliver?

Later, I came to understand those princess desserts and the beauty pageants my mother signed me up for as a signal: of the woman my mom wanted me to be, the beautiful woman who waited for her man to take the first bite of his meal before eating, who waited for her man to discipline the children, who waited for her man to make her happy. Just like she did with my stepfather. And when he walked out the door eighteen years after they married and never came back, my mom was lost. Forever.

"Think of your mother as a Venn diagram," Amanda, a caseworker for the Commonwealth of Massachusetts explained to me on one of our phone calls when my mother was released from the psychiatric ward once again. "One circle is your mom—bright and shiny, the one who always cracks jokes, who stands at the front of the bar leading everyone in another round of the "Electric Slide." The other circle is her illness—dark, unpredictable, raging at everyone and everything. Somewhere in the middle those circles meet, and that is your mother on any given day."

When I began thinking of having children, I thought of that Venn diagram, those overlapping circles. My mother made it crystal clear that motherhood was no guarantee of happiness. Having children is not a salve. Or a cure-all. But the way society portrays motherhood would have us believe that it is. We are told children give our lives meaning. We are told a baby will fix our marriages—and our minds. We are told we don't need to pursue our own dreams and desires because our kids will fill whatever empty spaces exist inside of us. But none of this is true.

All I knew was that all the mothers in the chain of mothers I came from were connected umbilically to each other—and to me—and I'd need to cut the cord.

8

Fuck-Off Fund

My whole life my mother had put her mother, Ruth, on a pedestal. But the story that gets left out, the one that's buried because it's a less tidy narrative, is that Ruth was a married woman with a thirteen-year-old daughter, Beth, when she fell in love with her doctor, the one who spent days (or was it weeks?) tending to her tuberculosis at Sunland, a sanatorium in Lantana, Florida. Instead of going home when she recovered, Ruth married her doctor Albert Reinherz in 1954 from her hospital bed and my mother was born that same year (followed by three more children). "I couldn't even kiss her until after we were married," I was told my grandfather said with an air of amusement and incredulity.

I imagine that on her deathbed, Ruth replayed the what-ifs in her mind. What if she hadn't left Beth behind with her father when she was just thirteen? What if she had decided to stay with her first husband for the sake of her child? If her thinking was anything like mine, she might have wondered if her breast cancer was punishment for not being the mother she was told she was supposed to be.

The 1950s were the decade my grandmother Ruth raised her children, yet the stories I heard about her life don't match up to the image of 1950s motherhood that are still the bedrock of the American ideal. There were suicide attempts, disappearances, and hospitalizations. There was a child Ruth didn't give birth to that she raised as her own.

It's easy to see that Ruth was deeply unhappy, an experience she had in common with many other women of her generation. In fact, in 1956, the *Ladies' Home Journal* devoted an issue to "The Plight of the Young Mother." By 1960, words like "trapped" were being used to describe American housewives. In 1963, Betty Friedan's classic *The Feminine Mystique* was published. "Is this all?" was the question Friedan asked in her book. "Is this all?" was the question that had been driving the restlessness of so many women of this period.

It was more than just the children that trapped women in those decades. It was the messages women were given, too. On the one hand, women were told they had to have children to be deemed normal, yet they were also not supposed to be too invested in their children, or too domineering, otherwise they'd be diagnosed as neurotic or even schizophrenic. They shouldn't focus on their children to the detriment of their marriages, or they'd risk alienating their husbands. When women weren't stimulated enough by their domestic duties, they were told there was something wrong with them. Some, like Ruth, took antianxiety medications like Miltown, also known as "Mother's Little Helper." Others underwent electroshock therapy.

Sitting here on my privileged perch as a woman who makes her own living, who am I to judge Kitty and Ruth or even my own mother on their failings as mothers and wives? I was born into the first generation of women who were no longer financially tethered to men. Only three years before I was born, the Equal Credit Opportunity Act of 1974 passed, giving every American woman, married or not, access to a credit card and/or a bank account in her own name. The idea of having my own money to "fuck off" with, as writer Paulette Perhach calls it, was powerful. *Fuck off* in the sense of doing whatever the hell I wanted with my cold, hard cash. And *fuck off* also meant I'd be able to tell any man who didn't treat me right to shove it. That was a privilege that wasn't afforded to the women in my family before my generation. That was a privilege that wasn't afforded to most women outside of my family either. I had the ability to choose whether I wanted to be a mother—and the financial wherewithal to create a good life for myself and my child—in a way that the women who came before me didn't. But that reality is also what left me deeply ambivalent. Just because I had the option to pick a different life from the women in my family, did I need to?

Kitty and Ruth had to make choices that I, thankfully, never needed to make. I dug up an article about Kitty's ten-day marriage to Harry Kay, the first man she married after divorcing her husband Irving in 1937. The first thing I noticed is that the article puts Harry's age at sixty, while Kitty was only thirty-five, a pretty big age gap even then. Just after getting married, Kitty allegedly informed Harry that she had a fifteen-year-old son, Bernie, and asked Harry for two hundred dollars to send to Bernie so he could come to live with them. When Harry refused, the claim continued, she "continually nagged your plaintiff day and night, incessantly and uninterruptedly," and then left him.

In Kitty's counterclaim she said that although Harry made

fifteen thousand dollars a year (over three hundred thousand dollars today), he "refused to give her money for food and other necessities, threatened to kill her with a chair, and told her in the lobby of the hotel where they were living that 'she would starve to death if she expected to sponge off him.'"

Maybe this is where the gold digger perception came from? Kitty married a man who was rich compared to her in the hopes that he would help support her son. But I see something else in this story, too. Kitty wasn't an American citizen at the time, and I can't find records of whether her first husband Irving was either. With anti-immigration sentiments on the rise in the late 1930s, mixed with antisemitism, Kitty may have been panicking, grasping at straws for any sense of security and stability. Marriage may have seemed like a decent enough option for a good-looking woman with no money and no education.

I'm not saying that either Kitty or Ruth should win any "Mother of the Year" awards. I'm just wondering if all those years I thought there was a glitch deep inside my DNA, a mutation that would predispose me to abandon my children, may have been a giant misunderstanding. Maybe I was judging my great-grandmother's and grandmother's mothering by a standard none of us could (or should) have to live up to.

The same with the British novelist Doris Lessing.

The story I'd always heard about Doris was that she abandoned her children to go to London to write. "The story that she walked away from her two eldest children and never looked back turns out to be, more or less, a fiction," writes the author Julie Phillips. The reality is that Lessing wrote hundreds of letters to two friends in the mid- to late 1940s, starting when she was twenty-five, where she talked about her desire to see her children, showed her concern about them, and outlined the arguments she had with her ex-husband in order to have more time with them. There was a part of her that wanted even more children and to live a traditional life. But then there was the other side that desired more: Doris wrote in a letter that she wanted to "run a newspaper, write novels, meet people, take part in the class struggle, etc."

Maybe what Doris was really doing was looking for a place where she could have some privacy, free from interruption. Maybe she just needed a few moments to herself. "If you say, 'I spend my mornings writing,' that will not prevent the furtive knock on the door, and then a moment later, the guilty, embarrassed, smiling face appearing around the edge of the door."

Maybe running away was the only way Doris could shut her door in peace. Maybe Kitty and Ruth planned to go back for their children once they had created a stable life for themselves. Maybe abandonment was just a label put on women who didn't follow society's straight and narrow definition of a good woman.

RECENTLY I SAT in my neighborhood bookstore listening to the author Claire Dederer read from her book *Monsters: A Fan's Dilemma,* and when it was time to submit questions, I wrote: *What if you abandon your children and you're not a genius? What if you don't write a* New York Times *bestseller? Or you're never recognized for your art? Does that make you a worse monster than someone who leaves their children to make a masterpiece?*

I needed to know whether women had permission to close the door on their children to write, even if what they wrote never turned into something deemed valuable by the larger world. No, writing is not the same thing as abandoning your child, but nonetheless it takes shutting the door against their cries. What I was really asking was: What if *I* toiled away year after year, not spending time with my child—or being fully present—and it all amounted to . . . nothing? How will I know if what I'm creating is *worthy* of my time, and in turn, my life?

"But I wanted to paint" is what Alice Neel said in 1928 when her daughter Isabetta was born. She had one puny life and she, like all of us, had to decide how to spend it. With her daughter, whom she loved with all her heart? Or painting, which she also loved deeply? And because her paintings now sell for millions of dollars, does that mean she made the right decision? Was it worth the trade-off? What about all the Alice Neels we don't know about? The ones who never made it into history books? The ones who died unknown? The ones who never made masterpieces?

How many great artists have been lost to the belief that we can't be mothers and use our minds? How much creative energy has been bottled up and buried in the name of motherhood? "How many Nobel Prize winners have we lost?" asked Rachel Yoder, author of the novel *Nightbitch,* when we spoke on the phone. "How much great science?"

And what about all the women who aren't artists, but have other ambitions, like those who just want to work and have some time and space to themselves? It's not just the individual who suffers when women aren't able to live to their full potential. It's all of us.

If Kitty and Ruth had abandoned their children to make art like Doris Lessing or Anne Sexton allegedly did, would that have made their choices any better?

What would I have done with my life if I knew deep in my bones from a young age that I didn't have to choose between being a writer and being a mother?

Instead, I only saw a forked road—and I believed I had to choose just one path.

I still believed that marriage and motherhood were *the* path to true happiness. Every Disney movie and rom-com that ever existed told me that. By the time I learned that there is an inverse relationship between marriage, motherhood, and happiness, I wondered if the problem wasn't marriage itself, but heterosexuality. I wasn't the first to come up with that idea. "I can't find a model, a female literary model who did the work she wanted to do and led an ordinary heterosexual life and had children," wrote the author Jeanette Winterson. "Where is she?"

Where is she? I wondered.

9

The Bogeyman of
the Childless Woman

The September morning after Evan and I officially signed our divorce papers, I woke up in bed crying. I didn't know what to do. I had nothing but time in front of me. Nowhere to be, no one who cared if, or when, I'd come home. I felt unmoored, like I was floating in outer space, with no gravity to tether me to the Earth.

I did the only thing I could think of: I walked. I walked through the brownstone-lined streets of my neighborhood, across the busy thoroughfare of Atlantic Avenue, to the blocks filled with double-wide strollers and candy-colored scooters ridden by kids of all ages. I did figure eights through the streets, passing dads carrying their infants strapped to their chests and moms carrying coffees like a lifeline. I thought about all the places I'd lived in New York City. Windsor Terrace, where I shared an apartment with my half-sister, Alex. Bed-Stuy with two film students and an endless army of cockroaches. Park Slope, alone, in a studio with a bathroom so small you couldn't sit on the toilet and close the door. Two apartments just blocks from each other in Harlem with Evan.

Eventually after weeks, and then months, my well-meaning friends started to ask an obvious question: Would you consider having a baby on your own?

It wasn't an unreasonable question and there were plenty of models. In a parallel life, I might have taken the same route as author Alyssa Shelasky, who writes about being a single mother by choice in *This Might Be Too Personal: And Other Intimate Stories,* and Shonda Rhimes, the entertainment powerhouse who's a single mother of three. Or I might have gone the route of Canadian singer-songwriter Feist and adopted a baby on my own.

I knew I *could* be a solo parent. I could go to a sperm bank, pick a man who on paper I'd love to date, and have a doctor knock me up. My feminist belief system told me that I should want to have a baby on my own—or at least I should think it was feasible (and it *was* feasible). But I didn't want to—and that made me feel even more ashamed. Why was I convinced I needed a man to have a family?

The obvious answer is that traditionally, the man has been the provider. But I was lucky. I could afford a baby on my own, as long as I was careful about my spending. No more eighteen-dollar cocktails and five-dollar lattes. No more tasting menus and designer sample sales. That's not what I wanted, though. I was searching for a teammate, someone who would help me to finally feel like I was on the inside next to the warm fire, instead of standing outside in the cold, looking in. Yes, I wanted a child. But I wanted a partner just as much.

Eventually, I signed myself up for a rest and relaxation weekend at a new age retreat center in upstate New York. On my first day there, a six-foot-two Swedish massage therapist gave me a massage in a dim room surrounded by crystals. Before I took off my robe he asked me what I wanted to let go of. "I need to know if I should have a baby on my own," I said. The words came tumbling out.

He motioned for me to lie down, and as I did he said, "Let's see what your body says." As he kneaded the muscles in my back gently I cried. It felt good to have someone's hands on me. It felt good to let all my pent-up tears out. It felt good to exhale.

"What about the baby?" I asked him after he was finished. I'd poked and prodded every inch of my mind and couldn't find a satisfying answer to my question about whether I should do this whole motherhood thing on my own. I read every book. Asked my friends. I'd even spoken to women I barely knew to see if they could help me decide. But everyone told me I'd *just know.*

Instead of words of wisdom, my masseur brought me a warm cup of tea, which was kind but far from satisfying. "Only you know the answer to the baby question," he said, clearly not knowing what to say. He was a massage therapist, not a *therapist* therapist. More than that, he was a stranger. How was he supposed to know what to do? I knew nothing about his life, just as he knew little about mine. Did he even have kids of his own? Did he have a partner? I felt like the baby bird in P. D. Eastman's book *Are You My Mother?* looking to everyone else, hoping to find my mother, but turning up empty-handed.

I knew my massage therapist was right: only *I* could answer my question. And I did know that having a baby without a partner wasn't what I wanted. But that meant finding someone to have a baby with right away. I had recently turned thirty-nine, and even though I had a batch of frozen eggs I could try to use someday, I understood they were no guarantee. I was terrified of dying alone. And the stats backed up my fears. The data shows there's a huge imbalance of single men versus single women as we move into our thirties and forties. I still remember listening to the *Dear Sugar* podcast episode when Paul Oyer, an economist at Stanford University and author of *Everything I Ever Needed to Know about Economics I Learned from Online Dating,* told Cheryl Strayed and Steve Almond the terrifying truth: "From a simple supply-and-demand point of view, women do have something to worry about, and it gets much worse as they age." I was heading into a forest without any trees.

There *was* one last-ditch effort I hadn't tried. A few weeks later, I called my closest guy friend from college to ask if he wanted to have a baby together, the same one who had cooked me Indian food all those years ago and told me that having babies was natural. He was still single. And I knew he'd make a good dad. Granted, the logistics of our co-parenting might be tricky, I allowed, since he lived in Nashville and I lived in Brooklyn and neither of us were willing to move. "But," I said with all the confidence I could summon when he answered the phone, "we can figure it out."

I'll save you the agony of not knowing: he said no.

I believed that being child-free, or a solo parent, would mean being willing to not belong. It would mean standing out. Being different. It would be a sign of failure, a sign something was wrong with me. I'd spent my whole life running after normal—and here I was considering making a decision that in my mind would forever relegate me to the margins. The voice in my head kept shouting: *What about being normal? Won't having a kid by yourself make you a perpetual outsider? And do you really want your kid to be considered a weirdo, too?* Of course

I knew that wasn't true. Of course my fear was irrational. But I lived in fear of not toeing the line. I lived in fear that by following my dreams in my twenties and thirties I'd irrevocably ruined my life.

I'D ABSORBED THE messages all around me. A woman's job wasn't to pursue a life of purpose and meaning. It was to wait to be noticed. To wait to be chosen. Adrienne Rich saw this truth so clearly. "Women have always been seen as waiting: waiting to be asked, waiting for our menses, in fear lest they do or do not come, waiting for men to come home from wars, or from work, waiting for children to grow up, or for the birth of a new child, or for menopause."

The women who don't sit around waiting for men? They end up childless—no man or baby in sight—living in a ramshackle apartment with only their cats to care for. Or at least that's the image, or "the bugaboo," as the psychologist Leta S. Hollingworth called it in 1916, that we are sold. Eventually these bugaboos "will lose their power to frighten," she said. Yet here many of us are, more than a hundred years later, still terrified of being labeled a spinster, or a witch, or, as then—vice presidential candidate JD Vance so poetically reminded us, a childless cat lady, still scared we'll end up alone with no one to care about, or care for, us.

I certainly felt that fear. Maybe because of my dad's mother saying that all the "good men" would be taken if I didn't get on it. Or maybe it was because as we started turning twenty-five and twenty-six my friends were getting married and having babies. Why couldn't I just be like everyone else? Why did I have to do everything the hard way? What was so *bad* about marriage and motherhood? Wasn't that the way of the world since the beginning of time?

"Women who put themselves first are villains in today's society, just as they were in the 1500s," writes Swiss journalist and writer Mona Chollet. But to be fair, I never considered my desire to backpack around the world "putting myself first." I was just doing what the men I'd admired had always done: wandered. Jack Kerouac, Ernest Hemingway, Bruce Chatwin, and Paul Theroux never had to explain their decision to go on the road or off the map. They just did it. They didn't worry about being persecuted or killed or labeled as crazy.

Throughout history it's always been the woman who doesn't follow the rigid rules of femininity who has been accused of witchcraft. Controlling, policing, punishing, and exiling the "bad" women who challenge male dominance is what misogyny is all about. And in turn society rewards the "good" women, those who get married, have children, and don't cause too much of a fuss along the way.

Then again, I already had an image in my mind of what true punishment was. It would mean turning out like my mother, or her mother, or her mother before her—women who may have been afflicted with mental illness or whatever you want to call it when a life shatters. Women who, as the story goes, all had abandoned their children in one way or another. In my mind there were two bogeymen: not having children *and* having them only to morph into my mother.

WHY DO WE have so few models for the shape a woman's life might take?

We're presented with a rigid timeline that urges us to "do

it all" by thirty-five—that is, establish a fulfilling career in our twenties, get married by thirty, and then have a baby before our thirty-fifth birthday. But if that doesn't work out, what then? What are the alternatives? And what if you try and don't quite get everything you want at thirty-five and you're now thirty-eight or thirty-nine. What does *that* mean? Does that mean you're a total failure and always will be? Does that mean there's nothing left for you and you're going to spend the next sixty years of your life in utter misery?

I remember reading the writer Rebecca Solnit's beautiful essay *The Mother of All Questions* for the first time and screaming "YES!" at the page. "We are given a single story line about what makes a good life, even though not a few who follow that story line have bad lives," she writes.

You don't have to look far to find examples of those who did all the "right" things, only to realize they weren't actually happy. I'm thinking of the high-profile mom blogger "meltdowns" in recent years. The stories of those like Natalie Lovin, one of the most famous Mormon mommy bloggers, whose husband she confessed dumped her after a dozen years of marriage. "I had to go back on my word and say, 'Just kidding, I was actually miserable, I just didn't tell you,'" she told *Elle* in 2019.

Social media reacted in horror to Lovin's admission. Brand sponsors that had adored her "content" when her life looked shiny and happy pulled out. She lost her career. Fell into a deep depression. The world seemed to turn against her for not fitting the model of motherhood she publicly touted. The internet felt betrayed by a woman who performed what it looked like to "have it all," and here she was admitting that her life wasn't as great as she pretended it was.

Meanwhile, after my divorce, as I cried alone in my bed

night after night, I scrolled through Instagram, mourning the fact that my life didn't look the way it was "supposed to." No, Natalie Lovin wasn't whom I aspired to be, but there were plenty of other women online who seemed to have figured something out that I hadn't. And their lives, at least the versions that popped up on my phone, looked downright glamorous. I blamed my failure of imagination—the fact that all my dreams for myself seemed to stop once I snagged the fantasy marriage and kid—on a personal flaw. But the truth is far more grim. It's not just me. It's all of us. We don't have many role models for what self-actualization looks like for a woman. It took reading Solnit's words for me to realize it: "We speak as if there is one good plot with one happy outcome, while the myriad forms a life can take flower—and wither—all around us."

Back then, as I kicked myself for every decision I ever made, I never thought to ask: What does a world look like where everyone wants, and goes after, the same things on the same timeline? I never thought to ask: Do I even *want* to live in that world? And if I don't, how could I opt out of this system without being pitied or seen as defective? Could making different choices be seen not as a personal failure, but instead expose a political failure to create a system that works for more people?

It was Taffy Brodesser-Akner's 2019 novel, *Fleishman Is in Trouble,* which was later made into a Hulu series, that captured the tension of the mental prisons women have been forced into. I watched Rachel (played by Claire Danes) and Libby (played by Lizzy Caplan) struggle under the impossible expectations of womanhood and motherhood. Rachel is the epitome of so many women I know. Even though I'm not a wealthy talent agent like she is, I understood viscerally the pressures she faced to be a "good" mother and a "good" wife while going full throttle in her career, too. And then there's Libby, the magazine writer who chose suburban life, only to wonder: "How did I get here?" Her internal monologue sounded a lot like mine: Is what I'm doing worthy of my time? Am I focused on the things I *should* be focused on?

I didn't have any way to answer those questions. I still don't. All I knew is that I wanted someone to show me the way.

10

Outlaw Mothers

If I wasn't going to be like my great-grandmother, my grand-mother, or my mother, and I didn't want to be like the "1950's mothers" that American society has fawned over and fantasized about for seventy-five years, *and* I didn't want to end up a mother who resented her children because of how they kept her from writing, what kind of mother would I want to be?

The truth is this: I had no vision for an alternative shape to motherhood. Which is one of the reasons why I'd been stuck for so long. But instead of looking for new shapes, instead of pushing to redefine the contours, I internalized the idea that *I* must be flawed. I figured since I didn't fit the mold—and didn't want to—that there must be something wrong with me. I'd missed the boat, gotten off track, not focused on the right things, not been strategic enough, not been nurturing enough, not been selfless enough.

And because in my mind everyone else seemed to be doing

just fine with society's rigid rules and expectations, I should just shut up and get on with it. So I did. I threw myself into the dating waters again, this time looking for a partner who wanted children, even though I had no idea what I wanted motherhood to look like, or that I could even ask that question at all.

Five years later, I'd crack open *Revolutionary Mothering: Love on the Front Lines,* to read Loretta J. Ross's words. "How do we get from a conservative definition of mothering as biological destiny to mothering as a liberating practice that can thwart runaway capitalism?"

Motherhood as a liberating practice? As a way to thwart capitalism? I'd never even considered it. At the time, I didn't believe I could find the space to really consider the type of mother I wanted to be. I was in my late thirties and I felt desperate, frantic. Motherhood at my age was a shot in the dark. In my mind, I would be lucky to be a mother at all. I couldn't *choose* the kind of mother I wanted to be. I *couldn't* mother with intention and agency. I just needed to find a partner and get knocked up. I'd figure the rest out later.

My whole life I believed that the decision to *not* have children was a radical act in a society that tried to force all women to become mothers. But as I started reading about revolutionary mothers, I wondered if there was a way for mothering to be a radical act, too.

The answer is yes.

In fact, from the 1970s to the 1990s, a group of Black and brown feminists, including bell hooks, Cherríe Moraga, and Gloria Anzaldúa, paved the way to redefine mothering as "investing in others' existence" and a "refusal to the violence" in a society that historically forced women of color to undergo sterilization and other forms of barbarism.

These women understood that they didn't have to let the politics of a sexist, racist, ableist, capitalist society determine their most personal decision: whether or not to mother. They understood that strict social norms are the last gasp of a patriarchy trembling in fear as it loses its power. These women understood that they could mother differently, that they didn't need to emulate or duplicate the images of motherhood they'd been force-fed their whole lives. They could decide what they wanted to replicate from the past and what they needed to transform.

What I couldn't see yet—or perhaps chose not to—was that there were already countless role models for mothering differently. Author Toni Morrison believed motherhood was an act of resistance that empowered her to truly be herself. Her children wouldn't allow her to perform—something she'd learned to do as a woman in a society that always needed her to be *something* to *somebody*. But her children needed her to live authentically. They didn't care what she wore or what she looked like. They didn't care if she was smart or sexy. To live authentically in a world that didn't see Black women's lives as worthy was radical. It was a "queer thing," wrote Loretta J. Ross, to choose to be a mother in a world that "conscripted 'Black' and 'mother' into vile epithets."

I felt greedy for more motherhood stories. Not just the fairy tales I'd ingested my whole life, or the influencers who showed up in my Instagram feed. But the women who defined for themselves the contours of motherhood. Like the author Barbara Ehrenreich, who didn't see a distinction between the spheres of work and motherhood.

You could do that? I thought as I read about how Ehrenreich brought her children along to protests and maintained a strict writing schedule after she dropped her kids off at school each

day. Ehrenreich didn't fit neatly into the motherhood roles and
identity prescribed by the dominant culture.

And then there's Angela Garbes, whose book *Essential Labor*
asks the reader to redefine the duties and indignities of motherhood as an opportunity to "craft meaning and—this is the
dream—contribute to positive social change." I didn't have to
accept motherhood as the patriarchy's version of motherhood
with a capital M. And once I could let go of those unrealistic
standards and expectations, motherhood could be liberating.

Beyond Morrison and Ehrenreich and Garbes were countless others, women who, whether quietly or loudly, were rejecting society's existing models in favor of alchemizing new
ones. The poet Adrienne Rich called such explorations "outlaw
mothering."

As I kept digging deeper into my reading list, I discovered
that outlaw mothering encompassed queer motherhood, too.
Before same-sex marriage and gay adoption became legal, the
author and activist Cherríe Moraga wrote about how the experience of being pregnant and birthing her son changed her relationship not only to her body but to her sense of herself as
genderqueer. Being pregnant and giving birth—the hormonal
roller coaster, the breastfeeding—revealed to Cherríe that
being biologically female didn't mean she had to present as
female to the world. Suddenly she saw the truth: "My anatomical sex wasn't wrong. The world is wrong about any gendered imposition on that sex, something intersex people have
long publicly asserted." Cherríe learned to define, and accept,
motherhood for herself, on her own terms.

She isn't alone. Black, brown, queer, and other marginalized communities have always been forced to create their own
version of motherhood outside of the dominant cultures' demands, oftentimes relying on kinship networks based on cho-

sen family rather than bloodlines. These women I was now reading about claimed a motherhood that didn't replicate what they'd experienced. Maybe it's because they never had the opportunity to embody the ideals of the Brady Bunch white family that they created their own. Even though I couldn't compare my heartache to Black, brown, and queer women, I wondered what I could learn about reclaiming a new motherhood legacy from tracing their footsteps. What would it mean if the word "mother" was an "action, a technology of transformation . . . ?" asked the writer Alexis Pauline Gumbs in *Revolutionary Mothering*. What if mothering was a practice like yoga or meditation, she wrote, "an alternative building practice of valuing ourselves and each other and creating the world we deserve"?

Here was what I'd been looking for. A role model—and a road map—for how to mother differently. But why did it take me so long to notice there was another way? Why had I gobbled up the image of the all-in, selfless mother so wholeheartedly? How come I didn't even consider whether there were different varieties of motherhood, or better yet, as many versions of motherhood as there are people?

These examples were around when I was deciding whether or not to become a mother, and I'm sure I had some exposure to them, but at the time any awareness I had was lost in the torrent of counterprogramming in our society. What's notable about this vision of motherhood is that it's one of women acting with agency and intention. This form of motherhood gives women an opportunity to see their role not just as fulfilling but as powerful. Motherhood as powerful is not something I'd really ever considered. To me, motherhood had always seemed weak, degrading, something to dismiss as small and unworthy of my time.

Now that I understood the *concept* of outlaw motherhood, I

needed to understand what it would take to *become* an outlaw mother. What would be required? How would I embody this new image? And if I spent my whole life striving to be normal, what would I do with those tortured parts of myself now that I was signing myself up for a new vision of motherhood altogether, a version of motherhood far outside the norm?

I wanted to follow in the footsteps of these self-professed radical mothers. And yet I also knew that outlaw motherhood wasn't easy, that it had its own challenges. I'd spent my whole life immersed in the bubble of the capitalist patriarchy. I knew deep in my bones what the self-sacrificing, identity-annihilating model of motherhood looked like. Now I'd need to figure out how to mother in reaction to that model. I'd have to break down my entire foundation of what I believed motherhood to be and rebuild it from the rubble. I'd have to wrestle with my great-grandmother's and grandmother's and mother's version of motherhood—cherry-picking what I wanted to carry on and tossing the rest.

Outlaw motherhood was just an idea. I'd have to figure out how to live into it, how to define it for myself. The mother code I desired to emulate went beyond the rearing of an individual child and focused on actively shaping my community. But I'd have to learn how to get there.

So how did my image of what motherhood had to be get so far from my desired reality? As I write this all these years later it hits me: the version of motherhood I, and all of us, have been sold is the version of motherhood that sees mothering and work, mothering and writing, mothering and self-actualization as incompatible. Whom does that benefit? My journalist training from my early days as a reporter at *Forbes* kicks in and whispers, *follow the money.*

It's all so obvious. How did it take me so many decades to

realize it? The capitalist patriarchy benefits from the tall tale that motherhood means self-sacrifice.

If women can be persuaded that mothering means giving up everything else in their lives, then that puts all the money and power and status in the hands of men. "When you are a woman, the things you like get used against you," Jia Tolentino reminds us in *Trick Mirror: Reflections on Self-Delusion*. "Or, alternatively, the things that get used against you have all been prefigured as things you should like."

So, because women "like" becoming mothers, the megaphone of the patriarchy bombards us with images and reminders around every corner of how impossible it is to mother and essentially *do* anything else.

What if it's simply not true? What if, as Black and brown and queer feminists and scores of other mothers of all colors and walks of life have shown us, we *can* mother differently? What if there's not one way to mother, and we've been hoodwinked into believing that motherhood needs to be all-encompassing to the suffocation of all else in a woman's life? What if we've been duped into believing that motherhood must mean a dead end to our dreams and desires?

"We don't have the luxury of living normal lives," the Black activist and artist Cat Brooks told Dani McClain in an interview in *Mother* magazine. Here I'd been attempting the high-wire act of cosplaying normal. But what if normality was a luxury? What if because of the fact that Brooks and others hadn't been allowed "inside" the American ideal, Black, brown, and queer families were forced to reimagine a mother code that values community over individuals?

"I tell my daughter all the time—and it's harsh—but we don't live for the I. We live for the we," said Brooks. The "we" is a rallying cry for marginalized people who see the world chipping away at their family unit. The "we" is a form of resistance.

The rigid norms and expectations of motherhood I grew up with were never true for women of color. The sexist idea that "men work and women take care of families" sounds great on paper, but the majority of women of color had to work outside the home, often in the "mammy" role to other women's children.

"There is no one-size-fits-all approach to what it means to be a mother, especially in an African American context," wrote Stephanie Buckhanon Crowder. "In many ways there is no norm. . . . There is no magical, maternal gene that gets turned on because a woman gives birth or adopts a child. Motherhood is a process. It is a journey. It may or may not begin with desire, but a part of becoming a mother is perchance growing into this state of being."

I'd been sold a story of white, middle-class, nuclear motherhood as *real* motherhood, perfect motherhood, the motherhood that is put on a pedestal and bowed down to by those in charge, where women don't have to work outside of the home and are dependent on male breadwinners. Or work outside the home in underpaid and undervalued roles.

Who benefits when women spend even more time mothering than at any time in history? Who benefits when women believe that they aren't good enough mothers? Who benefits when women don't have enough time for their kids or their work or themselves?

The patriarchy, of course. Or as Adrienne Rich calls it, "the machinery of institutional violence wrenching at the experience of motherhood."

It took Rich going on an extended vacation alone with her sons to feel what outlaw motherhood could really look and feel like. "Without school hours, fixed routines, naps, the conflict of being both mother and wife with no room for being simply, myself . . . we had broken together all the rules of bedtime, the night rules, rules I myself thought I had to observe in the city or become a 'bad mother.' We were conspirators, outlaws from the institution of motherhood."

I wanted to be an outlaw mother, too.

11

Sixty Dates in Six Months

I f I had to sum up the reasons for my divorce in seven words or less, I'd say: I didn't admit to my deepest desires.

Once I was single, I promised myself I would tell anyone I dated exactly how I was feeling from the get-go. Night after night I sat on the sticky stool at the bar just blocks from my apartment in Brooklyn and watch as men's eyes glazed over when it was clear I wanted more than just a fling. I could tell they thought I was needy, desperate. And looking back, they were right. I was. I was desperate for human contact. I was desperate for care and attention. I was desperate for love. But I was also desperate not to desire any of these things. I was desperate to go it alone. If I didn't need other humans, no one and nothing could hurt me, right?

My mask worked for a while.

I went on sixty dates in six months.

Here were the rules I set out for myself. No dinners unless

I'd met the guy first and already knew we had something to talk about. No more than one drink because of the law of diminishing returns—the more I drank, the worse I tended to feel afterward. No canceling plans with friends for a date. No going out of my way to meet a man where it was convenient for him unless it was also convenient for me. Quick coffees near my office or my apartment were a win. And so were walks. Both would give me an out if I needed one.

Most of the dates were forgettable, but here are a few more memorable ones:

There was the time I met two different guys in one night, saying goodbye to one, circling the block and then sitting back down on the same barstool to wait for the next one to arrive.

There was the man who was already on his second whiskey when I arrived on time for our date, who announced he'd signed his divorce papers just that morning. He then told me with a "Can you believe it?" look in his eyes that his ex-wife couldn't "get over her miscarriage." *Her* miscarriage.

There was the man who only wanted to talk about his "crazy" mother.

The doctor who wanted to buy a house upstate where his someday wife would live with their someday children while he commuted to the city for work. "But I love my career," I said, and he just stared at me blankly.

The sneaker enthusiast who only wanted me to send him naked photos of myself.

The guy who on paper seemed great but I felt no chemistry with.

The one who I felt a ton of chemistry with but stopped responding to my texts.

The one who helped me move my stuff out of my storage unit postdivorce but I couldn't imagine ever having sex with.

Two months went by. When I told my therapist about my dates she said, "You're not trying to fall in love with every guy. You just need one."

During the day, I continued working at my new job as a public relations executive so I could pay the bills and write at night. In the slivers of time between working and writing, I swiped on dating apps. I didn't use any special techniques. Instead, I did what all of my single friends did: try to meet in person with the men I matched with as quickly as possible to determine if there was anything there.

I couldn't help but see dating as an extension of the research I'd read on sperm and eggs. Look at any science journal and you'll see it, too. Sperm are rugged. Eggs are fragile. Sperm compete against each other for the prized egg. Eggs are a precious resource—only one per month!—passively sitting around hoping for the sperm to ask for the damn directions already so they can reach the finish line.

"It is remarkable how 'femininely' the egg behaves and how 'masculinely' the sperm," writes the professor and anthropologist Emily Martin. The egg is seen as passive. It's "transported," "swept," "drifts." Sperm, on the other hand, "deliver," "activate," "propel," "burrow," "penetrate." Eggs are like wallflowers at the dance, waiting to be chosen. Never mind that the egg is twenty times the size of the sperm! Sperm are racing to penetrate every egg—aka woman—they meet.

This seemed to be my mom's own understanding of the world. Men rode white horses and kept safety nets in their back pockets. Women smiled and waved and looked pretty. And so even as I grew into my feminism in college and beyond, there was at some unconscious level a part of me that wanted to be rescued. And then there was another part of me that wanted an equal—a life partner to have and to hold and to raise a baby with at the "advanced maternal age" (my doctor's words, not mine) of thirty-nine.

Intellectually, I understood that I didn't need a man to sweep me off my feet. But heads and hearts don't always agree. When I reviewed the past months of dating, I saw that I'd been waiting for a man to choose me, to see me as worthy of being his partner. I realized that I would have to start giving myself permission to choose the kind of partner I wanted. I would have to realize that I had the agency to decide what I was looking for—and to go after it.

Around that time, I invited my friend Amanda over for cocktails and asked her if we could swipe for each other. Amanda is gorgeous by anyone's standard. Tall and lanky with long legs. Long brown hair cut in perfect, face-flattering layers. An expensive, stylish wardrobe.

I told Amanda that instead of sitting on the sidelines, I planned on stepping into my power, so to speak. I would define what I was searching for. I would be interviewing the men I dated to be sure they fit my rubric. The men I had gone for previously were conventionally attractive mansplainers who never grew up. The only thing they had in common was that they all pursued me feverishly. Now I would focus on widening my options. Whatever I had been doing wasn't working. So what if I threw my requirements out the window?

"After sixty dates, I'm back at square one. I'm going to try something different," I confided to Amanda between sips of my vodka soda. "I'm gonna swipe right on any man who doesn't have an obvious red flag like a Trump sign or a tiger."

She seemed skeptical, but I was determined. "I'm convinced that there are men on these apps that don't take great photos or don't know how to have sexy banter and get passed up by most women," I said. "Those are the men I'm looking for."

She moved farther away from me on the couch. "I'm not letting you swipe for me then," she said, hiding her phone under her leg as I fake-grabbed for the device.

"Listen, I'm not saying you have to settle. I'm just saying you should go out on at least one date with men who may seem mildly attractive in their photos," I said. "I bet they just don't know how to take good pictures. Bathroom mirror selfies don't work for *anyone.*"

"No way," she said, shaking her head. "I have standards."

"I'll drink to that," I said, reaching out to clink her glass.

By the end of the night, we were sitting next to each other, drunkenly swiping on our own phones, occasionally showing each other someone's profile and asking, "Him?"

12

Ghosts

There's something I didn't mention about all those dates. Something that I planned to leave out. Something I never wanted to write about.

I tried to write around it. Believe me, I tried. I wrote myself into cul-de-sacs to avoid it. It's impossible to avoid, though. Because the narrative doesn't make sense—it doesn't ring true—without it.

So here it is: one of those sixty dates was a man named Daniel. From the first moment I met him he seemed familiar, comforting. He had blue-gray eyes, receding brown hair, and a stubbly beard that made him always seem slightly disheveled. He was kind, smart, but most of all we had fun together. We traveled to Spain and Oregon. We drank pinot noir and small-batch whiskey. We met each other's families. We hiked mountains and lay curled up in bed talking about our pasts and what we hoped for the future. Half a year after we met, he died by suicide.

I've thought a lot about what more to say about him, and here's what I've decided is important for you to know. That I thought Daniel and I were going to get married. That I believed we were on the road to starting a family together. That we had lived together, and then he broke up with me, and on the night he went missing I believed we were going to meet to discuss getting back together. I was already imagining our conversation. How he would say, "You're the best thing that ever happened to me" and that breaking up with me three weeks before "had been a big mistake."

But instead of making plans of where to meet with Daniel, I received a text from his father, asking if I had heard from him. When I told him I hadn't, I called Daniel's phone. No answer. So I raced to his apartment to see if he was there. He wasn't. I spent the rest of the night sitting on his couch reaching out to everyone who knew him to see if anyone had heard anything. At the same time, I felt ashamed that he was missing. *What kind of girlfriend loses her boyfriend?* The policeman who came to Daniel's apartment door that night asked me to search it for clues. His family wasn't in New York City, so I was the one who had to look in his closet to see if anything was missing. At the time I couldn't imagine that something was seriously wrong with Daniel. Instead, I scurried around his apartment with the eyes of a girlfriend who thinks she might find proof of another woman. I kept imagining him walking back in the door and asking me what I was doing there. I even practiced how I would say, "Oh, I'm so sorry to bother you. I'm glad you're safe."

I searched for Daniel for twenty-four hours, and I'll never forget that lost-keys feeling, that tingling like a phantom limb as I retraced my steps, certain that at any moment I'd find him. After the dogs were sent in and the helicopters, after I slept on his couch with my phone in my hand, waiting for him to walk in the door, I blacked out when the voice on the phone said, "He's dead."

I want you to know that Daniel took his own life by jumping off a mountain one hour and forty-five minutes from Brooklyn, where he lived. That he had a mother, a father, and a brother who loved him. That as I sat in shock at his funeral, and everyone discussed their surprise that such a laid-back, happy-seeming guy could do this, I felt sure that I knew why he had. I could remember every single conversation we ever had about having a baby—how I asked him when he thought he'd be ready, what kind of father he hoped to be, and, of course, what we would name our phantom child. I could hear my voice, nagging and prodding. Pushing. I stared at my hands, my dark funeral dress, listening to those around me cry and tell stories. I felt full of sorrow. But isolated, too, at a remove from the grief of his family and friends. I hugged people, made conversation, stood in the receiving line next to his loved ones. It's natural after a suicide to feel tremendous guilt, to think through all you might have done differently. Objectively, I know that. And still, all that week, and during the weeks that followed, I couldn't shake the feeling that I was uniquely at fault for Daniel's death. I now know I was just being hard on myself, but in my mind it felt like I was a woman whose desire for a child was so strong it could push a man from a mountain.

AFTER DANIEL DIED, I wanted to pause, to give myself the space to grieve. But three days later, I turned thirty-nine. There was no celebration. My birthday was a reminder that time was marching forward. That tomorrow would come and the day after and eventually I'd be forty, which is the age when I believed any eggs I had left would shrivel up and become useless.

To be a woman who is filled with desire is unseemly. To be seen as ravenous for motherhood is to arouse contempt. Women are supposed to take what they're given and like it. Women are supposed to be happy with the crumbs. Women are supposed to keep a poker face. To want, but not to show it. Don't be a try-hard. Don't show your cards. I've never been good at poker, though.

IN MY MIND, I didn't have time to wait to heal. I needed to push forward. I needed to keep dating. Within weeks of Daniel's death, I was back on the apps. There were dates when I could feel my lip tremble as I tried to hold back tears from whatever man was sitting across from me. There was the date where I told a man who had the unfortunate name of Daniel that my Daniel had just died.

There was an awkward pause during which, having started to cry, I told him I had to leave.

I look back and cringe. Why couldn't I give myself space to heal? Why did I always think I was running out of time? What was the rush? But of course I know the answers to those questions. Everyone and everything around me told me I was late to the game. That I'd gotten it all wrong. That I'd messed up. That I'd never be a mother.

AFTER DANIEL'S DEATH, so many people asked me if I'd seen any red flags.

As in, could I have stopped him?

As in, could I have known what was to come?

As in, what did I miss?

At the time my answer was no.

But now, I'm not so sure.

The truth is that there probably were red flags waving in front of my face, but I was so blinded by my desire for a baby that I saw nothing but green when I should have seen red.

I denied myself motherhood for so long that when it finally seemed in my grasp it was all I could see.

13

The Woman I'm Not

That night with Amanda when I decided to change my dating strategy once and for all came in the wake of Daniel's death. I felt unsteady, like a baby learning to walk. My legs felt new. My heart did, too. New and raw.

Amanda arrived at my apartment to be my support system as I waded back into the dating waters. She and others told me I could wait. I didn't have to rush. I could take time off. But I wanted to *do* something. I panicked. Momentum was the only way I felt in control.

I knew from my therapist that love was a numbers game. The more people you meet, the more likely you'll be to find the one person you click with. I figured if I opened up the pool of potential mates, I'd give myself more to choose from. And now I was the one who would be doing the choosing. I was no longer waiting to be chosen.

I'd watched friends like Amanda scrawl long lists of all

their requirements in a partner. One friend admitted to me that she was searching for a lumberjack in a tuxedo. Another that her future husband needed to be six foot five or taller. And still another that he had to be Jewish, but not *too* Jewish. I laughed at that one. At our age, trying to meet a man to have a serious commitment with at all felt like searching for a needle in a haystack. Jewish people are only 0.2 percent of the world's population. While I'm Jewish and would have welcomed a Jewish partner, that seemed like narrowing an already small pool into a miniscule one.

Instead, after that night drunk-swiping with Amanda I decided to make a list of my baseline requirements. Just like my entrepreneur friends created an MVP, or minimum viable product, to test out their ideas in the marketplace, I set out to look for another kind of MVP, a minimum viable partner. I didn't know exactly what I was looking for. I was more of the I'll-know-it-when-I-see-it type. But I knew, at the very least, he had to be kind, patient, smart, open to a committed relationship, ready to have children, and support my career and creative pursuits.

With that in mind, I was back on the dating apps pretending to myself and everyone around me that I was ready to fall in love again. In hindsight, even the bare-bones prerequisites I set out are hard to find. Yet night after night I swiped right on anyone and everyone who seemed like they could meet what I viewed as a very low bar for entry into my life.

So many of my friends complained that their match-to-date ratio was tiny. They'd match with five guys but three of those would fizzle out before they got to the first date, and one would ghost them. My idea was to increase my matches so I could in turn increase the number of dates I actually went on. Dates were something that wouldn't take too much time out of my already overscheduled life. Even so, dating felt like a full-time job. A dead-end one at that. One where there was likely no future.

Until I met Rob, six months after Daniel's death. Rob was one of those guys I may have missed out on in the past. From his profile, he seemed thoughtful, intentional, not the type who would have made the first move. Reaching out to him felt like sending a message in a bottle out to sea, but he responded quickly, and our banter became the anchor I'd been longing for in my life.

When we met in person, I learned that Rob is a drummer with long hair and holes in the right pocket of his jeans where his key ring pushed through the denim. He turned out to be everything I said I wanted—kind, patient, smart, supportive of my career and creative pursuits, and so much more—*except* he wasn't ready for a committed relationship. He was separated from his wife, not even divorced. I guess I could have run, but by then I understood just how hard it was to meet someone who met even *one* of the bullet points on my dating rubric. When I started dating, I thought almost anyone except the insane and insolvent could pass my test. Only now do I realize that love is a puzzle that takes two people to create. The pieces that fit with one person may not fit with the next. The parts of you that are round can become square and hardened when rubbed up against the wrong person. Your jagged edges get smoothed out by the right one.

I lay in bed ruminating about what my friends would say when I told them I was dating again, and a not-even-divorced-yet drummer at that. The drummer is the guy you date in college. Not the guy you try to have a baby with. Or at least that's what I imagined my friends would say.

But it didn't even matter what my friends thought I should do about Rob, because he didn't want to settle down. Not yet anyway. And meanwhile, my mind was telling me that I didn't have time to waste.

"I want to date other people," he said gently on date number three. He'd been with someone for the past seven years, and now they'd been separated for less than three months and there was no way he wanted to be locked into another relationship so quickly. He wanted to go out and listen to music at rock clubs. He wanted to play the field. Have sex with strangers. Drink too much.

"You should," I said. "I want the same thing." And a part of me did. I wanted to see who else was out there. To have uninhibited sex. To revel in postdivorce freedom. But I also had a voice in my head that screamed: *You don't have time. A baby is not just going to make itself, you know. Come on already. What are you DOING?*

I didn't let any part of that show, though. Instead, I said, "Go ahead," even though I hoped he wouldn't actually date anyone else.

In those early days, what registered most about Rob was that he seemed gentle, like he had a good head on his shoulders. We also had a lot in common. We both liked to travel, were well-read, and cared about the world around us. But how did I *feel* about Rob? I couldn't tell you. When it came to dating men, the formula had always been: Did *he* like *me*? Love had never been about what I wanted. It was about finding someone who would accept me. In many ways, I wasn't so different from the kid I'd once been, the one who felt she was always outside looking in. If someone—anyone—was willing to choose me as a partner, then I counted that as "enough." The only way that had changed after my divorce was that it had become about who might want to choose me as the mother of their child, too.

Looking back, on paper at least, Rob was all wrong for me. I was the first person he'd met when he joined the dating apps. He was three years younger than me and wasn't 100 percent certain he wanted children. He wasn't against them like my ex-husband, Evan, had been, but he wasn't ready to jump in either.

When I first told Rob I wanted a baby, he said what in retrospect seems smart: "But we don't even know each other. How do you know you want to have a kid with *me*?" Yet in my mind, I figured if we wanted it to work, we could make it work. He was from a small town in Ohio, with two parents who had been married since they were teenagers. Everything about him screamed "normal." And to me, that's all it took to start a family. Given the sets of parents I grew up with, normal equaled stable, normal equaled safe, normal was all that was needed. I figured Rob had good role models, so he'd know what to do when it came to maintaining a relationship over the long term while raising a small human. And as long as we were committed to the project of having a child together, we were way ahead of the pack. Thinking too much about the decision seemed detrimental. In fact, I worried that the more we thought about it, the less of a chance we'd have of actually starting a family together.

I'd read about an experiment conducted in the 1990s at the University of Virginia in which students were asked to select one of five posters—either an impressionist painting or a picture of an animal. Whichever poster they chose they could take home with them.

The crux of the study was that half of the participants were asked to analyze why they made the choice they did and write down their reasoning. It turns out that those who explained their pick in writing more often than not regretted their choice and wished they'd picked a different poster altogether. The conclusion? "The simple act of thinking about why you feel the way you do can change your mind about how you feel," said University of Virginia psychologist Timothy Wilson, who headed the poster study. "That can be very consequential."

I told myself that if Rob and I chose each other and sealed the deal with a kid, we'd be much happier than if we swam after all the fish in the sea, refusing to commit until we reeled in the perfect one. Ignorance, in my mind, could be bliss.

ON THE NIGHTS Rob wasn't at my place or I wasn't at his, I went out on dates with other men and imagined all of the women Rob was making out with at that very moment. Beautiful musicians with melodic singing voices. Badass drummers who expressed their emotions by banging out their favorite tunes. Smarty-pants sirens covered in tattoos.

He's going to find someone else, I told myself as I anxiously tossed and turned alone in my bed. But I couldn't let Rob know that. He had to think I was having the time of my life with other men. He had to worry he'd lose me if he didn't jump at the chance to be with me right that very second. Isn't that how the dating game works? It's a marketplace, after all— and the markets, I'd learned as a reporter at *Forbes* all those years ago, were all about perception.

I'd tried so hard to be the "cool girl" Gillian Flynn talks about in *Gone Girl.* "Cool Girls are above all hot. Hot and understanding. Cool Girls never get angry; they only smile in a chagrined, loving manner and let their men do whatever they want. Go ahead, shit on me, I don't mind, I'm the Cool Girl. And the Cool Girls are even more pathetic: they're not even pretending to be the woman they want to be, they're pretending to be the woman a man wants them to be."

Now to be clear, there's no question, I was pathetic. I'd been pathetic in my marriage and pathetic with Daniel and I was doing it all over again with Rob. I was pretending to be the woman I thought he wanted me to be. The one who dated around. The one who just wanted sex. Why? Because I always believed I had to force people to love me. Like if I didn't put them in a cage and trap them they wouldn't stick around. Niceness was my way to bait the trap. Being seen as good was, too. I had to be easygoing. I had to be chill. I couldn't just *be.*

Here I was just a little over a year after my divorce, and half a year since Daniel's death, performing once again. I now realize that performance is built into society's ideals around womanhood. If we don't perform, we're told (or made to believe), we won't have fulfilling careers. If we don't perform, no man will want us. If we don't perform, we won't have children. There's always a woman willing to give more, do more, *be* more, around the next corner. Capitalism tells us that if we don't shut the fuck up and do our jobs someone else will be waiting in the wings to do more for less. Relationships are no different. And the dating apps prove it. We swipe and swipe and swipe, convinced our perfect match is out there. I stayed with Evan for so long because I knew, even if what he had to give didn't feel like enough, there was another woman who would be glad to step into my place. And where would that leave me?

Later, I'd read Megan Stielstra's beautiful book *The Wrong Way to Save Your Life,* and wish I'd had a big sister/friend/mother figure/fairy godmother to come into my life and deliver the message Megan does there: "If you're hiding parts of yourself to look cool or make someone love you, please repeat after me: fuck that noise. You are perfect. You matter . . . Find people who love these things, too."

But I wasn't yet willing to bank on the possibility that someone might love me. I was instead willing to contort myself and hide myself—to be the embodiment of what America Ferrera talks about in her now-famous monologue in the movie *Barbie*. "You have to never get old, never be rude, never show off, never be selfish, never fall down, never fail, never show fear, never get out of line . . . And it turns out in fact that not only are you doing everything wrong, but also everything is your fault."

We have these cultural moments like in Gillian Flynn's *Gone Girl* and Greta Gerwig's *Barbie* in which these paradoxes of womanhood get named, but after the credits roll or the book falls off the bestseller list, we are left to ourselves to try to outrun the reality of living under the patriarchy. And when we can't, it's easy to revert to thinking that there's something wrong with *us*. Instead of remembering that the system is designed to make women feel like we have an open road ahead of us when, really, we're just hamsters on a wheel, we point our fingers at ourselves. As philosopher Kate Manne writes, misogyny polices women, coerces them, and demands they uphold the norms and expectations of the patriarchy. "A bit like the shock collar worn by a dog to keep them behind one of those invisible fences that proliferate in suburbia," misogyny upholds male dominance by telling women to be good and give men their due. And if they don't, they'll be punished.

That feeling that I was always being punished for some invisible transgression? That wasn't all in my head. It's the shock collar of the patriarchal system.

And yet I was still bent on "performing" being the impossible woman, someone who is able to transcend all the contradictions of the American feminine ideal, because in some way *that* felt easier than finding someone who might love what I loved.

Sitting here now, I can hear all those imaginary voices in my head mocking me for not being true to myself, not knowing whether I wanted a child until it was almost too late, not knowing whether I should stay in a marriage that wasn't right for me. Yet how could we as women possibly know what our true selves desire when we've been forced to perform our whole lives? How could we possibly hear our own voices when the white noise of the patriarchal machine drowns them out?

JOAN DIDION FAMOUSLY wrote, "It is easy to see the beginnings of things, and harder to see the ends," but if I had to pinpoint the moment I began to be more real, the moment I stopped performing, I couldn't. The seeds had been planted surreptitiously until I turned around and couldn't help but notice that something was different. A garden of tulips had suddenly bloomed where before there were none.

On my first date with Rob, in a now-defunct coffee shop a handful of blocks from my apartment, I felt something thaw (or at least that's how it feels in retrospect). He had been telling me about the decade he'd spent meditating as a way to release the childhood scripts that no longer worked for him, and a thought flapped like a butterfly's wings through my mind. It was barely there, not even fully formed. But in the haze of pleasure that hung over that entire first meeting, I wondered what scripts I wanted to let go of. I wondered what I had left to lose. If I showed Rob my true self, if I said to him in so many words, "Look, here's me. I'm thirty-nine, I want a baby, I'm exhausted from trying to perform for the world, I'm

divorced, I'm flawed, do you want to give this thing a try?"
What's the worst that could happen? He could run away? He
could say, "Nah, you're not for me?" Well, then at least I'd
know he wasn't right instead of wasting more time.

Typing these words all these years later, it seems so obvious.
The only thing that made sense was to try and be the real me
from the get-go. But I'd been faking it for so long I wasn't sure
what *real* even looked like anymore.

I'd spent my whole life telling everyone what they wanted
to hear. In elementary school the custody arrangement between
my parents outlined that I split each week between them
evenly. One week I'd spend Monday, Wednesday, and Friday
with my mom, and Tuesday and Thursday with my dad. The
next week I'd alternate. Weekends they passed me back and
forth, too. I became half a person. When I was with my mom,
I knew it would make her happy to hear that I wished I could
live with only her. And when I was with my dad, I told him
what he wanted to hear: that I wanted to live with him. My
friendships were filled with make-believe, too. I wanted to fit
in, so I contorted myself to become more palatable. In high
school I was a cheerleader even though I had no interest in it.
I hooked up with whoever asked me to, unable to untangle my
own desire from that of the boys who wanted me. By the time
I was a junior in college I was dating a guy named Billy, and
he had our whole lives planned out for us. When I graduated,
I would move to Ann Arbor, Michigan, to live with him while
he went to grad school. We'd get engaged, and when he finished his master's program, we'd move together to Wyoming
so he could get a PhD. We'd get married. Have two kids. It
sounded stifling, suffocating, a total snooze fest. I wanted none
of it. But I didn't have the heart to tell him. Instead, I had to
blow it all up. I started dating someone else I met while wait-

ressing at a pizza restaurant near campus, and when Billy and
I were making the cross-country drive to Ann Arbor to start
our lives together, I chose that moment to break the news: I
was in love with someone else. I watched his face crumple and
realized that I'd created this whole hurtful drama because I
couldn't tell Billy the truth. I didn't want to follow his dream;
I wanted to figure out my own. But why couldn't I just say
that?

The only time I was able to hear my own voice was when I
was alone, which is how I ended up spending my early twenties backpacking around Southern and East Africa. I could
push everyone else's desires far out of my mind only when I was
halfway across the world. On a rickety bus in Malawi or a dhow
sailing off the coast of Mozambique, I could disconnect from
the voices telling me what the world needed me to be (or
needed from me). I no longer worried about my mom's mental
state or the services Adam was or wasn't getting from Massachusetts. I was on another continent as my friends climbed
career ladders, got engaged, and made decisions about where
to live or what grad programs to enroll in—milestones that
might have made me more aware of how I was falling behind.
In the early 2000s, it was still possible to cut yourself off from
the world. My cellphone was a flip phone that I had to reload
with minutes whenever it ran out. I didn't give anyone back
home my phone number. The surface reason was because it
would cost them a fortune to call. But I also wanted to avoid
anything that would hook me back into the claustrophobia of
my family—make me conscious of all the ways my dad was
disappointed in the decisions I made, all the guilt I felt about
how my mom's life had turned out. If I wanted to email someone, I had to find an internet café in a big city like Nairobi or
Johannesburg, and then wait to receive a reply the next time I

was able to find internet (which could be days or weeks). It was in the quiet of my own tent at night or lying in a bunk bed in a hostel that I started to form the first sketchy ideas of who I wanted to be in the world.

But despite all of that, when I met Evan at thirty-one, I still let him paint the contours of our relationship. He wanted to be with me—and he was willing to offer me the stability and security I'd never had—but all of that came with the price that he didn't want kids. By then I was so used to believing that everyone else's version of reality was the "right" one. If Evan loved me, I should love him back. If he didn't want kids, I could make a child-free life work for me. It's impossible to know anymore if I really wanted the life Evan had envisioned for us or if I was just going along for the ride.

On that first date with Rob, I sensed that I wanted things to be different. That I wanted him to know who I really was. That I wanted to have a say in what this relationship was going to be from the start. And I wanted to know him, too. So on our second date, wandering aimlessly through the brownstone-lined streets of my neighborhood, I told Rob that there was something I wanted to share with him, but that I wasn't ready to share it yet. I wanted him to know about Daniel. I was headed to Australia for two weeks, so we wouldn't see each other until I was back. By then, I hoped, I'd get up the nerve to tell him. He would either stay or go, but at least I'd be living in reality instead of some fantasy I'd built up in my own head.

Rob and I texted every day while I was away. Funny jokes, long, winding conversations that would have been best left for when we saw each other again, but since two weeks seemed like two years, we awkwardly typed into those tiny boxes on our cellphones everything we wanted to say in person.

When I finally returned and we had our third date, we stood in my kitchen, unpacking boxes of misshapen vegetables from my farm share so I could cook us the dinner I'd been promising since before I left. Now felt like as good a time as any. If this was to be our last supper, at least we'd flame out with a good meal in our bellies. If it worked out between us, it would be a dinner we'd never forget.

"Remember when I told you I had a secret?" I asked, and Rob nodded. He looked like he was holding his breath, but I didn't want to pay too much attention to what he was feeling then, or I might lose my nerve. Instead, as the fading light streamed through my kitchen window, I blurted out the whole story. That after my divorce there was someone else. His name was Daniel. I thought we were going to get married and start a family together. "And then six months after we met, he took his own life. It was sudden. I didn't even know he was depressed. Or that anything was wrong. The truth is that I'm scared as soon as you get to know me, you're going to leave, too. Or decide you can't get far enough away from me and kill yourself."

I don't remember what Rob said in response. *I'm so sorry? Wow, that's a lot? Oh, Ruthie?* But what I do remember is that he took me in his arms and hugged me, and I hoped our embrace would never end. I didn't know if that meant he was sticking around, or if he'd decide later that this was all too much and leave. At that moment, though, it didn't matter. I felt seen. I felt heard. I felt like I was showing him the real me.

After that, we started cooking dinner. He chopped the onions and garlic for the stir-fry, while I made the couscous. By then it was dark, and the ice cubes in our whiskeys had melted. "I thought I knew what your secret was going to be," he said as I set the table. He was smiling. I stopped and looked up at him, confused. "While you were in Australia, I was googling you and noticed that your Google Plus profile said your gender was male."

Google Plus? Who uses Google Plus?

It took me a second to grasp what he was trying to say. I was thinking more about the fact that he had googled me and what he possibly could have learned about me from the internet.

And then it clicked.

"Wait? You thought I was a man?" I screeched, pushing his arm playfully for emphasis. We were both uncomfortably laughing now.

"Well, I didn't know," he admitted sheepishly. "The only friends we had in common on Facebook had both transitioned, so I thought anything was possible."

I was incredulous. Here I was, worried that Rob would bolt as soon as he heard about Daniel. That taking off my mask would be too much for him. And yet Rob had come to my apartment that night open to whatever I had to say, and if that included the disclosure that I was a trans woman, that hadn't sent him running. He was willing to stick around—to hear me out—to take whatever curveball I might throw at him. Unlike Billy or Evan, Rob didn't have hardened ideas about his vision for his life that I had to slot into. He wasn't easily scared off by emotion. He understood life was a river, constantly changing, churning, never the same from moment to moment.

ROB AND I had been dating for two months when I asked him if he wanted to come with me to Staten Island, the forgotten borough of New York City, for an off-the-beaten-path adventure. We are both big nerds for this city. I'd spent several years reporting in Staten Island, working on a book project about a group of Liberian refugees who had fled there after the civil war. Although the book I was writing had ultimately stalled out, I still had a special place in my heart for the streets and bus routes that had shaped so much of my early days as a journalist.

I now wanted to share that excitement with Rob. I figured we'd get up early, take the ferry over to Staten Island, and then walk through the neighborhood of Rosebank to Alice Austen's house, which is now a museum dedicated to the life of one of America's earliest and most prolific female photographers. I'd been to the Alice Austen House once years before, and I was obsessed with Alice. She never married, instead spending five decades with her partner, Gertrude Tate. Alice was the first woman on Staten Island to own a car, a big deal in the late 1800s. She was a woman who didn't follow the rules. She carried up to fifty pounds of equipment with her on her bicycle when she went out to take photos. Through her lens, she captured the private lives of her friends as well as strangers. A website for the Alice Austen House says Alice "was a rebel who broke away from the constraints of her Victorian environment and forged an independent life that broke boundaries of acceptable female behavior and social rules." She was everything I wanted to be. Though I wasn't a lesbian, I wanted an independent life that broke boundaries and flouted social rules, too. The problem was that I also wanted marriage and motherhood, two things that Alice had either decided against or had not been allowed to choose.

After wandering the museum, Rob and I held hands as we walked down to the sandy patch of beach in front of Alice's house. To our right was the Verrazzano-Narrows Bridge and to the left was water as far as we could see. But we barely noticed the beach in front of us until I looked down and a piece of bright green sea glass caught my eye. And then another. And another. Not just green, but blue and white and even some rare brown ones, too. Suddenly we were bent over collecting handfuls of sea glass—jagged, one-of-a-kind mementos that we ran to show each other, each one more special than the last. "You have to see this one," I said excitedly, holding a blue one up to the sun, a gorgeous shade of lapis lazuli.

"And this one," Rob said, showing me a flat one, green as the nearby grass.

By the time we got to the Sri Lankan restaurant where we planned to eat lunch, our pockets were full of bright-colored glass that had been weathered by life and made all the more beautiful because of it.

I'd already known long before then that I didn't want Rob to date other people, but that day on Staten Island I was ready to put my desire into words. I wanted to be exclusive. I didn't want either of us to date anyone else. Again, I felt that familiar fear rise up inside of me. I knew there was a chance I might lose him if I told him the truth, yet I also knew I couldn't continue not knowing whether he wanted to be my boyfriend. I felt silly—a thirty-nine-year-old woman wondering if the man she was dating wanted to go steady. But maybe life is not about growing up. It's about making the same mistakes over and over until we're finally ready to try something different and end up getting it right.

Later that night, when Rob and I were kissing in bed, I popped the question: "Will you be my boyfriend?" I held my breath, studying his face for clues as to his answer. Before he could say anything, though, I did what I always do when I get nervous, I kept talking. I felt bare lying there and used words to cover up my discomfort. "I don't want you to date other people," I said. "I want you all to myself."

He paused and I could feel my heart preparing to crumble. Then he said, "I want that, too."

It took me a second to realize that I had named what I wanted, and I had gotten it. I let go of the breath I'd inadvertently been holding. I was brave in a way I'd never been before. Instead of waiting for Rob to tell me what he wanted us to be, I had stated my desires clearly. As good as it felt, it also felt frightening. New. Like an old version of me had died. Like I was out on a limb with no safety net. If I fell, who would catch me? If I stumbled, who would bandage my scraped knees? Then again, maybe I didn't need a safety net. Maybe I just needed to trust that when I got knocked down, I would be able to attend to my own wounds. Instead of looking for someone else to swoop in and save me, I had to let go and see what would happen. I had to have faith that even when I fumbled, I'd get back up again. Suffering is not a blip. It's inherent to life. I couldn't stop myself from tripping no matter how hard I tried. I just had to believe that, in the words of the old song, I could pick myself up and begin again. I'd learned this truth before, but I needed to return to it. I was never going to be perfect. My family wasn't either. My whole life would be an ongoing negotiation with sorrow and suffering.

That night, when I fell asleep in Rob's arms, the bed and the room and our breath felt more solid than it ever had before.

14

Cowgirl SeaHorse

Rob and I spent that first year of our relationship in what I'd now call denial. I have a photo of us taken at my fortieth birthday party. I'm wearing a white and yellow eyelet shirtdress, surrounded by friends. I'm beaming, buzzing with the alcohol, yes, but also the energy of all the love focused on me at that moment. We're in the garden of a bar in Brooklyn. Too many of us squeezed into a picnic table. What the picture can't capture is that everyone is going around the table talking about what they love most about me. When it's Rob's turn, he waxes on about how lucky he feels to have met me. We'd only been dating half a year, but it felt like we'd always known each other. That finding each other was inevitable in some way, although, of course, it wasn't. I don't remember his exact words, but I remember the feeling: that after the boat rocking of the last year and a half, Rob felt stable. Rob felt right. The ghosts of his ex-wife and Evan—and of Daniel, too—still haunted us.

But it felt like their grip had loosened, even if it was just the tiniest bit.

Now I can see that those first six months with Rob felt like a honeymoon of sorts, but I also remember waiting for a wrong turn, a red flag I hadn't noticed before, or I had brushed aside, to make itself known. I was constantly peering at the horizon, searching for the first clues that danger was imminent.

There was also this: forty felt like a big deal to me. It was the age—the deadline really—that according to conventional wisdom was the bright line in women's lives. If something hadn't been accomplished by forty—children, marriage, a career you loved—it wasn't going to happen. In fact, a cover story published in *Newsweek* magazine in 1986 claimed that single, white, college-educated women over forty like me were "more likely to be killed by a terrorist than find a mate."

When it appeared, the *Newsweek* article detonated a bomb in women's lives, and its cultural shrapnel remains to this day. In 1989, *When Harry Met Sally* showed a thirty-two-year-old Sally crying to Harry after a breakup that forty was looming, a "big dead end." By 1993, *Sleepless in Seattle* called out *Newsweek*'s terrorism claim as fake news, but it was too late. When Meg Ryan's character, Annie, tells Rosie O'Donnell's character that the terrorism statistic is not true, O'Donnell says, "That's right—it's not true," followed by a reflective addendum: "But it *feels* true."

"*It feels true* is, in retrospect, a perfect way to sum up the thing that gave the grim statistic its staying power, both in the canonical nineties rom-com and in the culture at large," writes Megan Garber in *The Atlantic*. Thirty years after the original *Newsweek* article was published, feeling true was enough to send women everywhere running for cover in marriages that may or may not have been right for them. Few questioned that stat that was snagged from a single source, unpublished when the *Newsweek* article hit newsstands. Even though it was debunked twenty years later, after many of the women in the original study eventually married, it was treated as gospel. In fact, the terrorist line hadn't even been a part of the original study.

In 2006, Jessica Yellin of *The New York Times* reiterated what O'Donnell's character said in *Sleepless in Seattle:* "For a lot of women the retraction doesn't matter. The article seems to have lodged itself permanently in the national psyche."

And crazily enough, it still *feels true* today. For many of us, our inner critics carry the same finger-wagging blame that the *Newsweek* article carried all those years ago: It's our fault if we're single. Either because we've focused on our careers or we haven't measured up in a million ways, big and small. We've selfishly focused on being self-actualized to the detriment of self-actualization. Because while we may have accomplished our creative pursuits and career dreams (if we're lucky), we lost sight of that other more important North Star, love and family.

Now we would have to live with the consequences, society's rising levels of single, childless women. As if we hadn't understood it already. Men had been doing us a favor, choosing us as marriageable, and by doing so, bestowing upon us social status. Or as Wendy Wasserstein writes in *The Heidi Chronicles:* letting us have it all.

When I sat in the Music Box Theatre watching Elisabeth Moss play the lead role in *The Heidi Chronicles* in April 2015, just two months after Evan left me, I felt the sting of those two words: *letting us.* The cry that stuck in my throat was the powerlessness I finally understood. In all of the debates around whether women could have it all, what got lost sight of was that women didn't get to *choose* whether or not they could have it all. They had to hope that men would allow them to. That men would let them into the boys' club of good jobs and opportunities and money and power and, yes, even motherhood. Because if a man didn't choose us, then we'd be forever relegated to second-class status as single moms (if we wanted to have a baby alone)—or worse, childless women. All along I'd been waiting for the day that Evan would "let me" have a child. Now here I was waiting for Rob to let me have a baby, too. The anger I felt was actually a cover for a feeling of profound helplessness.

When I looked to the future, all I saw was a dark cloud of uncertainty, and I addressed it by booting it as far from my mind as I could. And they say denial doesn't work! But it did. For about six more months.

But as summer turned to fall, I could feel time passing more quickly. The yellow and red leaves scattered across the sidewalks of my neighborhood reminded me that life would relentlessly march forward—whether I wanted it to or not. The cool air on my skin whispered, *Remember me? Here I am again.* I'd been so worried about forty, but now I felt forty-one knocking on the door. The more I tried to stop time, the faster it flowed through my fingers.

That October, Rob moved into my apartment, the one I'd settled into after my divorce. It was less than five hundred square feet, and I liked it that way. At the time, my realtor asked me if I wanted to look at bigger places, but I feared that I'd become like an acquaintance I knew who bought an apartment for the life she dreamed of—with a husband and two kids—but a decade later, when that life hadn't materialized, the emptiness of those extra rooms reminded her of everything she *didn't* have. I decided it was better to buy the apartment for the life I was living now, and if and when the time came that I needed something bigger, I hoped I'd be in a position to purchase something with more space. The day that Rob moved in, though, I saw the folly of that decision. His boxes overwhelmed all three rooms of my already-cramped apartment. Not to mention that musicians come with lots of instruments that take up obnoxious amounts of space. There were guitars and electric keyboards, sure, but there was also a vibraphone that was almost three feet high and four feet wide. I eyed its hulking form against a wall. I mean, how could I not? It was bigger than a jukebox, and I had to walk around it to get into my kitchen.

When Rob and I had discussed moving in together, we promised that once we settled into our new life, we would begin talking about a timeline for trying to start a family. The vibraphone seemed like a small price for getting on the path to a future baby.

Rob thought we should wait to have a kid, get to know each other better and travel, something we both loved to do. That sounded wonderful to me, too—of course it did. But then I had to point out the facts: "Biology has a different plan for me." Rob could dillydally all he wanted when it came to baby making. He could take the next year and travel to Antarctica and Serbia, with a stop in Phnom Penh on his way home. He could have a baby at forty-five, fifty, fifty-five even. Alec Baldwin had just had his fifth child at sixty. He'd go on to have three more. As I type this, the headlines are full of stories about Robert De Niro becoming a dad again at seventy-nine and Al Pacino at eighty-three. But *I* couldn't wait. My body had me pinned against the wall, and that made me angry. More than that, furious.

Rob nodded. He understood my resentment and rage. His nods and understanding only made me more mad, though, which certainly didn't make him want to sprint any faster toward starting a family together.

On a crisp evening in November, about a month after he moved in, Rob and I sat next to each other on barstools, our beers standing guard in front of us. We were at Cowgirl Sea-Horse, a neighborhood dive bar in Manhattan's old seaport that feels like it's the last watering hole on the island before you fall into the East River. With its colorful Christmas lights, a raucous trivia night on Wednesdays, and frozen margaritas with blue plastic mermaids as garnish, this was the bar you'd choose to have a fun, carefree night. The place you'd go to escape the rest of the world. In hindsight, why Rob and I chose this bar for a serious conversation about creating a human together is beyond me.

At some point in the night, I asked Rob, "If it were up to you, how long would you wait until we started trying for a family?" as other patrons shouted out their answers to the trivia questions a few feet away from us. What I remember most was what I was really thinking, but not saying out loud: *Why can't we just have unprotected sex like they do in the movies, carelessly, swept up in the moment, and you knock me up? Why do we have to talk about this and strategize and plan and take all of the bliss and passion out of the moment?*

Rob picked up his beer, took a long sip, as if the answer was in the bottom of his glass. "I was thinking five years," he finally said.

Dear Reader, he wasn't joking.

Seeing my shock, Rob put his hand on my knee. "This isn't the end of the world, Ruthie," he said, or maybe looking back that's what I imagined he said.

"How long until *you* want to start a family?" he said.

I wish I had a picture of my face then, because I'm sure it

was a mix of surprise, incredulity, and anger. I felt like I was screaming into a black hole. "Yesterday," I squeaked. There was no amount of time I wanted to wait. In my mind all I saw was a dark, lonely future where I died alone, and it took days (weeks?) until anyone found me.

But Rob could see there were other paths in front of us. He saw compromise. He saw a way to meet in the middle. This was new to me. In my marriage, baby making was Evan's way or the highway. Daniel's death had left no room for discussion either. I'd been so used to living my life at an impasse with others. I had to either flee halfway across the world to find my own voice or contort myself to become what someone else wanted me to be. Not with Rob. His terrifying, and dare I say infuriating, way of being in a relationship was to intentionally, incrementally figure out a way to bring what we each wanted out of life closer together. To be able to see each other's points of view more clearly. My way was to bulldoze past each other's feelings until one of us got what we wanted. If I had a motto it would be: *There are no halfsies in war.*

"What if we split the difference?" Rob said. I looked around to see if the strangers sitting next to us at the bar were hearing him. I was flabbergasted.

"Split the difference?" I repeated slowly. I wish I could say I did this with an open, gentle curiosity about my partner's feelings, but that would be a lie. "And wait another two and a half years?" At this point I thought about flipping over my barstool and running out the door. "Do you know how old I am?"

Of course he did. He had sat next to me at my fortieth birthday party at that twee Brooklyn bar. He also knew I had frozen my eggs, and in his mind that meant there was no expiration date on my fertility. To him, frozen eggs meant we could take the time we needed to get to know each other and be sure we wanted to create a life together. But what I understood acutely, but Rob hadn't thought about, or if he had, he didn't seem to mind, was that we were both still getting older, and every month we waited to have a child meant one month less we'd get to spend with that kid once they were born. Time is a pie, you see, and when you eat the pie it's gone forever. I'd done the math. If I had a child when I was thirty-nine and I died at eighty, I'd have forty-one years with our child. But now that I was forty, I'd only have forty years. And so on. Any delay meant we were borrowing against our child's future with us.

Now it was my turn to touch Rob's leg. "If I were a decade younger," I said, "we could spend the next few years getting to know each other slowly. Meeting each other's families and friends. Traveling. I want that, too." I paused. The trivia game continued around us. There was cheering. Drunk men and women punched the air. "But I'm not thirty. I'm forty."

Rob didn't seem discouraged. "We can always adopt," he said, as if I hadn't already thought of that before. "The planet's on fire and there won't be a future anyway, so adopting a child that's already here would be a mitzvah." He looked to see if I was following. "Why bring another human into our already overpopulated world?"

I knew Rob was right. I loved the *idea* of adopting. But there was also this simple fact: I wanted to know what it felt like to grow a tiny human in my body.

I knew if Rob and I adopted we'd be great parents. Then again, I was wary of all that could go wrong when a child was placed with a new family. I'd read Joan Didion's *Blue Nights* and understood with every cell in my body the what-ifs Didion's adopted daughter, Quintana Roo, was left with even after being raised and loved by Didion and her husband, the writer

John Gregory Dunne. Joan writes about Quintana's anxiety, her alcoholism, and her history of mental health problems that started in childhood. Poignantly, Joan also writes about her own perceived parental failures.

My mother was plagued by her own set of what-ifs after her adoption, too. What if her parents hadn't both died by the time she was eleven? What if she'd been adopted by a loving family? Or what if, better yet, my great-grandmother Kitty hadn't arranged for all four children to be adopted by strangers but instead tried to keep them within the family?

Of course, I knew that plenty of adoptions worked out perfectly well. Adoptive families loved their children. Kids who were adopted turned into well-adjusted adults. But like everything else, my fears of the worst-case scenarios overwhelmed me.

That night Rob and I got no closer to figuring out *when* we'd have a baby. But we did leave with a promise: that we'd go to the fertility clinic where I froze my eggs to talk to the doctor about whether we could wait.

THE FERTILITY DOCTOR was pregnant. I eyed her belly, which made her look like she had an inflated balloon stuck to her midsection.

Rob and I sat next to each other, and she positioned herself across from us. Even behind her hulking wooden desk, you could see the swell of her midsection. She looked down at my chart. She looked up at me. "You have fourteen frozen eggs," she said, as if I'd somehow forgotten.

She continued. "That's great news. Not all women sitting across from me had as much forethought as you did, and it's a very different conversation I have with them." I turned to Rob, and we looked at each other smugly.

"If you thaw all your eggs," she said, "you could have two kids," and Rob and I laughed because we knew we only wanted one. We told her that. "In that case, you could just thaw half of them."

There was a conversation, some back and forth about whether to thaw all or just half of my eggs. There was another conversation about how we should try to have sex on our own for six months and come back if I didn't get pregnant. And then we left, back down the elevator to the street. Back to our lives, where we still believed science could give us the baby it had promised us.

I so badly want to freeze the frame right here. Freeze time when there was still hope that things would go simply. When I still believed I'd done something right by freezing my eggs. When I still believed that life was an equation, and if two plus two equals four, then if you're a good person plus you do the right thing plus you've already experienced some hard losses, then everything has to work out exactly like you want it to.

The truth is much more harrowing. Life is chaos. There is no certainty. No equation. No promise or guarantee that anything will work out. Bad things happen to good people. Good things happen to those who are terrible. No one *deserves* anything. As the Buddhists say, life is suffering. Not just occasionally, but at its core. I could do everything "right" and still end up with no baby. Or end up with a baby who suffered from a genetic mutation like my brother Adam. Or mental illness like my mother. Or any number of other ailments I couldn't predict or even point to.

MONTH AFTER MONTH, Rob and I sat on the rooftop of our building, looking from Brooklyn toward Manhattan, and I would think about my frozen eggs tucked away in one of those buildings and wonder about the day we'd be ready to use them.

It took a while, but just after Thanksgiving I convinced Rob that thawing my eggs didn't mean we'd have a baby *that* day. It was just the first step of many toward having a child someday in the future. We called the fertility clinic and spoke to our doctor, who told us that a few weeks later they would thaw my frozen eggs and mix them with Rob's sperm. One week from then they'd call us back to tell us how many of our embryos were viable. Those days felt like being lost in a dark forest. Like the world was happening outside of the thicket of trees, but somehow I couldn't find my way out. Writer Rebecca Solnit calls losing oneself a "voluptuous surrender . . . utterly immersed in what is present so that its surroundings fade away." But my surroundings didn't fade away. I didn't feel especially capable "of being in uncertainty and mystery," as she writes. The unknown terrified me. I wanted to *know*. I kept looking at the trees with apprehension, wanting one of them to suddenly start talking and give me answers.

The phone rang while I was sitting at my desk. Rob was standing behind me, his hand on my shoulder. I'd been living in suspended animation waiting for that call, but when it came it still felt like a jolt. Like every cell in my body was on high alert. When I answered I listened for clues. Did our doctor sound excited? Full of dread? Were doctors trained to modulate their voices, to reveal only facts and not feelings?

Here's what she said: only eight of my fourteen eggs survived the thaw, and only three of those eight became embryos after being fertilized with Rob's sperm. This was "slightly lower than we had hoped," she admitted. She went on to explain that, unfortunately, the egg-freezing technology in 2013 when I'd frozen my eggs wasn't as good as it is now. The lab once used a slow-freezing technology that they later learned allowed icicles to form, making the eggs more fragile. More recently they started using a faster freezing technology known as vitrification, where the egg or embryo is cooled so quickly that there are no ice crystals. This was great news for the industry and the thousands of women and families that would be freezing their eggs and embryos down the line, but it did nothing for me.

I'd have to wait another week to learn whether the final three embryos continued to divide and grow. "Frozen eggs are always unpredictable." This was the first time she'd mentioned that bit of information. When we were talking about thawing my frozen eggs half a year ago, she made the whole process seem predictable. In fact, she *predicted* we could have two babies with my fourteen eggs. Now it would be a miracle if we had one.

After the call, I couldn't move. I kept repeating the words *slightly lower than we had hoped* in my head. It wasn't slightly lower. It was devastatingly lower. It was so much lower I couldn't get up from my desk.

Doctors can genetically test an embryo once it becomes a blastocyst—a cluster of dividing cells with an outer layer that will eventually form the placenta and an inner layer that develops into the fetus. If any of our three embryos had turned into blastocysts, we'd find out the news over the Christmas holiday when we were in Ohio with Rob's family. But I wanted to be alone. I wanted to fall asleep and not wake up until we knew.

We were walking with Rob's mom near her house the day after Christmas when the nurse called. None of our three embryos had become blastocysts.

"None?" I repeated in disbelief.

"None," the nurse said.

At that moment, I felt like our stalled embryos represented my stalled life. Like my embryos hadn't failed me as much as I'd failed them somehow. Of course, whether our embryos succeeded in creating a baby said nothing about Rob or me as people. But the fact that I was a failure *felt true*. It didn't matter at that moment that whether an embryo is viable and able to develop into a healthy baby comes down to one thing, "dumb genetic luck," as *The Economist* put it.

I'd held on to the illusion of control, and with it some primal belief that doctors carried magic wands and could pull babies out of black hats. "Pregnancy is our first lesson in . . . surrender and submission," writes Angela Garbes in *Like a Mother: A Feminist Journey through the Science and Culture of Pregnancy*. But I didn't want to surrender. I didn't want to submit. Learning that life is beyond our control is hard for all of us, but especially for the generation of women like me who are so used to having a good deal of control over our time, our money, our bodies, and our fertility.

Looking back now, I don't know how I could have been so blind. I'd lived through the nineteen years that the doctors couldn't give us a diagnosis for my brother Adam. I'd lived three decades without a label for my mother's mental health issues. I should have been in a deep relationship with unknowability by now. But somehow I dug my heels in, seeking out certainty from life when it was clear there wasn't any. The reality is that doctors aren't all knowing. They couldn't tell me when or even *if* I'd get pregnant.

Now I understand egg freezing differently, though. Even when the procedure doesn't work, it's still a tool in the toolbox for women and couples who want the *chance* of having a baby. At least I knew I'd done everything in my power to give myself the option of having a child. I wasn't left with regrets. I took a gamble and lost this round. And if I hadn't tried, I may have had felt even worse knowing I didn't do all that I could.

As the psychologist Kathryn Paige Harden writes, there are seventy *trillion* outcomes when a sperm meets an egg. If I was lucky enough to get pregnant, there were seventy trillion ways that our DNA could combine to create the child I hoped for. "The genome of every person is the outcome of nature's Powerball," Harden writes. The child we ended up with, if we had a child at all, would be a roll of the dice.

IT WAS GREGOR MENDEL, known as the father of genetics, who, through his work with pea plants, discovered the laws of inheritance. He figured out that genes come in pairs and are inherited as units, one from each parent. Over the course of seven years, from 1856 to 1863, he examined parental genes and how they are passed down to offspring as dominant or recessive traits. By growing and studying over ten thousand pea plants, Mendel noticed mathematical patterns of heredity from one generation to the next.

I wished with all my heart that humans were as simple as pea plants. When Mendel bred pea plants there were three varieties—tall versus short, wrinkly versus smooth, and green versus yellow. All were determined by a single genetic variant. But in humans, there's no single gene for depression or anxiety or, in my mother's case, borderline personality disorder. "The human characteristics we care most about—things like personality and mental disease, sexual behavior and longevity, intelligence test scores and educational attainment—are influenced by many (very, very, very many) genetic variants, each of which contributes only a tiny drop of water to the swimming pool of genes that make a difference," Kathryn Paige

Harden writes. Intelligence, personality, and mental health are polygenic, meaning they arise from a combination of hundreds or even thousands of genes.

Mendel's ideas about inheritance and heredity came from his work with plants that "breed true." When he bred green plants with each other they formed more green plants. But humans don't breed true, no matter what stories we tell ourselves about family lineage. Children aren't always like their parents. Like doesn't always descend from like.

The truth is that having a child tests the limits of knowability. I would have to let go. I would have to embrace the unforeseen. The doctors couldn't tell us if we could have a child, and they also couldn't tell us whether our child would have an inherited genetic mutation or a spontaneous one or if there'd be a freak accident in childbirth. The truth is that there's no way to know what will happen when two people's genes collide to form a human baby.

"We lived in a world where we had control of so much," writes Ariel Levy in *The Rules Do Not Apply*. "If we didn't want to carry groceries up the steps, we ordered them online and waited in our sweatpants on the fourth floor for a man from Asia or Latin America to come panting up, encumbered with our cat litter and organic bananas . . . Anything seemed possible if you had ingenuity, money, and tenacity. But the body doesn't play by those rules."

When I hung up the phone with the nurse that day, I immediately made an appointment to meet with our doctor in person to discuss next steps. Sitting across from her, her last appointment with me before she went into labor, I realized that frozen eggs, like dating, are a numbers game. "On average only one in ten frozen eggs results in a baby," she had said. What she didn't say is that the science of egg freezing is still relatively new. Women over thirty-five years old are almost 45 percent less likely to get a live birth from egg freezing versus women between thirty to thirty-four years old. But I didn't know that when I froze my eggs at thirty-five.

While the number of women electing to freeze their eggs has increased exponentially since I had my procedure, the number who have returned to try to use their eggs is still quite small. What most don't realize is that the chances of having a child from frozen eggs are dismal at best. Yet clinics keep promising women that you can "invent your future" and that freezing your eggs is an "insurance policy" against your biological clock. Even now, no one really knows just how many women are expecting to thaw their eggs only to realize that the promise of fertility on our own timeline was always too good to be true.

Meanwhile, that January I spent months cursing myself, my marriage to Evan, and the field of fertility science for taking away my chance to have a biological child. I blamed myself for not having been strategic enough. But I also blamed the medical establishment and the media for jumping at the chance to offer women our own version of the American dream—the fantasy that we could have it all, anytime we wanted.

WHEN I FROZE my eggs, I spent close to fifteen thousand dollars on the procedure, which included the exorbitantly expensive medicines I had to shoot myself up with every night for two weeks. Then there was the twelve hundred dollars per year over six years I'd spent storing my eggs so I could use them at some unknown future date.

I joked with my friends that my phantom baby—the one I

didn't know if I'd ever even give birth to—was costing me as much annually as a fancy gym membership, with none of the benefits of exercising regularly.

The reporter in me told me to follow the money. When it came to egg freezing, the money led me to this question: Why aren't we talking about the Fertility Wealth Gap? Not just the gap between those who can afford to freeze their eggs and those who can't, though of course there's that, too. I'm talking about the fact that young women are forced to choose between freezing their eggs to give themselves a fertility "insurance policy" and saving for retirement (or doing whatever the hell else they want to do with their hard-earned cash).

We already know that women start off in their first jobs getting paid less than men, which means it's almost impossible to invest as much in their 401(k)s as men do. But what has been ignored is that young women are bearing the brunt of the financial burden to be able to have children later in life, even though men benefit from starting families later, too.

What would have happened if I had taken my initial fifteen-thousand-dollar investment and poured it into the stock market, which has an average annual return of 10 percent? With that average, I calculated that by the time I was sixty-five, I'd be sitting on over three hundred thousand dollars.

And still, I'm one of the lucky ones. I was able to scrape together the initial fifteen thousand dollars. I had access because of my skin color, education level, and the city where I live, which has great medical care on every corner. The research shows that Hispanic, Native American, and Black women disproportionately struggle with fertility issues. Yet the image we are shown when it comes to egg freezing and IVF is of a middle-class white woman like me. Everything from fertility clinic websites to news stories and social media posts focusing on infertility show white women. It's no surprise that when Regina Townsend, founder of The Broken Brown Egg, was going through her infertility journey she couldn't find other Black women like her for support and encouragement. Part of the problem is that the cost of assisted reproductive technologies in the United States is exorbitant. Unlike in other countries like Israel and the United Kingdom, which offer free cycles of IVF treatment, women in the US are on their own to figure out how to pay the huge out-of-pocket costs. Eduardo Hariton, a fertility specialist and VP of strategic initiatives at US Fertility, a network of clinics, shared in an interview with *The Economist* that for every patient who gets IVF in America, as many as four more women who want the procedure may go without.

I was already thirty-five by the time I "invested" in my fertility future. But these days, women at younger and younger ages are being sold the idea that freezing their eggs is a way to control their fertility. These clinics, backed by private-equity dollars, are using Instagram ads targeted at twenty- and thirtysomethings to coax women into believing that egg freezing is just another form of "self-care." Instagram ads for Extend Fertility, an egg-freezing startup based in New York, show a hand with manicured nails and the scolding caption: "If you can afford this"—meaning the manicure—"you can afford this," meaning the egg freezing. There's no mention of the costs beyond just the price tag for the egg freezing itself: the thousands of dollars in fertility drugs. The storage fees for the eggs on top of that. And then there's the money these women will need to thaw, fertilize, and implant the resulting embryo if they decide to use their eggs in the future.

Extend Fertility is not alone in their aggressive marketing

tactics. Another fertility startup, Kindbody, drove a van across the country to offer free hormone tests to women worried about their chances of having a future baby. And health company Trellis Health has partnered with cycling studio Flywheel to offer a spin class/information session on egg freezing to millennials.

Unlike the United Kingdom, which has a regulatory body called the Human Fertilization and Embryology Authority that oversees everything related to assisted reproductive technology and inspects all clinics providing fertility treatments, the United States' concept of regulation is haphazard at best. Unbelievably, there's no umbrella agency that regulates the fertility industry, an industry that is expected to reach forty-one billion dollars by 2026. But the Society for Assisted Reproductive Technology does set out guidelines for online advertising—and yet a 2019 study revealed that only 50 percent of fertility clinic websites followed these guidelines. Ads claiming that "When you freeze your eggs, you #freezetime" are not only dangerous, but just plain wrong. Success rates, meaning live-birth rates, for IVF in general, even for women under thirty-five, are around 50 percent per embryo transfer.

The fertility industry is not only glossing over what science tells us these treatments can and can't offer. It's also making a killing off of women's fears. This isn't a flaw in the capitalist system. It's woven into a system that puts profit over patient care and piggybacks on our society's stringent expectations of womanhood and motherhood. As women we are always told there is something wrong with us. Our bodies are broken. Our minds are, too. We're too fat. Too thin. Terrible mothers. Terrible for not being mothers. And now we're being asked to pay for the opportunity to potentially be biological mothers in the

far-off future ten or even twenty years down the road. What if
we don't? Then that's our fault, too. For not being strategic
enough. Forward-thinking enough. Smart enough.

Yet so few are questioning a fertility industry that sells
young women a sense of control that doesn't really exist. Egg
freezing doesn't stop time. Nor does it preserve a woman's fertility. As Dr. Emily Goulet, a reproductive endocrinologist
and infertility specialist, said in a March 2019 interview, egg
freezing is "an expensive lottery ticket."

It's a brilliant scheme: keep women focused on their bodies
and their fears of not belonging. Bombard them with images
of what single, childless women look like (spinsters, misfits,
cat ladies). Call them crazy, hysterical, unfit. Ignore their pain.
Dismiss them. All the while those at the top continue their
grab for money and power, and their counterparts in govern-
ment place more restrictions on women's bodies and roll back
more of our rights.

When I think about the ways women are coaxed into believing that their fertility future is in their own hands if they
just spend enough money and put their bodies and health at
the mercy of their doctors, I'm filled with rage. A woman is
never enough on her own. A woman needs men and children to
justify her existence. Time and again, a woman must put her
mind and body on the line.

15

Russian Roulette

Our new doctor, the one who replaced our other one while she was on maternity leave, spoke with a here's-what-we're-going-to-do certainty that I found calming. This doctor informed us that I had a "reasonable" chance at conceiving if we forked over an unreasonable amount of money for IVF, a procedure I later learned my insurance wouldn't pay for. Numbly, I wrote down the word "reasonable" in my notebook. In the world of IVF what's "reasonable" is both subjective and stupefying. Globally, up to seven out of ten IVF cycles do not result in a live birth. Yet I know women who have undergone eight, nine, even ten or more cycles hoping for that one golden egg. Any cost—both financial and healthwise—seems worth it if there's a baby on the other side.

That night after we got home, I opened up the tab on my computer for the Centers for Disease Control and Prevention's "IVF Success Estimator," an online calculator that asks you to answer a few questions and then spits out your odds at taking home a baby. I filled in my answers—age, height, weight, yes this was my first time doing IVF. After one egg retrieval, I had an 11 percent chance at becoming a mother by the time I was forty-two, the website assured me. After two retrievals, a 20 percent chance. After three, 29 percent.

I stared at the screen. Three retrievals would cost close to seventy-five thousand dollars, and we'd still have less than a 30 percent chance at success. It felt like opening a window and throwing money out of it. I wanted to run into the bathroom where Rob was washing up before bed and rage at the injustice of it all. But I also didn't want to scare Rob off with the reality—the cost, sure, but also the big boulder of energy and emotional effort this whole process would require.

Earlier that day, our new doctor had walked us through what IVF would entail. First, they'd remove a fresh batch of eggs from my body. Then they'd fertilize them with Rob's sperm to form embryos. We'd wait up to one week to see whether the embryos would divide and grow. Those that became blastocysts would be genetically tested. At each stage— egg retrieval, fertilization, blastocyst, and genetic testing—half would fail to make it. Given my age, my new doctor guessed we'd get about four eggs per round. "It's likely that only two of the four will fertilize," he said, sounding significantly more grim than our original doctor had when we were talking about my frozen eggs just the month before. "Of those two embryos, only one is likely to become a blastocyst." And then it was a roll of the dice whether that blastocyst would turn out to be normal once it was genetically tested.

"You only need one," he said, trying to sound optimistic. It was a strange echo of my therapist's words when I was dating. But even an embryo that was found to be genetically normal only had a 50 to 60 percent chance of turning into a baby in nine months. I held on to the idea that science could make it happen. But the stats for women my age told a different story.

No one talks about this part, though. I watched as countless friends in their late thirties and early forties had children. These friends plastered their photos all over social media. Some wrote public missives to their fertility doctors. I was caught in a loop of what researchers call "positivity bias," overestimating my chances of getting pregnant based on the fact that those around me all seemed to be doing exactly that. But those were the ones who were *talking about* their successes. The reality was that the women I knew who weren't getting pregnant weren't posting about it on social media. They were likely not getting out of bed. They were probably crying to their therapists. They weren't announcing their struggles with filtered photos of glowing partners and radiant landscapes. I'd been wooed by the tiny sliver of women who had won the baby lottery.

As our doctor handed us a folder with the clinic's motto Bringing Hope to Life stamped across the front, I wondered why humans couldn't be more like almost all other mammals— able to bear children until they die. Only five species of whale—including narwhals, belugas, and orcas—share the curse of diminishing fertility. Chimpanzees can get pregnant most of their lives. Elephants, too. But if I had to pick one mammal to magically turn into it would be a naked mole rat—forever fertile and unable to feel pain.

I LAY ON our couch and stared at the hanging pipes of Rob's vibraphone. It was like the vibraphone became my therapist, listening to my darkest thoughts and not-fit-for-the-world ramblings.

Even though I wanted to keep lying there, I knew I didn't have time. Rob and I had to make a decision about whether we were going to pursue IVF—and we had to do it quickly. Every day that passed felt like a death sentence for my remaining eggs.

Rob and I sat across from each other on the couch pondering the pros and cons of IVF. There were the obvious ones. In the pro camp, this might be our only chance at having a biological baby. On the con side: cost, emotional purgatory, and unknown health risks. Mostly I was obsessed with the injections. I'm terrified of shots and didn't think I'd be able to push the syringes deep into my belly fat or thighs. Rob wasn't worried, though. In fact, he offered to help me administer the injections. Night after night, we watched videos of women's bruised bellies as they stabbed themselves with syringes. I observed their hands, looking closely to see if they seemed shaky, any sign that they were as terrified as I was. But these women were matter of fact. They were clearly on a mission.

There were also the genetic tests that Rob and I would have to undergo to see if we were carriers of the two hundred–plus most common conditions. And once we were tested, we'd be able to test our embryos, too, to make sure they didn't have any genetic mutations.

After the disappointment of my frozen eggs, I'd renounced medical science as full of false promises of certainty. But now that we were considering IVF, I allowed myself to find comfort in all of the testing and the illusion of control that came with it—not only over whether we'd eventually have a baby, but whether that baby would be born healthy, too. Never mind that my local bookstore is filled with memoirs by humans just like me who were told their baby would be just fine, only to find out later that doctors missed something. In *The Still Point of the Turning World,* Emily Rapp Black writes about how her nine-month-old son, Ronan, was diagnosed with Tay-Sachs disease, a rare and fatal disorder, even though both she and her husband had been tested to see if they were carriers before she got pregnant. In Martha Beck's bestseller *Expecting Adam,* she learns that her unborn son, Adam, has Down syndrome and decides to continue with her pregnancy anyway. Everyone told her to end her pregnancy, but she insisted on giving birth to Adam. By the time he was born, she "had to unlearn virtually everything Harvard taught [her] about what is precious and what is garbage."

Each one of these books, in its own way, is about embracing the unknown. But instead of learning to live with the unknown, I doubled down on control. I spent day after day googling everything I could about genetics. Maybe there was some new study I'd never read before that would prove once and for all that mental illness could be traced to a certain gene. Then I would know for sure whether I could pass on to my child my mom's personality disorder or whatever other mental illnesses ran in my family.

I'm not a scientist. Not even close. I was just a desperate woman searching for answers to her deepest, darkest fears in the twists and turns of her DNA. I stayed up late studying everything I could about the twenty-three chromosomes that made up my molecular story. I woke up early to pore over studies like the one conducted by the Minnesota Center for Twin and Family Research. In an attempt to determine the impact of nature versus nurture, researchers examined over fourteen hundred pairs of identical and fraternal twins. Some were raised together; some grew up in separate homes. It sounded like a promising framework: in play were multiple permutations of nature (through the DNA differences of identical and fraternal twins) and nurture (for the twins who were raised in different homes). The researchers concluded that genes matter. Genetic factors have a significant influence on behavioral habits. Identical twins reared apart had the same chance of being similar as twins who were raised together.

I was particularly interested in whether mental illness is genetic or environmental. But even after decades of study, researchers still haven't been able to confirm a connection between genes and major psychiatric conditions. While psychiatric twin research *has* allegedly found a genetic basis for everything else—from the loneliness people might experience as adults, to their likelihood of believing in God, to the frequency of female orgasm—mental health conditions have stumped researchers. There was no way for me to read into this research whether the women on my mother's side of the family were more susceptible to inheriting mental illness than anyone else. Which also meant that the internet couldn't tell me if my someday child could inherit a devastating mental disease from me.

Around this time I came across the Stockholm Birth Cohort Multigenerational Study, which analyzed thousands of families with intergenerational histories of mental illness, and discovered that both bipolar disorder and schizophrenia had a strong genetic link. But it wasn't clear to me whether anyone in my family had either bipolar disorder or schizophrenia.

I learned that the tiny country of Iceland has an extensive database that allows people to learn more about their genetics— and even a dating app to ensure that Icelanders don't accidentally date their relatives. Genealogical tracking has also become increasingly common in the United States, with the soaring popularity of sites like 23andMe, but unlike Iceland with its national database, in the US it's a free-for-all. Consumers pay money to publicly traded companies that aren't necessarily concerned about providing a public good, just in returning shareholder value.

I was less interested in finding distant cousins—and I didn't even think that it was a possibility that my parents weren't *actually* my parents. My goal was to figure out how to stop the curse of generational trauma in its tracks. I combed through the website for The National Institute of Mental Health, hoping to uncover a datapoint, a factoid, a piece of evidence, *anything* that would tell me whether the variants of mental illness that ran in my family were passed down from generation to generation, like our brown hair and our fair skin. Had my grandmother Ruth inherited a gene, or genes, from my great-grandmother Kitty that made her susceptible to mental breakdowns? Had Ruth then passed that same gene (or genes) onto my own mother? Would my child be in danger, too?

Looking back I wonder what my plan was. If I'd found the smoking gun, the gene that could be blamed for my family's mental mayhem, what would I have done? Decided once and for all to give up on the idea of a biological child? Let fear push me toward not becoming a mother? Or would I have been willing to abort, or selectively choose, only embryos that didn't carry the offending gene?

I later read about Denmark, a country where universal screening for Down syndrome was introduced, and felt a chill of recognition run through me. Now that potential parents can screen for Down syndrome, the number of children being born in Denmark with the disease was less than two dozen in 2019. These parents are "faced with a choice—one made possible by technology that peers at the DNA of unborn children," writes Sarah Zhang in *The Atlantic.* "It was one of the first genetic conditions to be routinely screened for in utero, and it remains the most morally troubling because it is among the least severe. It is very much compatible with life—even a long, happy life."

My mind flashed to my brother Adam. If my mom could have screened for his genetic conditions, would he ever have been born?

In *The Atlantic* article, Zhang interviews Grete Fält-Hansen, a fifty-four-year-old schoolteacher, who leads Denmark's National Down Syndrome Association and has an eighteen-year-old son, Karl Emil, with the condition. Parents call Fält-Hansen regularly seeking information that will help them make an informed decision about whether to continue with their pregnancies. Most don't.

And Fält-Hansen questions the way the medical system encourages women to choose abortion.

Zhang describes the moment when the doctor presents parents with a long list of medical conditions associated with Down syndrome. Suddenly, in one fell swoop, all of a parent's hopes and dreams for their children are eliminated. "If you handed any expecting parent a whole list of everything their child could possibly encounter during their entire life span—illnesses and stuff like that—then anyone would be scared," Karl Emil's sister, Ann Katrine, said. But it is this line from Karl Emil's mom, Grete, that still haunts me: "Nobody would have a baby."

The truth is that I could have spent my whole life analyzing and pondering and attempting to control the myriad outcomes of what is essentially a crapshoot. If any of us thought too much about all the things that could go wrong in our future child's life, *nobody would have a baby*. Life continues because we remain optimistic, hopeful, focused not on all that could go wrong, but on all we dream about going right.

Now science can detect even more genetic conditions. Maybe one day in the future we will be able to know whether we can pass down a mental illness to our children. Maybe one day parents will be able to choose which conditions are deal breakers for them, and which they—and their children—could live with. The troubling question of *What kind of life is worth choosing?* will become the fundamental one facing all parents.

16

Grains of Sand

*A*bnormal.

That's the word the doctor used when she called after our first round of IVF.

As I heard her voice, I got up from my desk at work and went to the elevator, pressing the lobby button. I felt like I was pressing it in a dream. "Abnormal," I heard myself echoing back to my doctor. Once the doors opened, I went and stood outside, on the sidewalk. The cool spring air made me shiver. I noticed the sun trying to peek through the clouds.

All four of the eggs the doctor took from my body managed to fertilize and turn into blastocysts. We'd beat the odds. But then the odds caught up with us. All of our embryos were genetically abnormal, which meant that they were missing chromosomes or had extra ones, or even parts of chromosomes. By the time a woman is forty, six out of every ten of her eggs are considered chromosomally abnormal, our doctor informed us.

We'd gotten four that first round. If we could get another six, statistically speaking, one of them *should* be normal. That was how I understood the statistic, anyway.

So we did another round of IVF. Another two weeks of shooting hormones into my abdomen. Another two weeks of near-daily trips to the clinic uptown to have my blood drawn. And again, we got four eggs, which turned into four embryos, which turned into four blastocysts, which two weeks later turned out to be abnormal.

By now we'd spent close to fifty thousand dollars (not to mention the fifteen thousand dollars I'd already spent on egg freezing and storage), and still we were no closer to having a baby. Yes, we were able to swing it, but not easily. The money had taken me years to save up. Years when I was an entry-level reporter and then an entry-level editor, grinding out stories in newsrooms that treated us like bots, not people. Eventually I had a small sum that Evan and I used to buy a condo in Harlem. We knew nothing about real estate. But we managed to find a diamond in the rough, and then, lucky for us, we sold it just over four years later, for a lot more money, when we got divorced. I know how privileged I am to have had a job at all, let alone one that allowed my ex-husband and me to buy an apartment in one of the most expensive cities in the world. And I know how privileged I am that when I did get divorced I didn't end up like so many women in heterosexual divorces, where, as *Fortune* magazine reports, their household income spirals 41 percent.

By the time Rob and I made the decision to try IVF, the money we needed was right there in my bank account. Sure, the money was meant to be for an emergency, if I lost my job or got hit by the proverbial bus and couldn't work, or, ideally, our retirement, but the truth was that we had it. Meanwhile, the median annual wage for Americans that year was $34,248.45. The reality is that fertility treatments, like everything else in America, excludes those who can't afford the high price tag. And infertility doesn't just strike people of means.

I knew from talking to women in one of the slew of Facebook groups I'd joined that some women had borrowed from their 401(k)s or refinanced the mortgages on their homes to afford fertility treatments. Others took a second job at Starbucks, which paid for IVF for its employees. While it hurt Rob and me to dip into that savings pool, the fact is we were lucky enough that it was there for the taking.

Some states, like Massachusetts, require insurance companies to pay for up to six rounds of IVF. Other people have jobs that foot the bill for fertility treatments (up to a certain amount). When I was going through IVF I was still working at *Forbes,* and even though the company was headquartered in New Jersey (a state that requires companies to pony up for IVF), and I live in New York (another state that requires companies to pay for IVF), because my employer had a private health insurance plan they didn't have to follow state regulations. We were left to figure out the high price tag on our own.

In our case, I was the one with the money. Presumably, in more traditional, married hetero couples, the bigger income earner—usually the man—likely foots the bill. Whoever pays for it, it's a major financial investment, and negotiating the finances can take a toll on a relationship. And just because it was me with the larger bank account didn't mean I'd get to steer the ship. Our decisions about how to become parents would have to be joint. Just like our decisions on *how* to parent would need to be as well. If we ever got that far.

.   .   .

AFTER OUR SECOND failed attempt at IVF, I called an emergency meeting at our fertility clinic. Our doctor looked at my chart and recommended we try the same fertility medicines again.

"Can't we increase my dosages?" I asked. "Can't we try *anything* different?"

But just like in the financial markets where investors want to jump ship or change tactics as soon as things get bumpy, our doctor's recommendation was to stay the course. The truth was that the best path forward was the same thing we'd already tried twice before.

"You need one thing and one thing only," he said. "Patience."

By now I'd spoken to half a dozen friends who had all done IVF about the medication protocols their doctors were prescribing for them. Some were trying experimental new medicines that hadn't even been approved by the FDA. Others were on very high doses of medicines, or very low doses, depending on the clinic and their specific doctor's leanings. Still others were keeping up elaborate regimens of prescribed supplements, acupuncture, tinctures, and special diets to up the chances of success.

Over time, I came to understand that IVF was more an art than a science. There wasn't one way to bring home a baby. Doctors had competing ideas on what was right. And if you had the trifecta of time, patience, and money, you could talk to them all to find out whose regimen you liked best.

But I didn't have time, patience, or more money.

I insisted to Rob that we should find another doctor that I was certain would prescribe some new combination of medicines and poof! I'd get pregnant. Rob was happy to go along with whatever I thought was best, for which I was grateful. By the time we were sitting across from another new doctor in his tiny office, asking—okay, *begging*—him to prescribe a supplement or a cutting-edge new drug combination that we hadn't tried yet so we could have a baby, I was desperate for him, or anyone really, to wave their magic wand and cure me.

I'd asked everyone I knew for the names of the best fertility doctors in New York City. Asking a group of late-thirty-, early fortysomething women for the name of their fertility doctor is like asking for their signature lip color: everyone has an opinion and they're adamant about it. I was inundated with recommendations. I took to calling all the swashbuckling, messiah-like doctors that women in my social circle whispered reverently about, "cowboys." A part of me felt creeped out by their swagger, by their "I'll knock you up" nonchalance. But another part of me would have done anything to get an appointment with one of them.

Overwhelmingly, the fertility world, at least in Manhattan, was ruled by older white men. The most famous ones were untouchable—they booked up months in advance, cost ten times the normal copay just for the consultation, and refused to take insurance. The women I spoke to were in awe of these men, hanging on to their every word, telling anyone who would listen about the precise combinations of medicines they prescribed. The way these circles of infertile women I knew were wowed and wooed by these doctors felt sexual. It reminded me of NXIVM, the cult in upstate New York, where wealthy, mostly white women with all the privilege in the world were branded with the initials of their leader. And yet I, too, would have sacrificed anything for one of these doctors to impregnate me. I, too, hoped one of these doctors would deem me worthy of their time.

When I tried calling the office of one cowboy, I was told the wait for a consultation would be six months. When I called the office of another cowboy, this one featured in the Styles section of *The New York Times,* his receptionist said, "Our next appointment is in October." It was only May. By now, I was nearly forty-two, and I felt my age flashing in neon as I thought of waiting till October to speak to the doctor. No way. So I worked my way down the list I'd made of the best clinics in Manhattan and asked the receptionist at each one if there were *any* doctors in their practice I could see quickly.

One week later we were sitting across from Dr. Keller, watching him study my medical charts—advanced maternal age, a failed round of frozen eggs, two failed rounds of IVF. When he finally spoke, his words weren't the ones I wanted to hear. "Your doctors did exactly what I would have done," he said.

Silence.

"We can try again and hope for a different result," he continued. "But you know what they say about insanity, right?"

A smirk. Our doctor had a smirk on his face, but then, seeing something in me, he softened. "If you have the time and money, you could keep trying IVF."

But we had a finite amount of money. And we certainly didn't have the time, given my age. Dr. Keller knew that. We were at an impasse. Our choice was to try the same regimen again. *Or what?* I couldn't bear to ask.

I studied his desk. The photo of his wife and their three shiny children. The stacks of other women's files strewn in piles. The cup of coffee, now cold, leaving a milky ring on the wood below.

"Ruthie, let me tell you something." He paused, looking at Rob for a split second and then focusing his eyes on me. "If you want to be successful—if you want to have a child that you give birth to . . ."

I was leaning forward now, waiting to hear the special protocol we hadn't tried yet, but instead Dr. Keller said the words that would change my life forever.

He finished his sentence: ". . . you will seriously need to consider using donor eggs."

Donor eggs. I didn't know anyone who had used donor eggs before. Not only that, I'd never even heard of them. At that moment, all I wanted was for the floor to swallow me whole. My therapist's voice boomed in my head: *Is this hurting? Or is this helping?* And with every ounce of energy I could muster I repeated to myself: *hurting, hurting, hurting.*

My therapist intruded once again. *Breathe in for four seconds,* she commanded, *hold for seven and out for eight.* I did as she told me (four-seven-eight-four-seven-eight) and slowly I came back into my body, reminding myself to live in the present, reminding myself to find joy. The doctor wasn't saying I couldn't have a baby. The doctor was only saying that he didn't think it made sense to keep gambling away our life savings on what he deemed a less than 10 percent chance of having a baby with my own eggs.

When Dr. Keller saw the skepticism written across my face, he reassured us. "An egg is only one cell," he said. "Your body will decide how the baby's genes are expressed. Your blood will flow through the baby's body."

One cell from another woman sounded so simple. One cell, "smaller than a grain of sand," Dr. Keller said. *My* body would take care of the rest. "That's what's called epigenetics." I stared at my hands, the ones I'd always been proud looked just like my mother's and grandmother's. If we didn't use my eggs, would my child's hands look like mine?

But Dr. Keller wasn't thinking about my mother or my grandmother or our hands. He was thinking about data. "With donor eggs, your chances of success will go from the single digits to over 60 percent on the first try," he said, beaming. Rob nodded. I did, too. Those were decent odds.

Still, I wasn't convinced. He tried a different route. "Ninety-nine-point-nine percent of our DNA is exactly like every other human's DNA on the planet. The differences between us are miniscule. Your DNA. A donor's DNA. It doesn't matter. It will still be your baby."

And yet the doctor wasn't suggesting that Rob forego his genetics. He was asking *me*. If all humans are 99.9 percent exactly like every other human genetically, I wondered, why does our culture fetishize ancestry so much? Why was everyone I know buying 23andMe kits and building family trees?

On the sidewalk outside the clinic, Rob and I got into an enormous fight. Rob swore that if the tables were turned, he wouldn't care if we used his genetics or not. "It wouldn't matter to me," he said. "It really wouldn't. You heard the doctor. All human DNA is practically identical."

Except that the 0.1 percent difference between us and all other humans on the planet accounts for a whole lot. It accounts for the sound of my dad's laugh and the shape of my mom's smile. It accounts for the twinkle in my eyes and my wavy hair. There's also the part that the doctor never mentioned: that humans share 99 percent of our DNA with chimpanzees, too. By focusing on our commonalities instead of our differences, the doctor—and now Rob—was erasing everything that made us human in the first place.

"Yes, the genetic differences between any two people are tiny when compared to the long stretches of DNA coiled in every human cell," writes Kathryn Paige Harden. "But these differences loom large when trying to understand why, for example, one child has autism and another doesn't; why one is deaf and another hearing . . . Genetic differences matter for our lives."

I understood Harden's words intuitively, but I couldn't articulate them yet. Instead, as Rob and I rode the subway back to our apartment, I imagined grains of sand as far as the eye could see. Tiny cells, meaningless, negligible on their own. But I also understood that if we moved forward with donor eggs, there would be a stranger somewhere who shared half the building blocks of our baby. This didn't sound like a small thing.

Would our child have her smile? Her personality? At what point does a grain of sand become a beach?

17

The Tyranny of DNA

Before I met Rob, I sat on a bench in Central Park reading *The Gene: An Intimate History* and marveling at Siddhartha Mukherjee's description of Conrad Waddington, an English embryologist, who in the 1940s hypothesized that our environment could modify our genes.

Our environment could modify our genes? I thought with awe as I pondered the trees on the north side of the park and read and reread the story of Waddington's discovery. It wasn't nature or nurture, Waddington found. It was nature *and* nurture that mattered. And what constituted nature was much more complex than we'd ever before comprehended. Waddington believed that a layer of information was suspended above the genome, which could be changed, a layer he called "epi genetics" or "above genetics."

I always believed that DNA is literally a blueprint for life. I believed the alphabet of our genetic code is fixed the way the scaffolding of a building or the cement foundation is. Your body followed the instructions set out for it and voilà, you were created. Once Rob and I were trying to decide whether to move forward with donor eggs, I wanted to pinpoint how my body, the environment our baby would gestate in for nine months, could epigenetically change who our child would become. Would I take the jumble of this stranger's DNA and give it its own unique signature? Or was DNA destiny and I'd have little influence at all?

I knew a friend's husband worked with Siddhartha, and she offered to connect us so I could ask him about how epigenetics worked. But when Siddhartha appeared on the video screen in front of me—with his scruffy beard and dark, floppy hair— I suddenly felt silly asking this brilliant, fifty-year-old man to explain the science behind my body's impact on our future baby. I'd read the *Vogue* profile of Siddhartha and his equally impressive, MacArthur Fellowship–winning wife, the sculptor Sarah Sze, and felt downright intimidated.

"Hi," I said nervously, wishing I had never called him. But there he was, so I forced myself to tell him my dilemma: our doctor recommended we use donor eggs and I wanted to know if that would mean that my body would just be a vessel for our growing baby or if I'd have any imprint on our child at all.

Siddhartha didn't laugh at my question or make me feel stupid for asking it. He was real with me. "I think we don't understand enough about epigenetics to know the answer," he said.

It was a fair response. But still, I wanted someone to say to me: *if you choose this path, here is what will happen.* Maybe there was a diagram he could show me or a mathematical model that would explain all the ways my cells would mix and mingle with our fetus's genetic code to modify its DNA.

Instead of a diagram, Siddhartha offered a music analogy. "Just like when a score of a symphony is written, a musician could choose to play section one or section seven at different paces and in doing so would change the way the music is heard."

I nodded. With a partner who's a drummer, I'd heard enough about music over the past few years to understand that this was the perfect analogy. My body would be the musician, Siddhartha said. My womb wouldn't be able to change the notes of our fetus's DNA, but it could change the *expression* of how those notes were played. Played staccato, or short, certain genes would be turned on. Played legato, or long, others would be turned off. Played pianissimo, or very quietly, a certain gene may be less pronounced. Played fortissimo, or very loud, that same gene may be more pronounced. My body would decide.

But I still didn't know what that meant in a *tangible* way. Would my body turn on a gene that made our baby's hands look like my mother's and mine? Would my body flip the switch so our baby's sense of humor mirrored my own? How would changing the way genes are *expressed* change who our baby would become?

I finally got up the nerve to ask my question. "I know it's impossible to do an experiment like this in humans, but what I really want to know is if we put the same embryo into two different women whether the resulting children would be clones of each other." I paused, waiting to see his reaction. "Would the babies be exactly the same?"

I saw my question register on Siddhartha's face and I could tell he was taking it seriously. But I also knew I was asking an emotional question, and he was searching for a scientific answer. I wondered if the two could be compatible.

"We know the answer to that to some extent," was his reply. *We do?*

"The one thing we do know is that metabolic conditions in the mother affect the fetus strongly," he said. "In two different metabolic environments the fetus would be very different. So if one of these hypothetical mothers was using alcohol or one of the many drugs that cross the placental barrier it would impact the fetus. What we don't know, and what the psychiatric literature is full of, is whether psychological or mental states are passed down from mother to fetus, too."

I wrote down in my notebook: "Don't use alcohol or drugs while pregnant."

Siddhartha also mentioned one of the most famous studies of metabolic conditions, the Dutch Hunger Winter Families Study, also referred to as the Barker hypothesis or fetal origins of adult disease hypothesis. The results of this study are controversial, but some scientists believe that it proves that the body "remembers" trauma in the womb. That's because between September 1944 and May 1945 the Nazis blocked food supplies to the Netherlands and over twenty thousand people died of starvation. Paradoxically, women who were pregnant during that time gave birth to children who grew up to be *heavier* than the average adult. These children also grew up to have higher rates of obesity, diabetes, and schizophrenia. One of the researchers on the study reported that those who had been in utero during the famine died at a higher rate than those born before the famine or after. Some believed that this proved that our bodies remember the environment they're exposed to in the womb even decades later.

The next line in my notebook says: "Don't starve the fetus."

But other than using alcohol or drugs or not eating during my pregnancy, was there anything I could do to have an imprint? Preferably a *positive* one?

Before we hung up, Siddhartha told me about some epigenetic studies done on mice. One of the most fascinating was a study performed by Brian Dias at the University of Southern California's Keck School of Medicine. In it, male mice were introduced to a smell and given a shock to their feet at the same time. The result: the epigenetic markers in these male mice changed a smell receptor gene in their sperm cells. So when the male mice bred with females their offspring also became stressed by the same smell even though the offspring had never been exposed to the smell before. Dias repeated the experiment only using the sperm from the father mouse and artificially fertilizing the female eggs so the father mouse's anxiety around the smell didn't rub off on the baby mouse. And you know what? The baby mouse still inherited a sensitivity to that same smell, proving that trauma may be epigenetically inherited.

Which got me thinking: Could the trauma I inherited from my great-grandmother, grandmother, and mother *still* be passed down to our fetus epigenetically somehow even if we didn't use my genes? Could I pass down the genetic memories of the countries they left behind, the pogroms they fled, the mental battles they fought? And then I wondered: What pain and traumas might be embedded in a *donor's* DNA? My family's history was the devil I knew. A donor's, the devil I didn't.

Under "don't starve the fetus" I wrote: "trauma???"

AFTER SIDDHARTHA, I spoke to other doctors. Some referred to epigenetics as a switch that my body would flip on and off. Others asked me to imagine epigenetics as a volume knob that my body would turn up or down. But all I wanted was for somebody to be able to point to my future baby and say, "Look at that imprint you made!"

"Genetics is king," Charles Sawyers, the chair of the Human Oncology and Pathogenesis Program at Memorial Sloan Kettering Cancer Center, said to me. I sat on the floor of my bedroom on a Zoom call with Charles while in the kitchen Rob warmed up leftovers for dinner. Although I could still make out the cacophony of noises from the rest of our apartment—pots clanging, the NPR station playing in the background—I tuned into Charles's every word.

I wanted to know, and hoped he could tell me, what DNA really meant. With all my heart I wanted for him to play down the role of genes, to explain how *my* body, *my* uterus, *my* blood, *my* being, would be more important than any measly set of chromosomes.

It was not going well.

"We have all kinds of tools now so we can measure changes to DNA at the epigenetic level. What I think you're asking is whether the environment of your body, the environment the embryo is exposed to, chemically modifies the cells within the organism."

He was right. In my own way, that was what I was asking. But when he said it, it sounded so much smarter.

Charles was cautious. He didn't want to lead me astray. He knew there was no yes or no answer—the human body is too complex for that.

All these decades after Waddington's discovery of epigenetics, Charles explained, scientists now believe that a woman's womb can influence not only the brain development of her growing baby, but the metabolism, immune system function, and more. Our fetus would float around in my body and reap all the benefits of spending nine months there. My body would kick into action to nurture our fetus into a tiny human. I latched on to every word, but the truth was that everything he said seemed to double down on what Siddhartha had already told me. There wasn't anything new.

And then he said this: "There are all kinds of tools we can use to measure changes to DNA at the epigenetic level."

Here was something. If there were tools to measure epigenetic changes, then it was possible that there had been a study in mice where a mouse embryo had been cloned and placed into two different "surrogates," as Charles called the female mice. Once the baby mice were born, the researchers would have been able to examine their genomes and identify any differences between them. Since the mouse embryos had originally been cloned, any deviations between the baby mice would have been the result of the environment of their mother's wombs. Scientists would be able to see their mother's "imprint," the point I was most curious about (read: obsessed).

I felt excitement run through my body. Excitement mixed with fear. I knew we were just batting around hypotheticals. There was no control study for whether our baby would be the same if he or she was born from another woman's body. It was tantalizing, though, to wonder.

"It's not a complete black box anymore," Charles said. "We couldn't have done this kind of experiment five years ago, but now it's possible with mice." He paused, considering his words. "One thing I can say is that no matter which woman carried the fetus, the child would look the same. DNA is so powerful in determining appearances, at least early."

By the time I walked into the kitchen to tell Rob about my call, he was putting dinner on the table, and I couldn't contain my excitement.

"You'll never believe what I just learned," I blurted out, not waiting for Rob's reply. "There have been studies done in mice where they cloned mouse embryos and put them into two different mother mice to determine their epigenetic imprint."

I kept rambling on until something about Rob's body language—the way his shoulders sank in defeat, the slight grimace on his face—stopped me.

Rob listened and then he looked down at his plate. "I'm worried that you're going to miss out on the joy of being pregnant and raising our child by searching for some intangible, ephemeral thing that no one can give you. Of course you'll have an imprint on our baby! How could you not? I don't need to be a doctor to tell you that."

I felt stunned, like Rob had slapped me across the face. He must have seen my surprise because he pulled back a little. "I just don't want you to blow all this genetics stuff out of proportion and make our kid think it's a bigger deal than it really is," he said. "It will only be important if you act like it's important."

I knew Rob was trying to protect me. More than that, I knew he was trying to protect our future family. But I also felt leftover resentment roil inside me from our fight outside the doctor's office.

"It's like you're lighting matches and waiting to see if there's an explosion," he continued. "I think you should move on."

Move on? I wasn't ready to move on. And I didn't know if I'd ever be.

I didn't say any of that, though. Instead, I wanted to prove to him that my feelings mattered more on this issue than his since we were talking about replacing my DNA after all. I wanted him to see that I was right, and he was being insensitive. "Matches! Matches? Yes, I'm lighting matches. But I see them as lighting the way, not obscuring the view," I screamed.

I wanted Rob to understand how I was already grieving for my lost lineage even if that lineage was messed up, full of abandoners, addicts, and assholes.

He looked at me with sadness in his eyes, and in that moment something Charles said reverberated in my head: *We'll never know.*

Maybe Rob was right. Maybe Charles was, too. There would be no way to know who our baby would be once it was born or what impact I would have on him or her. We needed to decide whether we were going to have a child using donor eggs knowing full well that we had to leap without knowing where we'd land.

I SAT WITH my back against the bed, my laptop opened on my thighs. I'd been hunched over in one place for so long that the heat from the bottom of my computer had penetrated through my thigh fat, down to the muscle until my leg radiated with numbness. But I didn't care. I'd been meandering through the corridors of the internet like a bad dream, opening every door in the dark hallway, and when I didn't find what I was looking for, I slammed it shut and ran for the next one. And the next one. Until I was frantically opening and closing so many doors that I didn't remember which I'd already opened, and I was running in circles, spirals, figure eights, chasing I didn't know what anymore.

I landed in a Facebook group, one of several I'd found over the last few months. A common vocabulary carried across these groups, one that identified those who used donor eggs as "warriors" and "survivors." The language reminded me of cancer. The women who donated their eggs are "angels." The children born are "miracles."

It was as if these women needed to cheer themselves on, convince each other that they were not only just as good as other women who have babies "naturally," but better because they'd suffered so much to get to the land of motherhood. I empathized with them. I understood their need to prove they weren't imposters, fraudulent. I understood their need to prove they weren't selfish, that they hadn't worshiped their careers for too long and then suddenly scrambled to buy their way into motherhood.

As women continue to start their families later in life, egg donation will keep soaring. There will be even more women, like me and those I met in these online groups, who are considering donor eggs as an option and trying to understand what it means to carry a fetus created from someone else's egg.

Part of the reason that women are turning to these forums to seek answers to their questions is that the field of egg donation is so young. In fact, it started in my lifetime. Until 1983, when the first pregnancy from egg donation took place, the person who gave birth to you was the person who gave you your DNA. There wasn't a dividing line between biological mothers or bio-moms (the person whose body you come from) and genetic donors (the person whose genetic information is used to create an embryo). Now we have a whole new language, a whole new worldview, a whole new set of questions and concerns.

In those weeks when we were considering whether to use donor eggs, I read about how mitochondrial DNA has been passed directly from mother to child for thousands of generations and I suddenly felt sad that I would be cut off from this most human experience. I felt irredeemable, broken. Outside the warm hearth of humanity once again.

A few days later, I came across a forty-four-second video

from the University of Utah Genetic Science Learning Center that showed a mother rat licking her young. Some mother rats spent a lot of time licking, grooming, and nursing their pups. Others seemed to ignore them. It turns out that the nurturing behavior of a mother rat during the first week of life—her licking and grooming and nursing—shapes her pups' epigenomes. Through licking, the mother rats could change the way her babies' genes were expressed.

To my human eye, the mama rat's licking looked aggressive, but the hairless baby rats clearly couldn't get enough. They cuddled as close as they could to her. They nuzzled into her warm body. "New research shows we are natured by our nurture," author Belle Boggs writes. *Natured by our nurture,* I whispered to myself as I watched the mother rat's tongue soothing her babies. I liked that idea.

It had only been a few weeks since we left Dr. Keller's office and I felt like I was in free fall, like everything I understood about what it meant to be a mother was coming into question. I had no idea what the right decision was. Move forward with donor eggs? Try IVF with my own eggs one more time? Look into adoption? Give up on motherhood entirely? I just wanted to *do* something.

I wondered what others would do in my situation.

As I thought about the millions of strangers who walked the same city streets as me and sat next to me on the subway, I wondered how many of them were dealing with fertility struggles of some kind. In my own friend group, there were at least half a dozen who had recently been through their own version of reproductive hell. Then again, what about the women who got pregnant accidentally and didn't want to keep the fetus? Or those who were in the midst of IVF, heading to the clinic to have their blood drawn right at that moment? Or those who could only dream about IVF, but could never afford it? Or had given up long ago? The truth was that getting knocked up at the exact time that you want to be with the exact right person without any fuss might be the most magical thing of all.

I was the norm, not the outlier. The blissful images society shows us of motherhood without struggle do a disservice to all of us, erasing the bumpy paths most of us take to choosing when, and if, we'll become mothers at all. Even that word "choose" is rife with misunderstanding when so many women make choices with their hands tied behind their backs. They want children but can't find partners; they are terrified of parenting alone; there's no safety net; they can't find the money for fertility treatments; they want a baby but not yet, or not now, or not in this particular situation. There are as many narratives on the path to motherhood as there are people.

Before Rob and I sat down to talk about whether to use donor eggs, I had plowed ahead, calling all the top fertility clinics to find out about their donor egg programs. My journalism training means that even in my personal life, I can't take off my reporter hat. I pulled together a spreadsheet on my computer that outlined everything I'd learned so I could share it with Rob. Some of the clinics wouldn't allow us to see any photos of the donors. Some would let us only see baby pictures. Others worked only with fresh eggs from donors who had just had an egg retrieval. Still others only used frozen eggs. There was even a clinic with a money-back-guarantee program. I felt a bit grossed out even saying those words, like we were treating making a baby like a Black Friday deal at a big box store. This was a human life, not the newest iPhone, but there was something reassuring all the same that we wouldn't be spending still more money only to come home with no baby.

Late one afternoon, as dusk was gathering outside, I said to Rob, "If we're going to do this, it's really important to me to see photos of the donor." I had, you'll note, skipped over the part about whether we would use donor eggs at all and instead focused on the nitty gritty of the process. "I want the donor to seem real to me. I want to feel like I know her. Or at least feel that she's someone I'd like to get to know."

But Rob wasn't sure he wanted to know what the donor looked like. "I don't want to picture this other person every time I look at our child," he said. "We will be our kid's parents, not the donor."

By the time we were talking about all of this, I'd spoken to an acquaintance who had paid extra for donor eggs from a woman who had gone to an Ivy League university. But now Rob and I discussed how we were pretty certain that the education level—and the prestige of the college someone attended—meant nothing when it came to intelligence. Wasn't where most of us ended up going to school somewhat random or based on factors like wealth that weren't genetic at all? Would Ivy League eggs really guarantee us a more intelligent child? And if so, how important was intelligence to us?

Another acquaintance had paid thousands of dollars extra for eggs from a Jewish donor. I'm Jewish. Rob isn't. *Should I care about whether our donor is Jewish, too?* I wondered. *Would a Jewish donor mean our child would be that much closer to me genetically?*

By the time we'd finished our conversation and headed off to bed, my head was swirling with information. I only knew one thing for certain: we were willing to give donor eggs a try. Everything else—from how we'd make all of the decisions in front of us to whether we'd actually bring home a baby—was as mysterious as the night sky.

·   ·   ·

IT WAS THE middle of June and hot as hell as Rob and I sat in Dr. Sasson's windowed office at Shady Grove Fertility in Chesterbrook, Pennsylvania. Dr. Sasson was one of the fertility doctors I'd researched whose clinic offered a money-back-guarantee program for donor eggs. Now we were listening as he spoke slowly, writing every word down, so we would understand all of the complicated details he was laying out for us about the donor egg process.

"I know you've been through a lot to try and get pregnant already. Everyone who comes here has a story," Dr. Sasson said with a tenderness in his voice. He was humble, kind. Right away I trusted him. Rob seemed to as well. Dr. Sasson didn't try to wow us with how smart he was or with statistics on how many people he'd helped conceive.

"We don't believe the industry standard is fair. Patients going through fertility treatments do not have enough viable financial options," he said. "Instead of charging twenty-five thousand dollars and up for each treatment like other clinics, our base price is thirty-two thousand dollars for up to six rounds, but if you don't get pregnant we'll return your money, no questions asked."

I let his words sink in.

"So how does this work for you?" Rob asked bluntly. "How do you not go bankrupt?"

Dr. Sasson placed a blank sheet of paper in front of us and jotted down some numbers. "Let's see," he said. "Most women, upwards of 60 percent, get pregnant on the first try with an egg that has been genetically tested and is found to be normal. We can offer you your money back because we know that more than half the time you'll get pregnant in round one."

I nodded.

"For those who don't go home with a baby on the first try, the number soars to an 85 percent success rate by round two, meaning that 85 percent of our patients go home with a baby on the first or second try."

The numbers were great, yes, but we'd need to spend at least thirty-two thousand dollars, minimum, to move forward. This on top of the fifty thousand dollars we'd already spent on thawing my frozen eggs and the two rounds of IVF that went nowhere. If we decided to give donor eggs a shot, we'd have spent almost a hundred thousand dollars in less than a year—a crazy amount.

Before we began, I would have to undergo testing to see if my body was able to carry a fetus at all. And if it was, we'd have to think about how we would go about picking our donor. It was like we were running a marathon and we knew the finish line was a baby, but we were blindfolded so we couldn't see the road ahead. We'd have to stumble in the darkness, feeling our way through until we reached our destination. The part I didn't want to think about was what would happen if we never did. What would happen if after countless miles of struggle there was no baby on the other side?

Even as the wheels of my mind spun furiously, I was cognizant of the favorable odds in play here. Dr. Sasson wanted to help me bring home a baby on the first try. We'd pay a little more for the guarantee that if the worst happened and there was no baby we would get a full refund. Dr. Sasson was betting that we'd hit the jackpot quickly. It was his job to get us pregnant with a viable fetus, fast. We were on the same side. It seemed like a win-win.

As this new reality settled in my mind, I moved on to my next dilemma. "How would we decide on a donor?" I asked.

Dr. Sasson looked up, his pen no longer moving across the page. "I recommend picking a proven donor, a woman whose eggs have previously led to live births," he said. His answer disappointed me, but I guess it shouldn't have been surprising. It was his job to get me pregnant, and getting pregnant is a numbers game, not an emotional one.

Yet I wasn't sure how to separate out emotions from the process. I looked over at Rob. From the outside, he seemed like he was doing just fine at the whole emotional separation thing. He was nodding at every other word that came out of Dr. Sasson's mouth. There was no look of worry on his face.

I couldn't help but think about Faith Haugh, the Australian woman, who donated her eggs forty-one times, helping to create nineteen children with her DNA. And the donor whose sperm led to 150 children who are all now connected through a donor sibling registry.

I didn't have too much time to think about the distance between my emotional reaction and Rob's, because next thing I knew, Dr. Sasson was drawing three different tiers on his piece of paper. His pen hovered over the first tier—the least expensive—which was the thirty-two thousand dollars he'd mentioned. For that price, he said, "you'd be sharing one batch of eggs with two other families," and for a second I let myself imagine shadow families pushing our baby's half siblings—or diblings, as they're called—on the swings and helping them down the slide. Would we pass them on the playground? Or walking to the grocery store? Would our future child always wonder about his or her genetic heritage? Would we be messing up our child psychologically before it was even conceived?

The second tier cost forty-two thousand dollars, and for that price we'd be sharing one batch of eggs with just one other family. Each of us would get at least six eggs from the donor, which in our case would then be mixed with Rob's sperm. By sharing with just one other family we'd potentially end up with more eggs, so if we wanted to be certain we could have more than one child, tier two was the way to go. Dr. Sasson scribbled some math on his paper to make it easier for us to understand. If the donor produced twenty-eight eggs and we shared those eggs with two other families, we would each get nine eggs and one family would get ten. But if we paid for tier two and only shared with one other family, we'd each get fourteen eggs, five more chances at striking baby gold.

And then there was tier three, where for fifty-two thousand dollars we'd keep all twenty-eight eggs for ourselves and not share any with another family. The more money we had to spend, the better our chances at success.

Before we left Dr. Sasson's office that day, the nurse gave us a list of the documents we'd need to bring with us when we returned the following month. She also told us that until we completed the medical exams and submitted all the paperwork we wouldn't have access to the database of potential donors.

A few weeks later, I was lying on a bed in another's doctor's office as he performed a hysterosalpingogram, or HSG, on me, threading a thin tube through my vagina and cervix and injecting a dye into my uterus. A series of X-rays were then taken to see if there were any blockages that would prevent me from getting pregnant and to make sure that my uterus was a normal size and shape. Until this moment, the idea of donor eggs seemed so *theoretical*. We hadn't started to look at donors yet. We hadn't felt the sting of coughing up tens of thousands of dollars for this part of the process. It had been endless talk, with virtually no action. So far, I felt detached from the whole idea of my body as a vessel that could make—or not make— a baby. It was like I was a zoo animal and the doctors were pointing at my body parts, analyzing my reproductive capabilities and judging if I was fit to continue.

Somehow at that moment I couldn't fully process that we were moving step-by-step closer to using donor eggs to conceive our child.

18

The Procedure

July in New York City was as sweaty as a packed jail cell. I walked to work meetings at outdoor cafés through a wall of heat, met up with friends and acquaintances for iced coffees and cocktails, and didn't mention a word about the idea of donor eggs to anyone. Any whiff of contempt or judgment would have sent me into a spiral of self-doubt.

I didn't even tell my parents. In my mind, my mom would be upset, sad for me in the best-case scenario and, more likely, sad for herself. My dad would make a joke to try and make me feel better, but it would flop. I was afraid to tell friends, too. In the charged uncertainty of that time, I was sure that the friends I knew and loved would morph into the mean imaginary ones who lived in my mind—the ones who would hear the news that I was considering using donor eggs and immediately start texting back and forth about all the duds I had wasted my fertility on and how they knew my marriage to

Evan was never going to work even before I'd walked down the aisle.

I couldn't imagine that anyone would be supportive or encouraging. I never even gave them the chance.

I fantasized about what would happen once our baby was here, when younger women would say, "You're such an inspiration. You had a baby after forty." Would I smile and nod, or would I feel compelled to whisper, *Yeah, but I didn't get to use my DNA?*

I spent most of July—whenever I wasn't working or pretending everything was okay—crying inconsolably. I told myself I should be happy that using a donor egg—with its exorbitant price tag and cutting-edge science—was even an option for us. I knew plenty of women who didn't have that choice. I should feel happy I finally had a partner to have a baby with when so many women I knew didn't.

I should feel happy. But I didn't.

When I wasn't trying to bully myself into contentment, I would scare myself by forecasting that I was tempting the Fates by trying to have a baby. The universe gave me a maternal line full of God-knows-what issues, a half brother with a severe genetic mutation, two failed IVFs, and a batch of frozen eggs that failed. If I kept pushing for a baby, wasn't I asking for trouble?

On one particular day, I was digging through the filing cabinet in our bedroom looking for one of the many medical documents I needed to bring with me the next time we went to Dr. Sasson's office when a photo of me from when I was seventeen slipped out from between a stack of papers. I was wearing black jean shorts, a Keith Haring T-shirt, and my hair was swept in a side ponytail. My head was cocked slightly to the side. My arms crossed over my chest. I looked so young, so hopeful. Immediately the sides of my mouth began to quiver. Sorrow and disappointment bubbled up. I was staring at one of my many parallel lives. And even though I had no way of knowing where that road would have led, at this moment when Rob and I were struggling to get pregnant, that other life seemed like the one that got away.

I remembered exactly where that photo was taken and exactly who took it. It was in Maine where I was living for the summer before college, working at the drive-through at McDonald's. The other person in the photo was Jason, my then-boyfriend, and I didn't know it at the time, but I was pregnant.

Jason and I would spend afternoons drinking Budweiser in a coworker's living room and evenings over Zima at random house parties. I wore thick eyeliner curled up at the edges, the way Amy Winehouse would wear hers many years later, and Jason looked over at me one night and said, "What are you, a model?" and I nodded, because that had been my dream: for someone to recognize that I was beautiful, for someone to pay attention to me at all.

That's all Jason had to say. Next thing I knew we were making out on some stranger's couch, and he had his hand under my shirt. Maybe I'd seen it in a movie, or read it in a book, or maybe it was just in my head, but whenever a man wanted to have sex with me, I thought it meant he loved me. And when a man loved me, I loved him back.

Soon after, Jason and I moved into a house across town where we rented a room with a bed and a knee-high fridge for thirty dollars a week. The other tenants were mostly addicts and those down on their luck. The bathroom had blue tiles that were caked with black mold, and I forced Jason to stand watch, to ensure that the cockroaches that ran past my feet as I sat on the toilet didn't get too close.

The photo I now held in my hand was of Jason and me smiling, hand in hand, even though those months weren't a happy time.

I didn't realize right away that I was pregnant. Maybe it was because I was young and naïve and I didn't pay much attention to my periods, or because I was living on my own and just trying to make enough money to survive. By the time I walked myself to the Planned Parenthood clinic and plopped down across from the nurse, I hadn't bled in months. The nurse said, "You're lucky," and I wondered what luck meant in a situation like this. That I caught the pregnancy just in time to abort it? That I could scrounge up the five hundred dollars to pay for "the procedure"? That was what she called it, "the procedure"; the word "abortion" was never uttered.

The nurse told me to come back the next day and to bring someone with me, but I didn't have anyone to bring. I was scared to tell Jason that he'd knocked me up. I was terrified he would try to convince me to keep our baby, and that wasn't what I wanted. I was scared to tell my mom, too. She had moved a few months earlier to Chicago and we'd barely spoken since. If I called her now, I knew what would happen: she'd cry and say I got pregnant because she'd been a bad mother, and I'd end up feeling sorry for her when what I really needed was for her to help me.

I was scared of the disappointment in my dad's voice, so I didn't call him either. I knew he had tried to be a good dad, to stop me from dating Brad and Patrick and Lewis. And now this. Now I would call him to tell him I was pregnant? With some random guy's baby? A man he'd never even known about? I couldn't break his heart all over again.

Looking back now, I think about those years from fourteen to sixteen when I was a cheerleader for the soccer team. How after practice I never wanted to call my parents to ask them to pick me up. I always figured I was a bother. That I would prevent them from doing whatever they *really* wanted to be doing at that moment. That coming to get me was a burden. They'd huff and puff, be angry, whisper behind my back: *Ruthie's so needy. Can't she figure out anything for herself?*

So when it came time to get a ride home from practice, I asked for a ride from whatever soccer player was hanging around. And when they looked at me with a "what's in it for me?" look in their eyes, I thought about the one thing I could offer: a hand job. I traded hand jobs for rides home rather than calling my parents to ask them. When I think about how I didn't tell my parents about my abortion, or about our decision to use donor eggs, I remember all of those hand jobs and wish I could take them back. Why didn't I think I could call my parents like every other fourteen-year-old and ask them for a ride? Why did I feel like such a burden for something so simple?

And the worst part is: I didn't even try to ask them. I didn't let them know I needed them out of fear of what they'd think of me or what they'd say. I'd spent my whole life silencing myself when I could have just been honest. *Hey, Mom. Hey, Dad. I need a ride. Can you come get me?* And you know what? They might have.

But at my mom's house I had a version of survivor's guilt because Adam always needed so much. I was meant to be the easy one, the good girl who never asked for a lot. I didn't feel like I deserved something as small as a ride home because I didn't want to add to her burden.

And then there was my dad's house, which was filled with constant tension. Any time, attention, or money he spent on me meant less for his other family. I didn't want to deal with

the blowup fights, the jealous rages that would end with
slammed doors and cruel silences.

I don't doubt that my parents loved me, *and* I don't doubt
that I felt lost in the shuffle, unworthy of love and protection.
Or maybe it's just that they were so wrapped up in their own
lives—and I seemed so good at handling mine—that they
didn't know I needed anything.

Back at Planned Parenthood, I was scared the nurse
wouldn't let me have the abortion I so desperately wanted if I
told her that I didn't have anyone to come with me, so I said,
"Yes, of course, I'll bring someone," and that I'd see her the
next day. In the morning, I pushed through the picket line
filled with strangers reminding me of all the ways I'd already
fucked up my life even though, at seventeen, it had barely
begun. Inside, the nurse was there holding a paper gown and
telling me to put my feet in stirrups. As I lay there, she asked
me to fill out her questionnaire, "for statistical purposes only,"
she swore. "Your name won't appear anywhere." And as I filled
out the paperwork, I thought about all those researchers in
their white lab coats and wondered what they'd think of me
when they read the bubbles I'd blackened with my pen. I knew
they wouldn't understand what brought me here, all of the
stories inside of stories that led to this moment.

Once everything was over, the nurse handed me a brown
paper bag with directions stapled to it and told me to come
back in a few days to make sure they "got everything." Then
she walked me to the front and asked where my friend was—
the one who was supposed to pick me up—and I looked at her
without hesitating and said, "Don't worry, she's right out there
in her car. See the white Cadillac?" The nurse looked out the
window to where I was pointing, saw the car with the busted
fender and smiled. I thanked her and walked outside, right

past the white Cadillac, on my way back to the house, back to Jason and our merry-go-round lives that seemed to be going nowhere.

On my three-mile walk home, I came to understand why the nurse wanted me to be with someone. I was bent over in pain like I'd never felt before and there was blood clotting in my underwear and dripping down my leg. When I got to our room, I hid the brown paper bag with the meds and the directions, the words of warning I never read, so Jason wouldn't find out what I had done.

A few days later, I packed everything I owned into a backpack while Jason was at work and hopped on a Peter Pan bus down to South Florida to move back in with my dad. I never saw Jason again. A few more weeks went by, and an envelope arrived in my dad's mailbox. I had applied to one college, Boston University, and the letter in the envelope informed me that I had been accepted with almost a full scholarship. I held that piece of paper in my hand for a long time, just staring at it, unable to believe the words hovering in front of my eyes, unable to believe that someone, somewhere, thought I was worthy.

That was the closest I had ever come to becoming a mother. An almost-too-late abortion at seventeen. For decades I barely thought about that fetus. It wasn't until now as I was struggling to get pregnant—staring at that photo—that I began to wonder what my child would have been like if I had kept it. And then something else hit me: What would *I* have been like if I had that baby? Would I have gone to college? Would I have gotten married? Whom would I have married? Who would I be? What version of this book would I be writing if I'd had a baby at seventeen?

19

Playing God

If Rob and I had had a one-night stand and I'd gotten knocked up that first time we had sex, we wouldn't have had a choice as to which genes would become the building blocks of our child. My twenty-three chromosomes would have combined with his in mysterious ways, and when our baby popped out, we would have marveled at how his eyebrows looked like rainbows just like Rob's, or how the shape of her face looked like a mirror image of mine. We'd have eventually gotten over our fears of passing down to our child the mess and muck that lurked in our DNA. Sure, there'd have been nights that one or both of us would have tossed and turned, worrying about whether our baby would inherit my family's mental illness or a genetic mutation like my brother's or any number of quirks from Rob's side of the family. But that's the reality of bringing another human into the world. It's a gamble. The awe and magic of starting a family is that you don't know what you'll get. Becoming a parent requires surrender. It requires admitting that you have no control.

By the time Rob and I were sitting on a couch at a quiet café-bar in the East Village with a defunct fireplace and a dark wood interior, we had waited months for this moment. Finally, we'd gotten the call from the nurse at the clinic saying I'd passed all the tests. My body was deemed healthy enough to carry a child. We were eligible for the clinic's money-back-guarantee program. Before she hung up, the nurse promised to send me the code so we could log in to the clinic's donor database so we could choose not only the person our child would potentially look like, but the generation upon generation of molecular history our baby would carry as well.

The first thing that struck me, after I got over the fact that Rob and I were swiping on women as if we were perusing a dating site together, was just how few donors there were. My nurse reassured me that new donors were being added every few days, but the reality was that there were only about three dozen profiles. By the time we filtered those down to the women who looked even remotely like me—brown, wavy hair, brown eyes—there were less than ten. The truth is that I was looking for someone who looked familiar. And familiar, in my eyes, meant Jewish. The donor didn't need to be Jewish, but since I'm Jewish I hoped she'd at least *look* Jewish. The problem: there's a shortage of Jewish donors. Or even partially Jewish donors.

The situation is even worse for Black and brown women. I'd read about the scarcity of Black egg donors and understood there were many reasons for this. With our country's history of forced sterilization on Black and brown women, unethical medical research on African Americans, and the child welfare system and criminal justice system that separates families of color, it's little wonder that there'd be hesitancy to donate. But the clinics have also contributed to the problem with a lack of representation in literature, education, and outreach. While Black men and women are twice as likely to experience fertility issues, they are less likely to seek treatment.

And the situation has only gotten worse since the Covid-19 pandemic. The number of Black women looking for assistance with conceiving has shot up significantly. Yet Black sperm donors are fewer than 2 percent of the supply at the four largest sperm banks. This might have to do, as one expert hypothesized in *The Washington Post,* with the "highly selective process" for sperm donation, which involves exams, screenings, and comprehensive medical histories that create their own barrier to entry. Religion may keep people from donating, too. Whatever the reasons may be, there's no question that the options are limited.

When I saw the small pool of women from which Rob and I had to choose, I cried, "There's none left," barely bothering to conceal my distress from the twentysomething working away on his computer nearby us. But instead of matching my anguish, Rob looked over at me patiently and said, "Let's take a look at the profiles that *are* here."

Right away it was clear, though, that we were at odds. Rob and I couldn't agree on the basics of what was important to look for in a donor. I'll admit: I believed that what I wanted when it came to a donor should trump Rob's desires. I was certain that not using my DNA would mean I'd always feel on the outside of our family. Like I didn't quite belong. Rob would get to share his genes with our child, so in my mind that meant I should get more of a say on which donor we chose.

And then there was this: there was a fire raging inside of me that started as embers but was now threatening to engulf our whole relationship. I was angry that I needed to use donor eggs in the first place. If only we had thrown caution to the wind and instead of talking ad nauseam about starting a family for all that time we had just ripped each other's clothes off, I'd be pregnant already. Instead, we were careful, staying up into the wee hours to rattle off bulleted lists of the "right" time to start a family and sketching out the personas for the type of parents we would want to be. Instead of fucking we'd been futzing.

I told Rob all of this. And guess what? It didn't go well. "You have to remember that we met when I was just a few months out of my marriage," Rob said, pausing to let his words sink in. "I was technically still married, for God's sake. Barely separated. I didn't know what I wanted. And I felt like you just wanted me to slot into your life and make a baby with you. You didn't want to get to know *me*. You just wanted someone to start a family with." Silence. "Getting pregnant is the easy part, though. Don't you want to have a child with someone you actually *want* to be with?"

By now anyone who had been on the other couches near us at the bar had managed to snag another spot or quietly scoot away. I only half noticed. I'd like to tell you that as Rob ticked off the "facts" of our history together, my "feelings" of anger dissipated. The opposite happened, though. I insisted he had wronged me. He threw his hands in the air with a "Who me?" look on his face, which only made me more mad. I needed someone to point a finger at for my pain and there was Rob, right in front of me.

"You're going to blame *me* because you were with someone who didn't want a kid for seven years?" he asked.

He had a point.

"I didn't take away your most fertile years."

I rolled my eyes.

But if I didn't believe it was Rob's fault that we were in this situation in the first place, I would have had to face the far scarier reality: that no one and nothing was to blame. Or inversely, everything was. My family of origin, my marriage, my own ambivalence, my genes, and even biology were all factors that had collided to bring me to this moment.

I didn't say any of that. It took me many more years (and a lot more therapy) to reach that conclusion.

The night ended not with Rob and me peacefully deciding what we each were looking for in a donor. It ended with Rob slamming his laptop shut, getting up from the couch, and leaving the bar. Without me.

A FEW DAYS later, I did an experiment. I sat on the benches outside our apartment overlooking the highway and watched mothers and babies stroll by to see whether most women looked like their children.

I heard Charles Sawyers' voice in my head: "DNA is so powerful in determining appearances at least early." We had to find a donor who looked like me or I'd forever be relegated to the margins of my child's life. Everyone would know I was an imposter. A fraud. It would be written all over my child's face.

I noticed the woman with the bouncy curls, the just-right balayage, and the floral caftan holding hands with the little one with the same blue eyes as her and the matching crown of rotini spiraling out of her head. A mom with a toddler on a scooter walked by, and not only did they look like Big Me and Little Me, but they were wearing the same flowered maxi dress. But as I sat there longer, I observed that resemblance was a continuum. There were plenty of kids who looked nothing like their mothers. I knew this to be true from the people in my own life, too. Rob's sister's kids are dead ringers for their dad. If you stood a friend of mine, who I know used her own eggs, next to her kids, you'd think they were total strangers.

Then again, our other friends recently had a baby girl and she looked like a replica of both of them. And no one let them forget it. Every photo on Instagram someone commented on how she was their "#twin." I did it, too! We brought food to their apartment in those early sleepless days after she arrived, and I blurted out to her husband, "Wow, she has the same lips as you," and then a few seconds later, "And *your* eyes."

"DNA, it's an incredible thing," he said.

It really is, I thought.

I understood intellectually that whether or not my child looked like me meant nothing. I have plenty of people in my life who have adopted children or are stepparents and love their kids just as much as if they came out of their own bodies. But resemblance was the easy thing to point to.

My real worry was that by using donor eggs I would be cut out from my child's life, not only here and now, but for all the generations to come. This stranger's genetic code would not only live inside our baby and determine unknowable things about him or her, but would live on in our child's children, too, if they decided to have them. I wanted Rob to understand how sad I was that I wouldn't get to share every part of myself with our baby down to the cells that could only be seen under a microscope. I wanted Rob to know how scared I was that for the rest of our lives there would be a wedge between our offspring and me because we wouldn't share the same twenty-three chromosomes.

That night I approached Rob again about looking at the database of donors together. Before we even opened our computers, we each laid out what was important to us in choosing a donor. I knew resemblance had been an issue between us in the past, but I wanted to make sure he understood how important it was to me. "First and foremost is resemblance," I said firmly, hoping my self-doubt didn't show. Our donor didn't need to be an exact replica of me, but I hoped to find someone who resembled me enough that our child could pass as mine (even though of course there was no guarantee of that).

"I think the donor's family medical history and genetic tests should be our biggest concern," he said. In his mind, as long as the baby was healthy and was given a good runway for life, that's the most we could ask for.

"Of course, health and genetics are critical," I responded, speaking slowly so my voice wouldn't betray my anxiety. "But just as important is someone who looks like me. If we pick someone who has blond hair and blue eyes people might notice and make comments. I want to feel like this child I'll be carrying in my body is mine."

Rob nodded. "I know, I know," he said, half joking. "You might have told me a few times."

I also put a high priority on personality and intelligence, two things Rob didn't think about at all, or at least he hadn't mentioned. But how, from a few pictures and short essays, could we figure out how smart or funny our donor was?

I was stumped.

Sitting side by side on our couch, we scanned through the donors' photos. Some clearly posted the same pictures they used on Bumble or Tinder, their head tilted to the side, wearing a low-cut dress. One even had a picture of herself in downward facing dog on a deserted beach. Her profile screamed, "Pick me! I'll make all of your motherhood dreams come true!"

I'd gone out on enough shitty first dates to know that people lied in their profiles. They looked nothing like their photos. They twisted and cherry-picked the truth about their lives to make themselves appear better than they were. On the one hand, I was relieved not to be using my genes given my family history, but now I was faced with the uncertainty of someone else's genetic legacy. What if she didn't know that cystic fibrosis ran in her family? Or chose not to mention her father's clinical depression? Doesn't the system of self-reported medical histories encourage donors to lie if they want to get paid?

Suddenly my heart ached for all that would be lost by not using my genes. I'm funny. Is that genetic? Or how about my square-shaped face that I always attributed to my Eastern European ancestry? My genes aren't perfect, but at least I know what my genes hold (for better *and* worse). How was I supposed to feel about being in a position to "choose" the clay from which our baby would be molded?

Day after day, after grueling hours at work, Rob and I refreshed the clinic's database to see if any new donors had been added. The crassness—and awkwardness—of trying to choose our child's unique genetic signature from a few photos of a stranger as a baby and an adult, their medical history, a short essay, and answers to a series of inane questions like "What would you bring with you to a deserted island?" overwhelmed me. The fact that I wanted to be pregnant yesterday didn't help. The pressure mounted.

"If none of these women are the one, we'll wait for the clinic to add new profiles," Rob said, trying to be helpful. "There's new ones all the time."

"You don't understand," I said. "We're searching for my *replacement.*"

Rob put his arm around me. "No one's *replacing* you, Ruthie. You're still going to carry this baby. You're still going to breastfeed if you want to. You're going to change its diaper.

You'll wake up at three in the morning. You'll be the baby's mother. What else is a mother if not all of those things?"

I knew he was right. But I wanted to *feel* like our baby's mother. I wanted to feel the "strange double vision," as Louise Erdrich calls it, of "the you and not you of a genetic half replicated in the physical body of another."

I thought about the famous experiment that Harry Harlow did with infant monkeys. Harlow removed the tiny baby monkeys from their natural mothers a few hours after birth and gave them a choice between two different "surrogate mothers." One of the surrogates was a wire monkey with soft terry cloth that provided no food. The other was only made of wire, but a baby bottle was attached so the monkeys could eat.

Which "mother" do you think the baby monkeys spent the most time with? The terry cloth mother, of course. The one that was soft and nurturing. I wondered which mother I'd be. The one who offered tenderness and love? Or the jagged wire one who provided food and little else, never sure how to bond with her baby? What if, like the women in my family, I abandoned my baby, too? What if my shattered mind overwhelmed my ability to care for him or her?

Sitting in the living room of our one-bedroom apartment I read a study out of the University of Cambridge that found that women who used donor eggs didn't bond as easily with their babies. The eighty-five women in this particular study didn't smile as much at their child or respond as quickly—and because of that, the child was less likely to involve its mother by holding out or waving toys. My biggest fear—that I wouldn't feel as attached to our baby because we didn't share a genetic connection—was playing out in the research.

I scribbled in my notebook: "make sure to smile at our baby."

·   ·   ·

THE NEXT TIME we opened up the donor database, I studied each woman more closely. Rob and I were lying next to each other in bed as if we were watching the newest show on Netflix. Instead, we were looking for our "baby's mama," as we had begun to joke.

The majority of the women we scrolled by were just plain wrong. But this time through, I noticed a new profile, or maybe it was one we just hadn't paid attention to before. The woman in it looked like she could be my cousin. Brown hair, brown eyes, high cheekbones, wide smile, five six, 142 pounds, just like me. When I saw her profile, I thought: *this one could work.*

"There's something about her," I said to Rob, pointing at my screen. He looked over, pulled her profile up on his screen, too.

"What is it about her that you like?" he asked.

I didn't know how to answer his question. I still don't. I felt a sense of connection, a "this could be it" feeling. Now I just needed to get Rob's buy-in.

I clicked back over to the donor database. The clinic didn't give us the donor's name, for privacy reasons, so I named her Rachel. She looked like a Rachel.

Later that night, long after Rob went to bed, I stayed up lurking in Facebook groups for donor egg recipients. The women in these groups talked about everything. One flew to Eastern Europe to save money on the whole process. Another tried to give her baby a DNA test so she could track down her donor through 23andMe. There were scandals where clinics used eggs other than the ones they said they were using and they were caught. There were middlemen to help women and couples find the best matches. Some organizations brought young women over from other countries to donate their eggs in what, in some cases, seemed like egg trafficking rings. It was an unregulated industry, and a topic filled with deep shame. Few were willing to admit publicly that they needed someone else's eggs. Whenever there is silence, there is someone ready to exploit, to price gouge, to bend the rules.

"How did you choose your donor?" I typed. "Did you look for something specific? Did your partner help you choose? Was it important to you that the donor looked like you?"

I waited, hoping there was at least one other woman who was up late at night like me and willing to answer my desperate message.

As I sat there considering Rachel, the minutes ticked by. And then I heard it, a ding, letting me know I received a reply to my Facebook message. "Remember, your donor is not your baby," someone typed. "Look for someone who you'd want to get to know, who you'd want to grab a coffee with. No more and no less."

20

Sure Thing

I had felt something click inside me when I saw Rachel's profile, but I didn't trust it. This was the first donor I had liked, and what if that feeling was just relief at finding *someone*. It didn't mean Rachel was perfect. Another, better donor might be posted later that week. Or the next.

And so I analyzed and anguished. As with most important decisions in my life, I didn't have the confidence in myself to make it alone. I'd always believed that others knew the answers to my life's questions better than I would, like they had some special insight I hadn't been born with. But now I was starting to realize that it wasn't just important decisions where I relied on strangers for help, but life-altering ones about becoming a mother, too. In the absence of feeling like I could talk to my own mother, I decided to call a total stranger, the donor coordinator at our clinic, to ask her what to do.

As soon as I started speaking, I broke into tears.

"I know this is hard," she said to reassure me. Her name was Sara and she sounded young, like she was in her twenties. Maybe she had been a donor herself. "Tell me what you're searching for," she said gently. "I can be on the lookout for new donors that fit your description before they're put into the system."

Wow, I thought. Like with everything in life there was a loophole, a back channel that would allow me to skip the queue and get unfettered access to the new donors coming online. I listed my priorities. "Do you think it's weird that I want someone who looks like me? Am I being shallow?" I asked.

I cringed as I said those words, imagining her judging me. But Sara said, "Of course not! Most women want a donor who resembles them. You're perfectly normal. Then again, even if your donor resembles you, that doesn't mean your baby will."

I understood that. "Absolutely," I said. "But I want to be able to look into my baby's eyes and see myself in him or her. I understand there are no guarantees, though."

I couldn't see Sara's face since we were on the phone, but I imagined her nodding.

"Can you do me a favor and send me a photo of yourself?" she asked. "And then I'll circle back soon with some profiles for you to review."

As soon as we hung up, I sent Sara my picture, and then I clicked back to Rachel's profile. Something Rachel said in her essay caught my attention when I reread her words. She wrote that she wasn't sure if she wanted children of her own. Her honesty was refreshing. So many of the others had that I'll-do-anything-for-you-to-choose-me vibe. They seemed overeager. Pleading. Like they were pretending to be saints, contorting themselves into whatever they thought I wanted them to be. I understood innately why these women felt like they had to perform. Performance is something I'd spent my whole life doing. Twisting myself to fit society's mold is how younger me survived. Now I just wanted to be me, and I wanted my "baby's mama" to be unapologetically herself, too. I didn't want to pick a shapeshifter. I wanted someone who knew who she was.

Rachel was also the only donor who didn't speak in veiled religious tones about her desire to pass on a "precious gift" to another couple. She admitted she wanted to use the money she would receive from donating to travel and to get her master's degree in chemical engineering. She wanted a better life. *Good,* I thought. At twenty-seven, that's what she *should* want. At twenty-seven, that's what I wanted, too. Over the next few weeks I constantly refreshed the database to see if there was anyone new. Most days, one or two women would be added. But most were a definite no. At dinner one night, I asked Rob if I was being too picky.

"No, you're not. This is a big decision," he said.

It was on the way to visit Rob's family in Ohio for a long weekend that Sara called to let us know that she found someone she thought was "perfect" for us. We were still middrive, so I told her that as soon as we got there we'd take a look at the profile she was going to email. "That works!" she said enthusiastically. "I can give you the weekend to think about it before I upload this donor's profile to the database for everyone else to see."

Within minutes after we hung up, my phone pinged. Her email had come in. When I opened the donor's profile, I sat staring at it in amazement. It showed a petite woman with big bleached blond curls like Dolly Parton. The bio informed us that she'd graduated with a degree in theater and won a number of awards. The part Sara had emphasized when we were on the phone was that she was a "proven donor," who had donated five times before. There were already a handful of babies in the world with her genes. She was fertile to the max. "She's a staff favorite," Sara had said cheerily. "And Dr. Sasson gives her his stamp of approval."

I continued to stare at her teased blond hair. Had Sara not seen my photo? Didn't she know I looked like your run-of-the-mill Jewish girl? I named this donor Addison. Even though Addison's photos made me think of those Glamour Shots we took at the mall back in the eighties, her essay made me tear up. She sounded like a younger version of me. She wanted to save the world, head to Africa for a gap year to work in an orphanage. She mentioned traveling to India and Vietnam. She was a dreamer, which was both a blessing and curse, I knew. I wondered if being a dreamer was genetic.

I kept staring into Addison's eyes, but I felt no sense of recognition. Nothing that screamed: *she's the one.*

But I didn't want to disappoint Dr. Sasson by picking the woman who wasn't the proven donor. I didn't want to not get pregnant and then have Dr. Sasson and Rob say: "We told you to go with the other donor."

Then again, I knew that if I didn't choose the one my gut told me to and then I miscarried or never got pregnant in the first place, I would hate myself for not having listened to my intuition. There are some decisions that just aren't rational. And this was one of them. I heard the voice of the stranger in that Facebook group asking me, "Which one would you want to have coffee with?"

It could be as simple as that.

My answer: Rachel.

Rob and I called Dr. Sasson over the weekend to talk it out. There was very little cellphone service at the lake where we were staying, and we had to stand in a particular spot far from the cabin to get any reception. As we stood in the grass, we took in Dr. Sasson's words: "My goal is to get you pregnant, and looking at the data the proven donor seems to be a sure thing. The other one, we just don't know. She's never donated before, so you're taking a chance. It might work out. But if you're asking for my medical opinion, I'd go with the one that has a higher chance of making an embryo."

On our call, Dr. Sasson informed us that since Rachel wasn't a proven donor he couldn't be sure how many eggs they'd get. "Since we don't know, we're only going to allow two families to share her eggs instead of three." This meant that if we chose Rachel it would cost an extra ten thousand dollars, or forty-two thousand dollars in total. And the kicker, one other family had already chosen Rachel. If someone else picked her, she'd be gone forever. Or at least until she decided to donate again, which might be years, if ever.

We slowly walked back to the cabin. "I say we go with Dr. Sasson's pick," Rob said, his arm around me. "All that matters is that we have a baby, right? Isn't that the most important thing?"

But Rob's certainty didn't rub off on me. I needed to hold my feelings in my hand like a piece of sea glass, turning them over and over, holding them up to the light in different ways to see how the sun refracted the color at various times of day, throughout the seasons, whenever I felt like it. There was never an ending to my examination. I moved through, but I didn't move on.

ONE DAY, WHILE still hesitating over this decision, I took a walk around our neighborhood to clear my head and noticed all the moms pushing babies in designer strollers. They were wearing platform sandals and shapeless dresses in muted colors. Their hair looked perfectly cropped and sun-kissed. Their skin was dewy and their lips glossy. I couldn't help but stare. At the women. At their babies. Would these women and their babies get to experience something I never would?

By the time I walked in the door of our apartment my body was in revolt. I felt sucked dry. I let Rob stroke my hair. I told him how I'd been kicking myself for not realizing I wanted children sooner and for being so desperate to be loved that I allowed myself to marry a man who I knew didn't want a baby even though I didn't think I wanted a baby either. Then I voiced the cry I often had in the past, "Why do I always feel I'm being punished?"

Rob and I were lying on our sides, forehead to forehead, our arms wrapped around each other as my words settled over us. And then when I was sure he wasn't going to respond he said, "I don't believe that the universe punishes people, and I don't think you believe that either."

He was right. Deep down, I didn't.

He pushed my hair behind my ear gently, kissed my nose, and said, "We're going to have a baby somehow and you're going to be a great mom." And I believed him. At that moment I saw for what felt like the first time that I *could* rely on others. That I wasn't a burden. That I was lovable. I didn't need to make every decision alone. Rob and I were a team and being part of a team felt good.

The next morning, I sat beside Rob and told him I wanted to move forward with Rachel. He nodded. "Call the clinic and tell the nurse. I won't stand in your way."

He was offering me the freedom to choose. Together.

I inhaled the smell of his neck. Felt my body against his. This was where I wanted to be.

21

Are We Crazy?

As we sat across from Dr. Bernstein in a fancy office on the Upper East Side, I noticed her wire-rimmed glasses were held together by a piece of masking tape at the bridge of her nose. At first, she didn't say anything about the tape, and I was too shy to mention it, but as the minutes ticked by, I wondered if the masking tape was a part of the psych evaluation Rob and I were undergoing, a routine part of the donor egg process. I wondered if by ignoring the tape, this psychologist would note in her serious-looking doctor's notebook that I was going to be the type of mother who would hold back, not speak my mind, notice something was wrong but not voice it—and so determine that I wasn't ready to conceive using donor eggs.

Interestingly, I never once wondered whether Rob was being evaluated, though of course he was. But I was sure it was *my* performance here that was the deal breaker. That as the potential mother, I would be the one scrutinized more harshly. Rob didn't need to worry. Only I did.

Suddenly, Dr. Bernstein sat up straighter. She seemed to realize that her glasses were broken, and she proceeded to explain that she'd stepped on them the day before and just hadn't had a chance to get them fixed yet. As she reassured us, I could see that the masking tape on her glasses wasn't a test. I was being paranoid. My body flooded with relief.

It turned out Dr. Bernstein wasn't judging us. She was only determining whether we were planning to disclose to our child that he or she was created from donor eggs, and when. She encouraged us to talk to our child early and often—in age-appropriate ways—about where he or she came from.

I confided in Rob and Dr. Bernstein that I worried our moody teenager would stomp off angrily and say: *you're not my real mother.*

"Uh, yeah," Rob said nonchalantly, looking between me and Dr. Bernstein. "That's exactly what our kid will say." His matter-of-factness flooded me with rage. It was easy to be blasé when there was no question that your child belonged to you. When there was no *other* constantly looming in the background threatening your sense of self. My body would make our child cell by cell and yet I still felt threatened. Conditional.

Nonetheless, I was ready to move forward. My hope was that as my body made our child, I'd somehow make myself into a mother, too.

THE FOLLOWING MONTH my best friend, Laura, and I waited to board a ferry to Martha's Vineyard for our annual girls' trip. I didn't recognize it at the time, but there was a vein of sadness between us: if everything went well, this would likely be the last trip before I had a baby. I tried to push that feeling away. Deep down I knew that having a baby meant my life *would* change. There was no way around it. But so far, I hadn't wanted to acknowledge that part. There was also the loss of the person I was: in college, Laura and I had made a pact that we would never have children—and here I was, breaking our vow. I wasn't sure how I could be the fun, career-driven, adventurous friend Laura had known since college, and a mom. I wasn't sure how these pictures overlapped. Standing in line for the ferry, I realized that there would be loss as well as gain once I became a mother. Over the next few days, Laura and I drank Sancerre, ate oysters, and watched the sunset as if it was the last weekend of our lives. And in some ways, it was.

Laura and I were in the car together when I finally got the call from the clinic that we could transfer our first embryo in December. The calendar in my head finally had an X on it. But I was anxious that the big day was still three months away—an eternity in my mind.

SINCE ALL THE testing Dr. Sasson had done on my body months ago, my entire job had been to sit around and wait. The donor was now the one who had to inject herself with hormones. She was now the one who had to go to the clinic every morning at seven to have her blood drawn. She had to have an ultrasound every other morning to see if her egg follicles were still growing. I felt like one of the wives in *The Handmaid's Tale,* watching from afar as the handmaid nurtures and grows her baby, waiting for the day when the child will finally be hers.

The weeks passed, and Dr. Sasson called to congratulate us: the genetic tests showed that all six of our embryos had come back normal, which meant we had six chances at coming home with a live birth.

When the nurse called back to discuss next steps, Rob and I were on speaker phone with her in the kitchen. I was staring at the phone as it lay on the marble counter, her voice rising up to us as if the universe was speaking to us directly. Immediately, I blurted out: "How many are boys and how many are girls?"

It seemed like an obvious question. Rob and I had been going back and forth about whether we wanted a boy or a girl since we agreed that we both wanted to have a baby. I wanted a girl. He wanted a boy. There are some people who say things like, *as long as the baby is healthy that's all we care about,* but we're not those people. We both really cared. A lot.

I wanted a girl for reasons I'd categorize as both "emotional" and "rational" with a dash of ridiculous added for good measure:

I imagined I'd relate better to a girl.

I'd always fantasized about dressing up a little girl in cute clothes.

I'd wanted a do-over of my childhood.

I'd convinced myself girls were easier than boys.

The data showed that girls were four times less likely to be on the autism spectrum.

Rob wanted a boy because, well, you'd have to ask him. I'm still not entirely sure.

This disagreement continued through countless couples' counseling sessions with our ever-patient therapist. And now we were on the phone with the nurse and I was eager to learn the sex of our embryos and Rob said, "Wait."

"Wait, for what?" I asked, confused. It wasn't like we were choosing which embryo to implant. We were only finding out what we had in storage.

"I thought we didn't want to know," he said, equally confused.

"We never said that," I replied, not caring that the nurse was listening to us have a heated conversation. What should have been a happy moment—We have six embryos! They're all normal!—was quickly devolving. I wondered how many other couples had meltdowns in front of her.

"Why wouldn't we want to know? That makes zero sense," I said.

"Because then if it's a girl I'll be disappointed for nine months."

"You'll be disappointed my *entire* pregnancy if it's a girl?" I asked. "You won't get over it?"

I couldn't believe my ears.

Finally, the nurse spoke up. "Why don't you just give me a call when you guys agree on what you want to do? I need you to both be on the same page. I can't release any information unless I hear from both of you."

The writer Oliver Burkeman points out that the Latin word for "decide," *decidere,* also means "to cut off," which makes sense. When we decide on one thing, we are *cutting off* other possibilities. "Any finite life—even the best one you could possibly imagine—is therefore a matter of ceaselessly waving goodbye to possibility," he writes.

For Rob, saying he'd be disappointed for nine months was his way of letting me know that he didn't want to wave goodbye to the possibility of having a boy. When he'd fantasized about having a child, he saw an image of a boy in his head. We all say things we don't quite mean when we're supercharged, and for Rob it felt like he'd never get over the idea of not having a son. To mitigate his disappointment, he decided he'd rather not know the sex of our embryos and just wait for our baby to be born. He would be so excited the moment I gave birth that he'd fall in love with our baby—no matter the sex. But he wasn't sure he'd be falling in love with our baby slowly over my pregnancy. And he worried that if he found out the sex and it was a girl, then that nine-month slow burn might lead to a lot of hemming and hawing and getting in the way of intuitively and fully experiencing the moment of childbirth.

But for me, finding out the sex meant finally being able to imagine our future child. Until now, the idea that we were going to have a baby felt as real as the oxygen we all breathe. I knew it was there, but I couldn't picture it. It was invisible. I'd been immersed in the hope that we would be able to conceive a baby, but it all felt as thin as air. Knowing the sex, somehow, would make it all seem more definitive. Like the embryos were more real. Like this whole baby thing was actually going to happen. Of course, there were a lot of steps between knowing the sex of the embryos and giving birth to a healthy child. But it would help me feel like I could reach out and touch that reality.

In the end, we decided to find out the sex. Five girls and one boy. But we agreed to let the lab technician play God and pick which embryo Dr. Sasson would transfer into my uterus. We wouldn't know the sex of the embryo the lab technician actually chose until the baby was born. And by then we'd feel our baby kicking in the middle of the night. We'd sing songs. Whisper to him or her our hopes and dreams. The baby's sex would no longer matter. It never did. It was just something we could pretend to control.

We'd made so many decisions already. So many choices that at the moment felt impossible. Now we could sit back and let the lab technician decide which of our six embryos would have a shot at life and which would stay frozen. Stashed away in a vat of liquid nitrogen.

When I imagined the lab tech choosing our embryo, I flashed back to sitting in the audience at Radio City Music Hall to see *The Nutcracker*. It was dark and the toy soldiers were all standing at attention, eyes closed, silent. And then suddenly their eyes shot open, they were alive, their rickety bodies jerking this way and that. In this fantasy, Rob and I play God, waving our magic wands to give the lab tech permission to pick the sack of cells that would one day come alive.

But I don't like playing God. I gain comfort from the notion that the world is chaos and yet beauty, joy, and awe still find their way into my life. This idea that our potential child, and his or her diblings, are like a stack of toy soldiers sitting in a dusty theater, plagues me. I believe in science to my core—and I understand the difference between potential and actual. Yet science doesn't address the thorniness of what to do with the feeling I have that our embryos are tiny people lying in wait. Despite the fact that my brain laughs at the idea of a homunculus, or "little man," who lives inside our sperm and eggs, a term credited to Paracelsus in the fifteenth century, at times my heart feels like a fool, living in the pre-Enlightenment era. Why does it *feel* like our embryos are alive even though I know they're not? Why does it *feel* like I'm already a mother to these six balls of undifferentiated matter? Why does it *feel* like if we discard them or leave them in storage indefinitely that I'd somehow be abandoning our children?

The next time Dr. Sasson and I were on the phone, I told him how I was feeling about our leftover embryos and asked him what he thought. "I joke with my patients and say, 'I missed that day in medical school when they taught us when life begins.' Is it at implantation? Is it just when sperm meets an egg? No one knows."

No one knows, but I kept pushing anyway. I knew that embryos weren't children, not even close. "But then why do I *feel* like my embryos are our potential children?"

Dr. Sasson didn't hesitate. He didn't even pause. He acted like a man who considered these questions so many times that by now he was on autopilot. He'd seen so many embryos with all the potential for life in the world not make it for one reason or another. They never implanted. Or implanted but never grew. Or grew, but stalled out. Or made it so close, to twenty or twenty-five or even thirty-one weeks, but then for some reason just stopped. Until that embryo was living, breathing on its own, it was all just potential.

"Your word 'potential' is really important," he said. "Potential isn't actual. This is your cluster of cells that has the *potential* to be a child if like a bazillion things actually work out properly."

"Yeah, a million things would have to work out," I said wistfully.

"Not even a million," he said quickly. "More than a million things have to happen just on the first day. You're growing a person. Think about all the things that have to occur for that to work out properly. There's a *potential* that it could happen, but it's not actual."

As I hung up the phone, I imagined the distance between the two plains of potential and actual. Sometimes that distance was vast. And sometimes it was so, so close. But either way they were never one and the same thing. Rob and I would have to exist in the limbo of knowing our embryos weren't alive, but they weren't *not* alive either. Potential is to actual what fantasy is to reality. I'd learned that I needed to be real in order to have the intimacy I craved. Now I'd have to learn my next big lesson. I'd have to embrace reality. That would mean giving up control. That would mean giving up certainty. That would mean letting go.

22

What If?

"There's your embryo," Dr. Sasson said, beaming, as if he had created it with his own hands. "Isn't it perfect?"

He was pointing to a screen in the operating room where I lay naked from the waist down on a bed with just a paper blanket across my bottom half. Rob stood next to me holding my hand as we both looked toward where Dr. Sasson was pointing. We watched as the doctor was handed our embryo, which had been loaded into a small catheter that looked like a tiny straw, and which he was inserting into my cervix as he spoke. "Look over here," Dr. Sasson said, even though we were already looking, and before he even finished his sentence we saw a white speck floating into my cylinder-shaped uterus.

Earlier that morning, Rob had made coffee and granola for the two of us like he did every morning. For so long I'd been waiting for this day, never sure if it would come. As I spooned granola into my mouth, it seemed unimaginable that today I would be leaving the clinic with a secret in my body. I would have an embryo inside me. Whether or not the embryo would implant and eventually become a baby was another story. But for now, I told myself, I should take this step as a small victory. I would beg the universe to make my tiny embryo grow. I don't believe in God, and I certainly don't pray, but that morning I made my case to the universe like someone appearing before a king hoping to have their wish granted.

"You know that whether or not you get pregnant today, everything will be okay, right?" Rob said a little later as we sat in the waiting room.

I didn't know everything would be okay, but I appreciated that he was trying. I looked around at the other women. Some looked my age, but many—most—looked much younger. I wondered what they were doing in a fertility clinic. I wondered in what ways their bodies had failed them.

Finally, a nurse brought us into an area in the back we never knew existed and opened a curtain to reveal a changing room. "Both of you should put these on," she said, pointing to a blue hair cap, a blue paper gown, and blue paper slippers to place over our shoes. All I could think about was that I needed to go to the bathroom, but she told me I couldn't go until after the transfer. "You must have a full bladder," she said, "to help with the visualization of the uterus." I breathed deeply and tried to forget I had a body at all.

When we arrived at the cold, bright operating room, a new nurse I had never seen before asked me to tell her my name and birth date. This was the first of many times I would repeat my name and birth date over the next few hours. There was nothing inside the room except for a bed with stirrups, where the nurse asked me to place my feet, and a chair next to the bed for Rob.

A few minutes later Dr. Sasson walked in, turned off the

lights, and told us that on the other side of the wall was a lab technician with a petri dish. "Inside that petri dish is your embryo," he said. I noticed on the wall there was a whiteboard with my name and birth date on it. So many layers of verification. I wondered how many embryo mix-ups there had been before they put all these protocols into place. How many times had the doctor accidentally put an embryo into the wrong woman's body?

Before I had a chance to think too much about nightmare scenarios, the sonographer placed the transducer on my abdomen and Dr. Sasson inserted the speculum. Suddenly, the ultrasound screen above us revealed my insides. Another screen lit up and showed us our embryo.

"Have you ever seen anything so perfect?" Dr. Sasson said. I hadn't. There on the screen was the ideal embryo, circular, magnified to the size of a small cake.

"Oh, wow, it *is* perfect," I said.

Rob put his hand on my shoulder. "How big is the embryo in real life?" he asked.

"As big as a period at the end of your sentence," Dr. Sasson said.

Next thing I knew, we were watching the doctor impregnate me in real time. He picked up the embryo with the catheter and inserted it deep inside me. I forgot about everyone else in the room and just focused on Rob and me and the spherical organism that we hoped would one day become our baby. We looked into each other's eyes and back at the screen. There was nothing sexy about this moment—we weren't alone in a room, in a bed, our bodies connected physically and emotionally—but it was magical, nonetheless.

BEFORE WE LEFT, Dr. Sasson told us that we would need
to wait twelve days for a blood test to tell us if I was pregnant.
"Don't jump to any conclusions based on your symptoms," he
warned in the hazy, dreamlike moments after the embryo
transfer. The progesterone and estrogen I was taking could
make me bleed, feel bloated, have sensitive breasts, urinate
often—all the signs of pregnancy. "Whatever you do, don't
take an at-home pregnancy test," he said. "They could be
wrong. I've seen it happen."

Dr. Sasson was trying to protect us. He didn't want us to be
disappointed. He had seen the devastation of false positives.

Rob and I had booked a hotel room in Philadelphia, a short
drive from the clinic, so we could spend the day resting after
the embryo transfer. I'd lurked in the clinic's Facebook group
for long enough to know that everyone had a different idea of
what a woman should do to increase her chances of implantation. Some said to orgasm immediately after the transfer because the uterus's contractions would help the embryo burrow
more deeply. But at that moment an orgasm seemed both bold
and unrealistic. Where would Rob and I go to get it on? The
clinic restroom? The operating room with the lab tech behind
the wall? I'd been through enough poking and prodding for
one day, thank you very much.

Others said to eat asparagus, avocados, and other anti-
inflammatory foods. There were those who believed a woman
should lie down, countered by those who swore it was better to
remain active. Everyone agreed, though, that stress was the
worst thing for embryo implantation. But how could I *not* be
stressed with all of these contradictory ideas of what I should
and shouldn't be doing? Haven't women gotten pregnant since
the beginning of time? During the Holocaust? The Rwandan
genocide? Those certainly qualified as stressful times. And yet

they managed to get pregnant. Did they all orgasm? Eat avocados? Worry about whether they should stay in bed or remain on their feet? All of this preciousness was driving me crazy.

The next day when Rob and I got home, I had barely sat on the couch when I realized it was only day two, and Dr. Sasson told me I would have to wait until day twelve to know whether I was pregnant. How would I get through another ten days? The following day we'd both be going back to work, but I couldn't imagine doing anything else but sitting on our couch and waiting for the day I could know for sure whether I was pregnant.

That night, when Rob was busy doing other things, I looked at Facebook to see what the other women in my group for donor egg recipients were writing to each other. And that's when I saw it: streams of photographs of pregnancy tests. Barely-there pink lines followed by comments like "Can you see anything?" and "Am I crazy?" and "I gave it five days and then I took a pregnancy test." I wasn't the only one jonesing to know if I was pregnant. These other women weren't waiting almost two weeks like their doctors had cautioned them to.

I knew what Rob would say if I told him I was thinking of taking a pregnancy test. He would tell me to wait for the blood test like the doctor recommended. He would try to protect my heart. But I wasn't him. I needed to know.

So I didn't say anything. I would wait three more days then take a test. The next day I raced to the pharmacy to buy a pack, feeling the whole way as if I was heading to a secret hotel room to meet a lover. I'd promised myself and Rob to always be honest about my needs. And instead of coming clean to my partner and simply saying that I desperately needed to know if I was pregnant, here I was skulking through a CVS with the pregnancy test in my hot little hands. I snuck in the apartment with the test in my *New Yorker* tote and closed our bedroom door behind me. The only place I could think to hide the tests were in my drawer behind all of my tights that I never wore. *He'll never look here,* I thought.

That box in the back of my drawer burned a hole in my brain for three days. I couldn't even look at Rob. I knew I had betrayed him. Yet I felt compelled to follow through. After dinner that night, while Rob was working on his computer in the living room, I tiptoed into the bedroom, pulled out a stick from the box, and slipped it into my pocket. I then nonchalantly strolled into the bathroom, peed on the test, and placed it gently on the rim of our sink. I didn't think about what I would do once I knew the results. Where would I go with my devastation if I wasn't pregnant? Where would I go with my excitement if I was?

Two minutes later the test was lying in my palm.

I couldn't believe it. There were two red lines pulsing in front of me. I looked at the directions that had been in the box, the ones that I'd slipped into my pocket, too, and confirmed. Yep, two red lines meant I was pregnant. I crept back out of the bathroom and hid the stick in the box it came in, in the back of my underwear drawer this time, and didn't say anything to Rob. *What if it was wrong?*

The next day, I took another test. The two red lines looked a bit darker now.

In a few minutes I'd tell Rob everything—about the sticks and how I couldn't wait and can he believe it, I'm pregnant. I would eagerly hand the stick over to him. My body shook with relief and exhaustion and fear all at once. I had convinced myself for so long that I would never have a baby. I had convinced myself I was cursed. But here I was pregnant. I repeated it to myself every few seconds. *I'm pregnant. I'm pregnant.*

It was only a pregnancy test, but those two red lines represented more than just a new life: one red line was the road that brought me to this moment, my life with Rob, and if all went well, a baby in nine months. The other, the road not taken, the one where I stayed married to Evan or married someone else and there was no baby. I opened my eyes and closed them again just to make sure that when my pupils focused there were still two red lines in front of me.

There were.

When I finally told Rob, there was no crying or hugging, no proud happy looks. Later, I'd realize my expectations had been set by what I'd seen on TV. "While commercials for home pregnancy tests still offer the same predictable scene—a young, overjoyed woman, tears running down her cheeks, emerges from the bathroom and falls into the loving and outstretched arms of her husband—the picture has changed for many of us," writes Angela Garbes in *Like a Mother.*

Rob's arms weren't loving or outstretched. He was angry.

"How could you go behind my back and take a pregnancy test?" He was fuming. "I thought we agreed to wait for the official test."

I nodded. "We did. But I couldn't wait. It was too much for me. It was all I could think about."

He didn't soften.

"Well, I don't believe it. It could be a false positive like Dr. Sasson warned us. I don't want us to get our hopes up." He didn't want our dreams to be dashed and for me to end up back on the tile floor in our bathroom, crying, like I had after we found out our frozen eggs weren't viable, and our first two rounds of IVF were a bust.

Now I can see that what Rob wanted was for me to bring him into the process. It was *our* baby after all. And he wanted the intimacy and connection of being in it together. It was everything I'd longed for as a kid, for someone to want to be with me in this way. And even as I'd wanted it, I'd gotten used to seeing myself as someone who needed to operate solo. The person who figured her own way out of problems. Indeed, I was so used to believing that no one would be there when I needed them that I couldn't see Rob waving his arms saying: *here I am.*

ONE WEEK LATER I marched into the clinic to get a blood test to confirm what we already knew: I was pregnant. A few days later, a friend called to ask if we wanted to video chat with another couple who was also using donor eggs. I imagined the camaraderie and connection of finally having someone else who would understand the mixture of shame, awe, and uncertainty I felt. When their faces appeared on my screen, all I could think about was how I wished I could reach through the computer and hug them both. They looked like they could be our friends. Like we'd known them forever. The way she talked a lot to tamp down her anxiety reminded me of myself. The way he tried to soothe her by rubbing her back and putting his hand on her knee made me think of Rob.

As soon as they started telling us their story, though, I knew this was all a mistake. To hear how this other couple put into action all the choices we *didn't* make filled me with anxiety. As they kept talking, my body flooded with cortisol. My hands shook. My mind was screaming, *Run.* Meanwhile, I sat staring at the screen with a smile frozen across my face.

Had we made all the *wrong* choices? Had we rushed into the most critical decision of our whole lives? Should we have splurged and come up with an extra five thousand dollars or ten thousand dollars to ensure our child had the best of everything? If we were richer, would we have had the option of a "better" baby? Had we been cutting corners in places where it was vital not to? Racing to have a child while forgetting that once our kid was born the decisions we made in those early days could haunt us forever?

I could barely breathe. I could see from the screen in front of us that my cheeks were flushed. It was too late. I was pregnant. What was I going to do, time-machine back and make different decisions?

And then the woman said something else. I leaned in closer to make sure I heard her correctly. The agency they worked with had given them the option of paying extra for a video call with the donor. A video call! Why had we gone with the clinic that wouldn't let us do a video call with the donor? I wouldn't take a job without meeting my new boss first. I wouldn't marry someone I met on a dating app if I only swiped on their profile and never actually met them in person. We had to be the dumbest people in the whole world! Why hadn't we chosen a clinic that would allow us to meet our donor over video?

"It's so obvious," I cried to Rob once we finally hung up from the never-ending call. "It's so obvious."

My mind raced. Again, I wished for a time machine so we could do it all over again. This time we'd consider all the "right" things when we chose our donor. This time we'd spend even *more* money to make sure our donor had gone to the best schools. The truth was that our donor, the one I'd named Rachel, hadn't graduated from college. We'd decided at the time that didn't matter. But now I wondered: Were we setting up our future child for a lifetime of defeat? Was where you went to college, or whether you finished college, a sign of how smart you were after all?

I'd imagined myself going to coffee with Rachel, but it had been just that—an imagined scenario based on what I'd gleaned looking at a few photos and reading her essays. How could we be expected to make decisions about our child's life if our only knowledge of genetics was from eighth-grade science class? How much control do we actually have? How much control do we actually *want*?

The next few nights I curled up next to a slumbering Rob and read Doris Lessing's *The Fifth Child,* a horror story that reveals what happens when a monstrous child is born to a perfect family. I tried to imagine what would happen if our baby turned out to be a monster. Would I be able to bring myself to touch it? To love it? Would I be the jagged mother or the terry cloth mother from Harlow's monkey study, the one providing only sustenance or the one who could comfort and protect, too?

As I sat in bed, my mind went to other monstrous babies, and it landed on Mia Farrow's character in *Rosemary's Baby.* In the film, Rosemary had been impregnated by the devil, and in the hothouse of my worry I began to wonder if I'd been, too. *Rosemary's Baby* is the "cautionary tale of a woman's body being completely consumed by the evil intentions and powers of others," writes the author Lyz Lenz. Except in my case, I'd actually chosen the devil whose egg would be used to create my baby.

It's no accident that movies and books find fertile ground in the horrors of pregnancy. There are so many unknowns in bringing home a new baby. In the *Alien* movie the "fetus literally bursts out of the chest of the host, subsequently killing the host in the process leaving a deep open cavity." Back in college, when my roommate suggested that pregnancy was like being invaded by an alien, I'd immediately rejected the idea. Now that I was pregnant, her words felt like a prophecy.

Only later would I learn the ways in which science has shown that pregnancy is literally an invasion. David Haig's research in evolutionary biology at Harvard has revealed that there's a real-life tug-of-war between a fetus and the mother. In reality, a mammal's placenta is not a maternal organ that nurtures the fetus, but a *fetal* organ designed to drain the maternal blood supply. The placenta bulldozes its way into the mother's blood vessels, forcing them to dilate and then produces hormones that raise the mother's blood pressure and blood sugar. The mother's body then must raise her insulin levels to save herself. A mother and fetus both want to keep the fetus alive, but how much of the mother's body is her own in the process is up for grabs.

"The placenta does not, technically, belong to the mother," writes Angela Garbes in *Like a Mother*. "Our bodies may create it, but it is part of the developing child, which means it is also made up of 50 percent genetic material from the father."

Not only would the blueprint for our baby be a combination of Rob's DNA and our donor's, but the placenta, this foreign object that would feed off my body, would be made up of Rob's and this stranger's genetic material, too. Rosemary was onto something. Growing a fetus can feel like growing a monster inside of you. Even more so if you're growing a fetus with someone else's egg.

It doesn't help that in the current political climate, where access to even lifesaving abortions is not guaranteed, there are new implications for women in getting pregnant. There have been many recent cases where women carrying fetuses with severe abnormalities not compatible with life have been forced to carry their pregnancies to term, because doctors are too scared of crossing the delicate line of what constitutes a "medically necessary" termination.

At the time I didn't know that two and a half years later *Roe v. Wade* would be overturned, and this nightmare would become a reality, hindering access to abortions for those who most need it. In 2024, as more states moved to strip women of their reproductive rights, two movies arrived in theaters that, as the film critic Bilge Ebiri points out in *New York* magazine, expressed the anxieties of this new reproductive era. The film *Immaculate* is about an American nun impregnated by the Catholic Church, which is bent on creating a biological heir to Jesus Christ. And then there's *The First Omen,* also about an American nun, but this time she discovers a plot to birth the Antichrist. Both movies, Ebiri points out, sprout from our palpable "need to make our anxieties tangible."

All of this time I'd been haunted by the idea that I could be a monster passing down who knows what terrifying unknowns to our child. But now the pendulum had swung in the other direction—my fetus unknown, threatening, possibly monstrous. I knew this paranoia wasn't real, but I felt it all the same.

And yet, what peeked through the fog were rays of contentment, connection to the larger human family. During this time, I had tracked down research by a group of evolutionary biologists in Germany that revealed that every single species— from bacteria, insects, and birds to plants and humans—has a common ancestor, which has been named LUCA, or last universal common ancestor of all living organisms. Billions of years ago there was a unicellular, bacteria-like organism that existed from which all of us humans living today are descended.

This fetus didn't come directly from my DNA, but somewhere billions of years ago our ancestors emerged from the same bacteria and archaea living in the deepest, darkest parts of the ocean. If our fetus was a monster then I was, too. *And maybe that's exactly it,* I thought as I touched my belly. *We're all a mixture of good and monstrous and everything in between. We're all a part of the human family.*

23

More Than Just DNA

At our first ultrasound a few weeks later, a bald man I'd never met before wearing a white lab coat excitedly told us that he saw the yolk sac and the fetal pole, two terms I'd never heard before.

"See that," he said, pointing at a blurry dot on the ultrasound screen. "That will grow into your baby."

My organs looked like stars, like an intergalactic moonscape, like our fetus was floating in some alien world so different from our own even though it was inside of me. A few minutes later, the doctor turned a knob and the room filled with a whooshing sound. "That's the heartbeat," he said, and Rob and I looked at each other in awe.

"It seems so fast," I said.

"It's 147 beats per minute," the doctor replied. "Totally normal."

Rob smiled. As a drummer, he knew the speed of 147 beats

per minute. He began tapping on his legs, tapping out the beat of our baby's heart, and for the first time in a long time I let myself breathe.

I was ecstatic. And wary, too. While our friends had given their fetuses nicknames in utero—"strawberry," "bunny"— Rob and I decided not to give ours one. In the ultrasound photos that day we saw an organism; a blob. So that's what we called it. Blob was factual. But that was also a protective maneuver—a way to keep from getting attached in case something went wrong.

After pondering the pros and cons of having a baby for so long, there was a part of me that didn't believe it was happening—that was still very afraid—even as I told people how happy I was. And I *was* happy! And excited by the life that Rob and I were building together. That night, though, I jumped out of bed at three in the morning and ran to the bathroom covered in sweat. My body was rocked by chills. My hair was wet, my cotton pajama dress stuck to me. I looked in the mirror. *Am I bleeding? Do I still feel pregnant?* I thought about waking up Rob. I said his name softly a few times before getting out of bed, but he had his blue earplugs in and I knew he couldn't hear me. I moved closer to his side where the sheets were dry and he turned over. He hated being woken up. I told myself to go back to sleep. Of course, everything was fine. I should just close my eyes.

Back in bed, another wave of chills. I counted them—*one-two-three*—wondering if they were contractions. I kicked the blankets off because I was so hot, but then the sweat made me cold and I shivered again. *One-two-three.* The storm outside blew cold air through our cracked window, the tree *tap-tap-tapping* a terrifying beat.

In my half sleep, I wondered if our fetus was dead. I wondered if it had disappeared. In one of my panics, a few nights before, I'd read about "silent miscarriages," the term for when a woman doesn't bleed or show any signs of miscarriage, but her fetus suddenly stops growing. The idea that I wouldn't even know whether our fetus was still alive or dead haunted me. I grabbed my laptop and googled my symptoms.

Every worst-case scenario appeared before my eyes. Chills and sweats can be a sign of miscarriage. Fever, too. One minute your fetus could be growing and the next it could be gone.

The next day I was back in the doctor's office where a doctor I'd never met before walked into the room and smiled, encouraging me to do the same. "Now that you're ten weeks pregnant you can have a noninvasive prenatal test, also called a NIPT, to help determine the risk that your fetus will be born with certain genetic abnormalities," she said.

I thought about my mother's pregnancy with Adam. Amnios weren't used routinely until the 1970s, and the first CVS test, another common test used today, wasn't performed until 1983. All of the options we now had weren't widely available for my mom's pregnancies. She had no way of knowing whether the fetus she carried had any chromosomal abnormalities. She didn't have the choices—as hard as they would be to make— that Rob and I now had to abort a baby with a fatal condition if we chose to. (Of course, if I'd been pregnant just two years later, at the time of the *Dobbs* decision, I may not have had the option to abort either. I may have been like Kate Cox, who was forced to sue the state of Texas to allow her to receive a court-ordered abortion, to protect her own health.)

The doctor listed off some of the syndromes the NIPT would be on the lookout for: Down, Edwards, and Patau, to name a few. Then she explained that the test was called noninvasive because it could be done by drawing my blood and analyzing small fragments of the fetus's DNA that were floating in my body.

"But we used a donor egg," I told her sheepishly. Rob put his hand on my back. Our baby wasn't even born yet, and I was already feeling othered.

"Oh, that doesn't matter," she said matter-of-factly, and I suddenly wanted to hug this doctor I had only met a few minutes before. "Even though your DNA is different, your baby's DNA will still be floating around inside your body."

Diana Bianchi, I'd later learn, is the reason pregnant women are able to have a NIPT at all. Her research on cell-free DNA allows doctors to screen for genetic abnormalities, like Down syndrome, Edwards syndrome, Patau syndrome, Turner syndrome, Klinefelter syndrome, and triple X syndrome.

But it's her research on microchimerism, the two-way flow of cells between the fetus and the mother, that I was even more intrigued by. What most of us don't realize is that pregnant women receive cells from their developing embryo and vice versa, creating a long-term biological connection. When Bianchi was at Boston Children's Hospital and later at Tufts Medical Center, she discovered male DNA (those with a Y chromosome) in women who had been pregnant with boys.

I was so excited by this possibility I decided to give Bianchi a call.

I loved the idea that our fetus's stem cells were like seeds taking root and becoming part of my body's landscape. What I didn't realize until a few weeks after my NIPT test, when I called Bianchi to speak to her myself, was that my cells would also take root in our fetus and become part of the landscape of our baby's body, too.

"You have a bigger imprint on your child than just DNA," Bianchi, who now works for the National Institutes of Health, told me. Fetal cells have been found to stay in a mother's body beyond the time of pregnancy, she said, and in some cases for as long as decades after the birth of the baby. A mother's cells also stay in the baby's blood and tissue, and the mother's cells are used to help the fetus's immune system learn how to operate.

"That happens in donor-egg pregnancies, too?" I asked skeptically.

"I wondered the same thing," Bianchi said excitedly, and so her team studied egg-donor pregnancies specifically. "How can a woman accept a completely foreign fetus?" she wondered before she did her research. "If someone gave you a completely unrelated kidney your body would reject it. What is it about a fetus that stops that from happening?"

I had no idea.

"Well, we looked at placentas and afterbirths from women who used egg donors and found that mothers did recognize the fetus as foreign, and yet their bodies didn't reject the fetus." She opened her eyes wide in amazement on the computer screen in front of me. "You see, motherhood is much more than cells. Familyhood is much more than cells. We're just starting to understand that."

Bianchi's research is just the beginning. At the Mount Sinai Hospital lab run by a cardiologist named Hina Chaudhry, Chaudry's team simulated a heart attack in mice that were pregnant and discovered heart cells with DNA that didn't match the mother's own. These cells belonged to the unborn mice that tried to repair the mother mouse's wounded heart. The study revealed that fetal cells transfer to the maternal myocardium during pregnancy and might help repair injuries to the mother's heart. Keeping the mother mouse alive is a win-win for the mama and her fetus. She wants to live and the unborn mouse needs her to survive.

It's no different in humans. Fetal cells have been found to increase the mother's immune response and even repair some tissues. In cases of rheumatoid arthritis, an autoimmune condition that causes severe joint inflammation, fetal cells can help the mother's body heal.

In one study of humans, Bianchi told me when we spoke, more than half of adults still had maternal cells in their blood. It turned out, our baby *could* carry my DNA in their body after all. And I'd likely carry theirs.

I was coming to understand that genetics was not a simple black-and-white equation. Yes, we get 50 percent of our DNA from each of our genetic parents. But our bodies can also carry cells from the body of the woman who birthed us—and from the developing embryos we carry. Some researchers even believe that we carry the DNA of our maternal ancestors within us: our grandmothers and great-grandmothers and so on. "It's like you carry your entire family inside of you," the evolutionary biologist Francisco Úbeda de Torres told *The Atlantic*.

When I hung up the phone with Dr. Bianchi, I sat in awe. I'd wanted more than anything to share a genetic connection with our child—and in some small way I now knew I would. The deep bond I'd develop with my baby would live on in our cells.

24

Defect

A few months later I went for my twenty-one-week ultrasound, and as I lay on the table watching the technician tick off all of our fetus's body parts—arms, legs, spine, kidneys—I smiled. "Everything is exactly where it is supposed to be," she said—and I lay, happily secure in the knowledge that my body was deciding how our fetus's genes would be expressed. My body was creating the music of our fetus's microscopic body.

I decided to post a photo of our sonogram on Instagram to finally let my community know I was pregnant. Only our closest friends and family had known up till then. We were all in lockdown because of the pandemic, so it's not like anyone had seen my growing belly. But as soon as I added the photo to my feed, I began to feel like a fraud. As the messages flowed in from friends and strangers, waves of women in their late thirties and forties DMing me to ask how many rounds of IVF it took before we got a positive pregnancy test, I cringed. They thought I was one of the lucky 5 percent of women my age who did IVF and snagged the golden egg. *Look, she did it,* I imagined them thinking. *She had a baby in her forties. It can happen to me, too.* I imagined question marks in women's eyes. *Which doctor did you use? Which medications? Did you do acupuncture? Did you take supplements? How long did it take? How much money? Why you and not me?*

I fought the urge to start typing in messages like: *This isn't what you think it is.* And: *Our baby isn't even from my egg.* And: *You can't just wait until you're good and ready—established in your career, settled in with the perfect partner, your life lined up just so— and have a baby with the snap of your fingers.*

"Stop with the shame," Rob said as he saw me staring listlessly at my computer screen. "Stop it now before the baby arrives. Otherwise, he or she is going to pick up on your shame and feel ashamed, too."

And I knew he was right.

That night Rob and I headed up to our roof to eat dinner. "Will you grab the orange glasses?" he asked as I placed everything we'd need in my tote bag to climb the three flights of stairs. But all I could do was stare at him in disbelief because the glasses he was pointing at weren't orange. They were blue. Rob is colorblind, and sometimes when I don't catch myself, I feel frustrated that his perception of color is so different from mine, that he doesn't see the world the way I do, he doesn't perceive the shades and shadows that are so obvious to me. He sees orange and I see blue. I see shame everywhere I turn, and he sees none. I see danger lurking around every corner and he's carefree, the wide-open road spread out in front of him.

·   ·   ·

THE FOLLOWING WEEK I was back in the doctor's office for a fetal echocardiogram, the test to make sure that the baby's heart is growing normally. I could see our baby's heartbeat on the screen as I lay there, so I knew it was alive, but when the cardiologist stepped into the room, she brought a different kind of bad news, something I'd never imagined.

"Your baby has a hole in its heart," she said slowly. "Just a tiny one," she added, smiling at me, as if that would somehow soften the blow. She took out a piece of paper with a crude drawing of a heart on it and drew the smallest circle I'd ever seen right where the hole in our baby's heart was. She explained that 50 percent of the time these holes close up before the baby is even born.

"But what happens the other 50 percent of the time?" I asked.

She put her hand on my hand, reassuring me that the baby wouldn't have to go to the NICU, that it wouldn't need surgery, that she or he could still play sports and do all the things that other kids do. But what I was upset about, what I was already kicking myself for, was that I hadn't even thought about the possibility that our baby's heart could malfunction. I'd considered every other scenario but not this one. If this was beyond my imagination, what else was out of my control?

I believed that as long as I faced all the worst-case scenarios, I could protect myself and everyone I loved. Of course this was magical thinking. Of course I had no such power. Still, my mind clutched at these illusions, that if I gripped hard enough I could bend the universe by the sheer force of my worry.

When I called Rob after leaving the doctor's office, he seemed calm. "I bet the hole will close up before the baby's born," he said after asking a few questions.

"How are you so sure?" I said, surprised at his confidence.

There was a fifty-fifty chance. Why was he on the side of life and I was always on the side of death and disaster?

After the appointment, I became obsessed with the baby's kicks. Those powerful jolts were what made me feel safe. If I felt a kick, I knew our baby was still alive. Before I left the office, the cardiologist reminded me what my doctor had recently said: "If you notice a decrease in your baby's movement or kicks, go to the emergency room immediately."

Wait, what? I was in charge of making my sure my baby was still alive? Did I need a spreadsheet? Was there a special app for that? The days crept by. Every hour felt like another opportunity to miss some kind of sign as the baby pushed and poked against my body. On Sundays, I sent photos of my belly to my family and Rob's. I no longer just looked like I gained weight. Now it was obvious I was pregnant. Each week my baby—and my belly—got bigger. Now there was more to lose. There was more at stake.

Around that time, I decided to write a letter to our baby so I would remember this moment, a letter that I could look back on and laugh at myself when our baby was finally here and the doctor assured us that he or she was perfectly fine.

Dear Baby, it began.

And then: *You're not even here yet and I already have so much to tell you. If any one thing was different, you wouldn't exist. Or you'd be a completely different person. The flap of a butterfly's wings changes the trajectory of the entire world. And so it is when a baby is conceived, deep inside a woman's body or in a lab under a technician's microscope.*

I didn't always know that I'd be able to have you. I didn't always know that you were a real possibility. Back then, I looked into my crystal ball and my future was murky. I was married to a man who didn't want a baby. And yet, one day I woke up with a feeling—some might have called it a vision—of a little girl holding my hand as I walked down the street.

I had no idea how I was going to have this baby or if she'd really be a girl or a boy or who this little baby's dad would be or if this baby would even have a dad or if I would somehow muster the courage to have a baby on my own, but that feeling was there and it didn't go away. So much has changed since that day, and now I look down at my growing belly and know that in a few short months you will be here. I wonder what games we will play. What secrets we will whisper to each other as I lay you down to sleep. What songs I will sing. The one my mom sang to me about being her precious firstborn?

Your dad and I are getting ready for you. He built bookcases in the living room to hold your stuff and measured the room so we know exactly where your crib will go. Friends brought us books to read about how to take care of you and gave us clothes for you to wear. We're already dreaming about who you will be when you grow up, but then the idea of you growing up makes me sad because I want you to be my baby forever.

At my appointment recently the doctor told me you have a tiny hole in your heart. I cried. I didn't want there to be anything wrong with you. But now I'm starting to think it sounds poetic. You're already brokenhearted. You're already human. Your cracks are already starting to show.

Don't worry, I have cracks, too. Someday you'll see them. And together I hope we can heal.

Love,
Your mom

25

Body Snatcher

Over the next few months, the fetus's invasion of my body turned into a full-on takeover. None of my clothes fit. I could no longer sleep comfortably. Walking took effort. I had to use the bathroom every few minutes because the fetus was pressing on my bladder. I already couldn't go anywhere because of the global pandemic that had descended on the world. But now even if I wanted to take a walk outside I couldn't because public restrooms were closed, and no restaurants or stores would let me inside to use the bathroom. My pregnancy felt never-ending.

I wondered what my great-grandmother and grandmother's pregnancies were like. I wondered about my mother's pregnancies, too.

Rob brought home a book of songs, and each night we picked a new song to sing, Rob with his beautiful voice and me, always out of rhythm. "You Are My Sunshine." "Yellow

Submarine." "Oh My Darling, Clementine." We lay in bed, my belly against Rob's back, the baby's kicks rocking us to sleep.

As my due date drew closer, Rob and I drove from Brooklyn to Boston to take Adam to lunch. We wanted him to see I was pregnant—to be a part of our child's life from the very beginning. But as we sat down together at a restaurant, I saw how much worse Adam's condition had gotten. His involuntary tics forced his hulking frame to suddenly squat to the ground. Even after we were in the booth, he slammed his chin against the table every few minutes or threw his cellphone into the air.

"You're going to be an uncle," I said. When I said the word "baby," Adam seemed to jolt into focus. "Congratulations!" he said, and leaned over to hug us.

My mind flashed to the conversation I finally had with my mother, the one where I told her that we were going to use donor eggs. I'd worried that she'd make our decision to use donor eggs about her—about how sad she was that her genes were not being passed on to our child. But she seemed genuinely happy for us—for the fact that I came around to the idea of being a mother, and in turn, she'd get to be a grandmother. If there was any inkling of disappointment or doubt in her heart, she never let on to me.

The two people I was most anxious about sharing my pregnancy with responded exactly as I would have hoped, if I had let myself feel hope. Instead, I'd been filled with fear and panic and then felt guilty for being worried in the first place. From now on, I told myself, I would start looking for other ways to see the world.

After we ate, Rob and I made sure Adam had some money in his pocket and had gotten on the correct train, and then we

sat in our car. Our family was taking shape, and we were leading the way. I was carving out the path I wanted—creating the
contours of a life of safety and belonging—just like I always
hoped someone would do for me growing up.

It was possible to sit next to the warm fire. I just had to
draw the circle, delineating inside from out.

IN THE FINAL week of my pregnancy, Rob and I sat on our
couch and watched videos about what to do if I went into labor,
which items to pack in the hospital bag, and how to count
contractions. A few days later, the doula we'd hired sat on our
roof with us and pointed at a plastic uterus to show us what
would happen to my body during childbirth. We watched as
she opened the mannequin's cervix and gushed over the beauty
of the pelvis, how each section came apart like puzzle pieces
and then fit back together perfectly.

The next morning, we went to the clinic for an ultrasound
to make sure the baby looked like it was ready to make its way
into the world. There were ten doctors in the practice, and we
were told that we would see all of them before I went into
labor so that whenever the baby was born, we would feel com-
fortable with all of them. But here we were just days before my
due date, and we hadn't met the doctor who had just walked
into the room.

This new doctor marched in, barely said hello, and man-
splained to us why he thought I should be induced on my due
date.

"But the ultrasound technician told us this morning that
the baby seemed perfectly happy," I said. "I have enough amniotic fluid. The baby's in position. I don't understand."

He looked at me like I was an idiot. He looked at me as if to say, *I'm the doctor. Don't believe everything you read on Google.*

"At your age," he said, and I knew this was going nowhere good, "we're worried about the risk of a stillbirth."

Stillbirth? He had my full attention.

"When you're over thirty-five, every day past the due date is a danger to the baby. The amniotic fluid could dry up and we can't tell the exact line between enough fluid and not enough. Things change quickly, and we wouldn't want to take that risk."

I stared at him in disbelief. "Why did no one ever mention this before? I mean, I've been here every week over the last month and none of the other doctors said anything like this."

I turned to Rob. He looked angry, too. We'd read that women are forced into inductions so doctors can control the flow of patients on the maternity ward. Uncertainty is inconvenient. And as anyone who has ever been pregnant knows, babies come when they're good and ready.

Rob had had enough. "Ruthie shouldn't be induced unless she really needs to," he said. He'd done the research. Inductions can be more painful, and they can make the labor take longer.

But now I felt torn. I should obey this doctor. Wasn't he the expert? If he told me what to do, shouldn't I listen?

The doctor raised his hands in the cactus pose, signaling that he'd given up. "If you don't want to be induced it's your choice, but there's a one percent chance your baby could be stillborn." Meaning: *you decide if that's a chance you want to take.*

Over the last nine months, I'd let the internet seep into my brain. The internet said I should create a birth plan. I should advocate for myself. I should have the birth I'd always dreamed about. Unless, of course, there was a risk to the baby or my-self. And until that moment my pregnancy had been pretty uneventful. There'd been the bleeding that scared me so much in the beginning, but that had resolved itself and everything had been normal since. There was the hole in the baby's heart too, but the cardiologist assured me that it wasn't life threat-ening.

The doctor's arms were now crossed over his chest. He knew he had won. The idea that I had a choice in how my labor would go was always an illusion. Unless I wanted to blame myself for the rest of my life if something did go wrong.

I'd met men like this doctor on dating apps. Arrogant and rough. The ones who tell long-winded stories about them-selves and never ask about you. This doctor ordered me to lie back against the bed and put my feet in the stirrups. He pat-ted the cushion next to me and the paper made a crackling sound.

"Move your hips down," he commanded as he pushed his hand inside me and I twisted in pain. "You're two centimeters dilated," he said, snapping off his blue gloves. He didn't ac-knowledge my squirming. He didn't acknowledge that his forcefulness had hurt me.

"But I was two centimeters last week," I said. "And I've been bleeding and cramping, which the doctor on call said was likely from dilating more. Are you sure?"

He looked at me as if to say, *Do I really need to explain this?*

"It's all subjective," he said, dropping his gloves into the garbage can next to him.

Is inducing me subjective, too? I wanted to ask. But I didn't dare. I didn't know how else he could hurt me or our baby.

He left the room, but not before telling me I could get

dressed. Rob and I walked slowly, dazed, to the front desk. I wanted to make sure this doctor wouldn't be the doctor delivering our baby.

"What's the OB equivalent of a waitress spitting in your food?" I asked Rob. "That's what I worry he'll do to our baby."

"I won't let that happen," was all Rob said.

I didn't want the arrogant and patronizing doctor to be there in my most vulnerable moment. I didn't want him to have our baby's life in his hands. I didn't want him to taint our first moments as a family.

The woman at the front desk said we could go home and think about whether I wanted to be induced. She smiled sweetly and said maybe the baby would come on its own.

As soon as we were outside, I turned to Rob and said, "We have to induce. Even if there's the tiniest risk of stillbirth, we have to induce. We can't lose this baby now."

Rob hugged me.

We went home and ate spicy foods and eggplant and Chinese food just like the internet and my friends and family told me to. We listened to every myth and superstition because what other choice did we have? I pumped my breasts until blood dripped out of my nipples and had sex until semen ran down my legs because breast pumps and semen supposedly make the uterus contract. This is the body of a woman about to bring life into the world. Bleeding from her vagina and her nipples. Semen dripping down her leg.

But still no baby.

THAT NIGHT ROB and I were talking—again—about whether our child should have my last name or his. We both loved the idea of giving the baby my last name. It seemed like a fitting act of rebellion, since only 4 percent of babies take their mother's last name. And I saw it as a gesture of inclusion. Even though I couldn't give our child my DNA, we could share a lineage through my name. I imagined Rob and our baby would feel some ephemeral connection our child and I would never feel, and somehow sharing a last name would tilt the scales back toward even. Sure, I carried our child, but I was still grasping for the feeling that I mattered. Yet I also worried that if we gave our baby my last name, Rob would feel left out. I couldn't live with that idea either. I wanted to be cautious that not sharing a name with our child wouldn't feel like a kind of erasure for Rob.

"I wouldn't feel that way," he said, and for a moment I felt reassured. But as our conversation continued something just didn't feel right. Even if Rob swore he would be fine with the baby having my last name, I worried a seed of doubt would always be lodged in my heart.

"What if we combine our last names?" I said.

"Like with a hyphen?" he responded.

We went back and forth. Ackerman-Heath. Heath-Ackerman.

"I worry that a hyphen will be clunky. What if we just have one of our last names as the baby's middle name?"

He paused, thinking, then said, "But won't whoever's name is the middle name just get lost anyway? Isn't that like having just one last name? And how would we choose which last name goes in the middle?"

He had a point.

There was also the baby's first name. Way back when I was married to Evan, Olive was the name that floated into my mind. Olive had always felt right. Real. But now that our baby was about to enter the world, I balked. Olive was the name I had chosen in another lifetime. Olive was the name I'd chosen on my own. I wanted our baby to have a name both Rob and I picked together.

Clementine, we decided, if it was a girl. Rye for a boy.

In the end, we chose to combine our last names. Heath and Ackerman became Heathman, and as we lay in bed that night, I hoped that Baby Heathman would join us before morning.

26

It's a Baby

When I imagined giving birth, my biggest worry was something happening to our baby. I understood that America's maternal death rate was abysmal, one of the worst in the developed world, but in my hormonal state all I could fathom was that our child was fragile, and I was invincible.

By morning when I still hadn't felt any contractions, I dutifully got ready to head to the hospital to be induced. As I sit here now, somewhere in my feminist brain is a little voice that says: *You should have trusted yourself! Your baby was fine! You didn't need to be induced! Let the baby take its sweet old time! Mothers and babies know better than doctors!*

But at that moment I was terrified. If something went wrong, I would never have forgiven myself. "We choose powerlessness over the potential for self-blame," as journalist Allison Yarrow put it. And there's no question that's what I did.

My mind played tricks on me. There were times when I felt

like "real" mothers wouldn't need to be induced. Their babies and their bodies would work in perfect synchronicity. At those moments I told myself it was because we used a donor egg that my body wasn't getting the message to go into labor. It was all my fault my labor needed to be kick-started in the first place. Doctors know what they're doing. That's why they give them the white lab coats.

"Real" mothers also give birth in bathtubs and without pain meds. They're crouched down, never lying prone on a bed. Even Adrienne Rich wrote that she didn't feel like a "real" mother because she was unconscious through her three deliveries when she *should have been* "awake through it all."

Even in childbirth women question themselves. And I was no different. I performed. I obeyed. I didn't want to make the wrong decisions. I didn't want to pay the price. I didn't want to be one of the difficult ones.

So I consented to being induced. But the one thing I did insist on was that the fury-filled doctor would not be the one to deliver our baby. I didn't want our first moments as a family to be tainted by his aggression.

The hospital obliged.

When we arrived with our duffel bag that we'd packed months before—including tea light candles for ambience, special postlabor underwear, and a birthing gown Laura bought me—Rob and I were giddy, like this was just another New York City adventure we were going on. I'd been terrified that I'd go into labor in the middle of the night and give birth in a taxi because we'd get stuck in traffic and not make it to the hospital on time.

Instead, we took a lovely ferry ride from Brooklyn up the east side of Manhattan. Our doula, who had been my yoga teacher before I got pregnant, met us there. We took the elevator to the labor and delivery floor, where the nurse had the nerve to ask, "Why are you being induced?"

I wanted to say: *I don't have any fucking clue.*

But instead I said: *Because my doctor said so,* and shrugged.

Once they started me on the Pitocin drip, I imagined I'd go into labor right away. But four hours later I felt nothing. The kind of nothing where Rob and I lay in my hospital bed watching Anthony Bourdain episodes to keep ourselves busy and our doula scrolled on her phone.

"What's going on here?" I asked Rob jokingly. "My whole life I've heard how painful labor is, and I'm so tough I can watch TV shows and not feel a damn thing."

The nurse smiled a knowing smile and increased my Pitocin. But before she did she asked me if I wanted the anesthesiologist to come in and give me an epidural. Let's stop here for a second. This was something I'd thought long and hard about. I understood deep in my bones that all childbirth, no matter how it happens, is *natural*. I'm grateful for the invention of pain management so humans don't have to suffer. I don't believe that because Eve ate the apple that I need to endure pain. Yet when the nurse asked me directly if I wanted meds I said, "Yes, but can I wait? I just want to see what it feels like." A wee bit of pain never hurt anyone, right?

I'm still ashamed of those words. Because what happened next is seared into my brain forever.

Once my contractions started, the waves kept coming. I was knocked down over and over and I couldn't catch my breath. Twenty minutes in and I had enough. The problem (and this is the part I didn't understand at the time) was that there's a gap between when you ask for the anesthesiologist and when he or she arrives at your room. By the time he arrived, I'd been screaming, "Help me! Help me!" over and over, and I'm absolutely certain the nurse was thinking, *honey, I told you,* but she didn't let on. I looked and sounded nothing like those women I'd seen in videos becoming one with their bodies, channeling their pain, opening themselves up to some kind of otherworldly connection to the eternal mother.

To make matters worse, the anesthesiologist couldn't locate the right spot to insert the needle. He kept stabbing me repeatedly in my spine as my contractions surged. But because I have scoliosis and my spine is curved, the place he was poking wasn't the correct one. I tried to crane my neck toward him to get a closer look, as if I could have helped him somehow, but all I saw was blood. I shook Rob's arm. Stared into his eyes in fear. "Can't you help me? Can't you get another doctor?" The anesthesiologist ran out of the room to get help just as another contraction broke over me. Eventually a third anesthesiologist came into the room, and she was able to insert the needle. All in all, it took an hour and a half *after* I asked for pain medicine to get it.

By then my pain had been ratcheted up to such a level that I couldn't get it under control. Someone came in and handed me a computerized pump that attached to my IV and released pain medicine every few minutes at the push of a button. But as soon as I pushed down on the button, I begged for more.

A doctor I didn't know came in and broke my water, but because he never asked me, I thought I'd peed on myself. A half hour later I was certain the baby was about to come out, so I sent our doula to grab a nurse. But the nurse didn't want to check because now that my water had broken, she said there was an increased risk of infection. "My baby is coming!" I screamed, and all I remember is the nurse saying, "You're right," and running to get the doctor.

The young doctor with long, straight brown hair whizzed

into the room bringing in a huge mirror and propping it at the end of the bed. "So you can see your baby," she said gently.

"Are you ready to push?" she asked, and I thought, *what choice do I have?*

"Yes," I said, knowing that was the answer she was looking for. She looked satisfied and then she got a serious look on her face. "Push only when I tell you to so you don't tear."

Within minutes I saw the top of my baby's head, before it slid back inside me. "Again," she called out, and again I pushed, squeezing my eyes shut. I couldn't tell how much I was pushing or where I was pushing from—everything was throbbing, and with all the pain medicine floating in my body at that point I felt numb. But my doctor kept telling me I was doing a good job. Rob kept squeezing my hand. Our doula kept snapping photos.

Another half an hour and the doctor placed a sticky, wriggly, purple being onto my chest.

"It's a baby, it's a baby," I cried. "It's a baby," I said again, looking directly at Rob this time. It was as if I hadn't understood that after nine months of carrying this fetus it would one day arrive as a full-fledged human.

"*She's* a baby," our doctor said, smiling. And that's when it hit me: not only did we have a baby, but we had a baby girl.

At that moment our doula snapped a photo of us—Rob smiling, a look of relief on his face; me, staring into Rob's eyes dumbstruck; and Clementine, sweet Clementine, lying there puffy, eyes shut, her tiny fingers curled around mine.

A few minutes passed like this, and all I remember is the doctor calmly leaning over my hospital bed and telling me I was bleeding a lot, losing too much blood quickly, and she was about to call in the troops. Well, she didn't really say, "call in the troops," but she did say that many doctors were about to descend on my room and not to be scared, they were going to give me a shot in my thigh and a special pill to try to stop the bleeding.

She'd also informed me that the blood transfusion team was on its way now and the head of labor and delivery, too—an official-looking person who would stand off to the side and make sure I didn't die on the hospital's watch.

Next thing I knew, there were arms. Lots and lots of arms, like octopus tentacles grabbing at me. Checking my blood pressure. Pumping medicine into my veins. Injecting me all over my body. Scurrying around the room. Someone lifted our baby off of me and handed her to Rob. As the army of strangers worked to save my life, I couldn't take my eyes off the life that had just shimmied out of me.

Someone in blue scrubs weighed her—eight pounds, two ounces. Someone else put a stethoscope to her heart. She was wrapped in a blanket, a pink and blue striped hat placed over her tiny head. And then, finally, she was ensconced in Rob's arms, lying on his bare chest as he sat in a chair a few feet away from me, and the doctor whispered that I'd lost 1.25 liters of blood, a quarter of the total amount in my body. But all I could think was: *There she is. She's finally here.*

I'd been warned that my labor could take days. Our doula harangued us with stories of fifty-six hours of pushing. The internet was full of cautionary tales about how the hormones injected into a woman's body to induce labor often slow down the process. There were too many scary scenarios to count. Emergency C-sections. Husbands who were forced to leave the room right after their wives gave birth because of Covid-19. Babies born with umbilical cords around their neck. Jaundice. Complications from not getting enough oxygen to their brains.

But Clementine arrived in five hours—and as far as anyone could tell us she seemed perfectly healthy.

Once the doctors all left—off to tend to other emergencies— Rob scanned the room. "I can't believe how much blood there is," he said. "You probably don't want to look, but the floors, the bed, the chair, everything is covered in blood."

All I could think, though, was: *she's normal.* She has ten fingers and ten toes, and even though we wouldn't know for another few weeks whether she still had a hole in her heart, right now her heart was beating just fine.

Over the next few months, the trauma of those hours would approach and recede like a wave. Sometimes I was back there again, in that bed, as the anesthesiologist fumbled trying to insert the epidural. Sometimes I closed my eyes and heard the doctor whisper about how much blood I'd lost, the footsteps of the team of other doctors approaching. Sometimes I was in limbo—straddling between life and death—between hemorrhaging and healing.

Sometimes I thought: I almost didn't become a mother. I almost stayed married. If I had continued to contort myself, Clementine wouldn't be here right now. I almost gave up after my frozen eggs failed. I almost buried myself under the rubble of grief when my IVF cycles didn't work. I almost didn't allow myself to have her because I thought if we couldn't use my eggs then I didn't want a baby at all. And then once we knew we'd be willing to have a baby with donor eggs, we almost picked a different donor. There are so many ways Clementine almost didn't exist.

WHEN LIFE BEGINS to form, the very first cell divides into two perfectly identical copies, which divide into two more copies that are identical, too, and so on. Despite the fact that the copies are exactly the same, one cell will become a brain cell, and another a blood cell, and so on. Somehow each cell knows its special role. It is one of the many wonders of nature.

Somehow, as the story goes, the women in my family didn't know how to perform their special roles as mothers. My father tells me about how when I was six months old and they'd just gotten divorced, my mother left me alone in my crib at night while she went out with her friends. Another story: my mother kidnapped me while my dad was at work and moved us into another apartment where my dad couldn't find me.

My father wasn't trying to be cruel—or to disparage my mother. Instead, he was making a point. Mothers don't leave their children in cribs while they go out at night. Mothers don't steal their babies away from their father. What kind of mother would do such a thing?

There was another story passed down from my dad. This one was about my grandfather, Al, my mother's father, and how he had an affair with a "young dancer" whom he'd gotten pregnant around the same time my grandmother was pregnant with my aunt. Apparently, my grandfather was a doctor and he didn't want to cause a stir. He didn't want the neighbors to whisper that he had impregnated another woman, a woman who wasn't his wife. He didn't want the congregants at the synagogue to gossip. So he brought home the baby he had with the young dancer for my grandmother Ruth to raise as her own. These two babies were born six months apart, but no matter: my grandparents told everyone the two babies were twins, a six-month old and a newborn, my Uncle Charlie and my Aunt Daisy.

Through the years, whenever my father told me that story we would laugh. At the foolishness of my extended family to believe that those two babies could possibly have been twins. "Had they never seen a newborn and a six-month-old before?" we'd joke. "How could they not have noticed that Charlie was so much bigger?"

We laughed at the brazenness of my grandfather to bring another woman's child home for my grandmother to parent. We laughed at my grandmother for not kicking him and that blond baby who looked nothing like the rest of our family to the curb and finding herself another husband who was faithful.

And then as the years passed, I heard a different version of the story from my mother. "Who told you that uggy story?" my mom asked. "Uggy" was the word she used for ugly, to show me that my version of events hurt her. She wanted to correct the record. She wanted me to know that my *Harvard-educated* grandfather was a doctor, as if men who were doctors and went to Harvard would *never* cheat on their wives. My grandfather, she told me, vacationed in Haiti where he fed "the poor children." And, according to my mother's version of history, the woman, the dancer, was a patient of my grandfathers who got pregnant and was too poor to take care of her child. "Grandpa Al was helping her out," my mother said, by adopting her son and bringing him home as his own.

Over the years, I begged my Uncle Charlie to get a DNA test. Now that Grandma Ruth and Grandpa Al had been dead for so long maybe he could find out who his biological mother was. Maybe she was still alive. Maybe he could meet her. But he refused. He'd already lost two sets of parents. Ruth and Al died when he was five, and then his adopted parents died when he was in his twenties. He didn't need another parent to lose, too.

So I let it drop. I didn't want to push Charlie. *Maybe knowl-*

edge isn't everything it's chalked up to be, I told myself. *Maybe knowing where we come from isn't the be all, end all.*

Recently I learned that my Uncle Charlie did finally have a DNA test, and what he learned was this: he's 99 percent Scandinavian. My family is 99 percent Ashkenazi Jewish. Charlie could not have been my grandfather's biological child.

My mom was right. The "uggy" story about my grandfather wasn't true. Maybe he *was* just a nice Jewish doctor, as my mother always said, and he adopted his patient's baby because she couldn't afford to raise him on her own.

All I know is that when I found out about the DNA test Charlie took, I called my father and told him about it. I excitedly explained that Charlie wasn't the product of an affair between my grandfather and the dancer, whoever she may have been. I had a can-you-believe-this-turn-of-events tone in my voice. "I like my story better," my father joked. "And I'm sticking to it."

I knew my dad was just trying to be funny. He wasn't trying to hurt anyone. But these family legends of affairs and abandoning babies in cribs leave an imprint, an emotional trauma that gets passed down, even if there's no genetic trauma to speak of.

When Clementine was a baby and I walked into a room and saw her in her chair all alone, my mind would flash back to my dad's story, that image of me alone in my crib crying for my mom, who wasn't there. Even when Clementine was sitting in her red bouncy chair playing, contemplating her hands or cuddling her stuffed lamb, I wondered if she felt abandoned. When she cried at night, I jumped. I never wanted her to feel like there was no one to run to her. I never wanted her to feel like there was no one to answer her cries.

Maybe if Clementine shared my DNA I wouldn't have felt

like I had something to prove. I would have known deep down inside that I was her mother and that would have been that. Or maybe this is what the system does to us: makes mothers feel inadequate no matter what we do. We're cold and rejecting, or we're hovering helicopters. We work too much or not enough. We're a biological mom, but not a genetic mom.

"If it wasn't about your DNA, you'd feel unworthy about something else," Rob told me back then. "Maybe you're just obsessed with DNA because it's the easy thing to point your finger at. But the more you focus on DNA and wonder if you're connected enough to Clementine, the more you suck the joy out of your time with her and the more disconnected you feel."

"You could be right," I said, but how would I ever know?

OVER THE YEARS, my mother has repeated a story about how when she was a child her mother, Ruth, would dye her hair blond. She still remembers her scalp burning as the chemicals seeped in, and with it, the feeling that if her mother thought she and her siblings were beautiful, she wouldn't feel the need to fix them by changing their appearance. And then there's the part my mother didn't say, or maybe didn't need to say, that as Eastern European Jews my grandmother may have had a complicated yearning to erase the biological destiny she saw in her children.

My mom didn't dye my hair blond, but the beauty pageants of my youth stick out in my mind. My younger self, walking across those stages in suburban shopping malls, waving and smiling. The trophies that still sit in a box collecting dust in my mom's apartment, a prize for performing femininity well. One could say that by not dying my hair, my mother created her own mother code, her own set of boundaries as to the relationship she wanted to have with her children.

Each generation of women made mistakes, yet they *also* tried to improve on the errors of their mothers. Maybe my mom was, in her own way, doing her best to love me and prepare me for the world. And now I held my baby in my arms, wondering what mother code I would end up writing.

27

Baby Blues

When Clementine was just a few days old, I held her in the crook of my right arm while I struggled to dial Adam's number with my left hand so we could video chat. My living room felt like a coffin—claustrophobic, stale—the August heat beating down just outside our window. I spent the past five and a half months there, on that gray couch, staring at those walls. Between being pregnant and being in the middle of a global pandemic, I didn't get out much. One day marched into the other with nothing to differentiate them.

Not only was I crying and then crying about crying, but to make matters worse, Clementine refused to breastfeed. But Rob and the lactation consultant at the hospital reassured me that we just had to keep practicing. In the meantime, we were sent home from the hospital with donor breast milk, which only made me feel worse—I needed a donor egg and now I needed donor milk, too.

The internet called my sadness "baby blues," but it felt like the whole world was crashing down on me. I had no idea whether baby blues was the same thing as postpartum depression. All I knew was that I suddenly understood that if my great-grandmother and grandmother actually did flee their families and abandon their children—traveling and looking for the high of new love instead of being anchored to a baby that needed so much every second of every day—I wouldn't blame them. Babies are hard. Babies are relentless. Babies don't care that you're tired and teary.

At that moment all I wanted was for Adam to meet Clementine right away. Even though he couldn't see her in person because we all—strangers and loved ones alike—were dangers to each other, I wanted him to understand what it meant that he was now an uncle. An uncle to the little girl Rob and I had wanted for so long.

To make even a phone call with a child that small is an accomplishment. In those first days I was viciously exhausted. I sat on the couch, now covered in spit-up and breast milk, and desperately tried to get Clementine to latch on to my breast while fighting to stay awake. When we both ended up frustrated and in tears, I finally relented and pumped my breast milk into bottles for her to drink every two hours. Feeding took almost an hour, so with only an hour in between feeding her and needing to pump again, I had to figure out how to feed myself, shower, change her diaper, and put her down for a nap. What I didn't know was that even flamingos lose their pink when they feed their chicks, turning a paler peach or even white until the chicks learn to eat on their own. Life was being sucked out of me. I wasn't the same person I had been only days before.

The baby books and websites—and all those well-meaning

friends and family—told me to make sure I slept while the baby slept. But sleep seemed impossible. If I was sleeping, how could I eat? If I was sleeping, how could I brush my teeth? And by the time I finished shoveling food into my mouth and lay down to rest, she was crying again, that wail that rattles a mother's bones, that wail designed to make mothers jump out of their skin, stand at attention, give their babies milk—or anything, really—except my baby, our baby, wouldn't eat from my breast no matter how hard I tried.

I texted friends, and finally set up a video chat with a lactation consultant who for $150 showed me videos of women in Africa breastfeeding. It looked so easy, so *natural*. The baby in the video practically jumped onto its mom's breast. Except we couldn't do it. "You're both learning," the consultant reassured me. "Try not to force it," but that's hard to do when your baby's not able to eat and is crying hysterically.

"It's like dating," she said. It's a dance. "Act nonchalant, like you don't care if she breastfeeds or not, and she'll change her mind."

But I don't have a nonchalant bone in my body.

The second lactation consultant asked me to lie down on the couch naked and put Clementine on my stomach. "Let her come to you," she cooed.

But she never did.

Whenever I would take my breast out of the special nursing bras I bought for too much money for the breastfeeding sessions I fantasized about before she was born, Clementine would swing her head back and forth as if she was screaming "no." Our pediatrician laughed when I told her how our baby rejected me.

"That's the way newborns look for your breast," she said.

But how was I to know that? I thought I was torturing her. I thought I was forcing my breast into her mouth, which went against everything I thought I knew about consent from my women's studies classes in college. I was fried, frazzled, fragile.

There was a third lactation consultant. The one we met at the hospital where I gave birth. Two days after we brought Clementine home, we got a call from her. "How are you guys doing?" she asked, and before I could form words, I broke down crying into the phone. When I finally calmed down, I said, "She's crying every twenty minutes for food," before choking back more tears.

Her voice was soothing like those meditation teacher voices in the apps I barely listened to while I was pregnant. "How much are you feeding her?" she asked gently, which only made me cry more.

"Exactly what you wrote on the chart we brought home," I said, exasperated. "Ten milliliters per feeding, sixty milliliters per day."

Rob was standing next to me, but somehow I felt responsible for the fact that our baby was screaming at the top of her lungs. I felt like I had done something wrong. Like not being able to soothe my baby was a sign that we'd never bond.

"Oh no!" the consultant said. "It's not sixty milliliters per day. It's sixty milliliters *per feeding*." We were supposed to be feeding her eight times a day.

My eyes widened. I spun around to look at Rob. I couldn't believe what I was hearing.

"What? But we read the chart. It says right here." And when I looked again, pointing at the numbers so Rob could take a closer peek, too, we saw through our fatigue that the chart wasn't clear at all. There was no way to know that we'd been starving our child. I was horrified.

"The good news is that she's going to be a whole new baby once she starts eating the right amount," the consultant said.

Rob watched as more tears rolled down my cheeks. I wanted to wail into the abyss right alongside Clementine. I wanted to know how others survived being sent back into the world with a baby and no real idea of how to keep it alive.

SO IMAGINE HOW important it was to me to call Adam if with the few precious moments I had when Clementine wasn't crying and I wasn't crying and one of us wasn't sleeping that I picked up the phone to dial him.

The screen lit up and I saw the ceiling and part of Adam's forehead before I heard his voice. And then he came into focus: his head taking up the whole screen. His wispy beard. His crooked teeth.

"Hey!" Adam said excitedly. He was squinting. "Is that my niece?"

"It sure is," I said, trying to hold her up so he could get a better view. "This is your niece. You're an uncle now."

She squirmed and opened her mouth and closed it again and Adam and I laughed. He sang her several rounds of "Oh My Darling, Clementine," and when he hit the high note and said her name, we laughed some more.

"She's adorable," he said, and then he smiled a faraway smile before going silent for a few seconds, just long enough for me to wonder what he was thinking. And then he said it, he said what may have seemed like an innocent enough question to some, but broke my heart. "Is she okay?" he asked, and I knew what he really meant was, *Is she like me?*

I blurted out the only truth I knew: "She's perfect just the way she is," and I smiled. And then I went back to the foggy, dark tunnel of those first fuzzy days of motherhood.

28

Ghosts in the Nursery

At our six-week wellness checkup, Clementine's pediatrician handed me an iPad with a survey for postpartum depression. "Here, fill this out," she said nonchalantly as I sat in a chair in the corner of the room and cried.

Rob walked over and put his arm around me while holding Clementine carefully against his left shoulder. "In the last seven days, have you been able to laugh and see the funny side of things?" the question on the screen asked.

I clicked on option three, "Definitely not so much now."

"In the last seven days, have you been anxious or worried for no good reason?"

"Yes, very often," I responded honestly.

"Postpartum depression is very common," the pediatrician said when she saw my tears. "Fifteen percent of new mothers have it." Fifteen percent didn't sound very common to me, though. I asked my friends who had young children and none of them admitted to having postpartum depression. If it was so common, why did no one else have it? Why wasn't anyone *talking* about it? And if 15 percent of new mothers had it, that still meant 85 percent didn't. I didn't need to have been a reporter at *Forbes* to know that I was in the minority.

In my mind, I heard the pediatrician's diagnosis of postpartum depression as an indictment. *You are your mother,* were the words I heard. But I wanted to stand up to the "ghosts in the nursery," as child psychoanalyst Selma Fraiberg so beautifully referred to the relationship between how a parent was raised and their own parenting style. Sure, those who were abused can go on to abuse. Those who were traumatized can go on to traumatize. These "ghosts" can reappear even generations later. But there was another possibility: I could make different choices and try to keep the ghosts at bay.

I didn't need to drop my daughter or scald her in the bath or fall asleep while she was on my chest and suffocate her when I rolled onto her tiny body. All I had to do was live alongside her to mess her up by showing her all of the ways—big and small—that I was flawed. If I didn't get help for my postpartum depression, the risk would be a double-edged sword: I would miss out on Clementine's infancy, and she'd miss out on having a mother that was able to be present and engaged for the first months of her life. I wanted to get help. Within days, I had an appointment with a psychiatrist who prescribed me Zoloft.

When we got home, I sat on our couch and scrolled quickly through all the photos I'd taken over the last month and a half until they turned into a flipbook, and I watched Clementine grow from a tiny creature into an infant. I stared at the motion picture I created in disbelief. I watched her so closely every day and yet I missed all of the changes as they happened before my eyes. I'd been looking for connective tissue inside our bodies instead of in the bond we were creating together.

I thought of something that the psychologist Kathryn Paige Harden said to me when I interviewed her: "It's not because you love your child that you take care of them. It's because you take care of them that you love them."

The truth was that as I nurtured Clementine, I *grew* to love her. It didn't happen all at once, but over minutes and hours and days and months until I didn't notice the increments anymore, just the overwhelming feeling I'd learn to call love. I'd always believed love was automatic, tidal. That it had to bowl me over, knock me off my feet. But now I understood love as a process of commitment, and as I committed to the mothering the love followed. I didn't have to lose myself. Through the act of caretaking, I could find myself—and my daughter, too.

A FEW WEEKS before, I'd taken Clementine back to the cardiologist for her one-month appointment to check on the hole in her heart. It was the same doctor who had done the echocardiogram when Clementine was still inside me. I'd wanted Rob to come with me, but because of the high number of Covid cases in New York City at the time, hospitals and doctor's offices were only allowing one person to bring a child to appointments.

"So, listen," the doctor said as soon as I sat down, but she didn't need to say that because I was already listening. "As you know, Clementine's heart had a hole in it that we saw in the ultrasound before she was born. Fifty percent close up before birth, so we're hoping that's the case here. But if not, the majority close up in the first year of life."

She nodded to show me how certain she was, then she

walked me into the other room where the technician waited with his instruments to tell us my baby's future. I hoped his ultrasound machine was a magic wand that could take away anything that may have been wrong with Clementine. I hoped the electrodes he stuck to her tiny chest, which were connected to a hulking machine by multicolored wires to measure the electrical activity of her heart, would zap the holes out of her body once and for all. But I also understood that these were just diagnostic tools, and this man in his white coat with tortoiseshell glasses and floppy hair and a name I couldn't pronounce wasn't a magician.

Clementine didn't like the electrodes, and as the technician stared at the silent machine, she began to claw at the wires and the pads, and he asked me to hold her hands down so he could concentrate on the blurry black-and-white screen in front of him.

Everything will be okay, my love. Mom is here. You are safe. I said all of these things and I meant them.

I looked over the technician's shoulder as he worked to see if I could find any holes in Clementine's heart. I noticed the little fist-like organ thumping, and I turned back to the tech for any signs of worry.

But he was stone-faced. His blank face was even more terrifying than whatever could possibly be wrong because I read into it my worst fears. His features became a Rorschach test, shapes that shifted between menacing and neutral and everything in between. I wanted to scream: *Just tell me what you see! Is she going to be okay? Is she going to play sports and run and live a long life?*

As I held Clementine's hand, I begged the universe to show mercy on me and my child. *I'm a good person,* I chanted to myself, *so please protect my daughter.* This wasn't a religious belief. It was a *wish* for the world to be right and just and for my struggle to become a mother to count for something. Now nothing else bad could happen to us. Ever.

The testing took over an hour. One hour of holding my baby down as she cried and squirmed and I anxiously tried to decipher whether she would have a future or whether she'd be snatched away from me.

Before this moment I never imagined Clementine as an athlete, but now that I feared that door was closing, now that the chance could be taken away from her, that was exactly what I wanted for her. I suddenly saw her as an Olympian, stepping up the white cube to receive her gold medal. She could be a ballerina, an astronaut, a fighter pilot, president of the United States for God's sake. She could be anything she wanted to be.

Suddenly the technician stood up and gave me a blanket to cover Clementine with so she wouldn't be cold. He left the room and told me the doctor would be back soon, and I sat there in the rickety chair while Clementine lay on the bed, her tiny fingers clamped around my finger, whispering to her: "I know this seems scary, but you are going to be all right."

A few seconds, or minutes, later the doctor came back in and sat down. I wore my hypervigilance like a cloak, noticing her every move. "I know this is not what you want to hear," she finally managed to say. "But we found two holes in Clementine's heart. They are very small, and I still think they have a 90 percent chance of closing up before she turns one. But they are there."

The doctor turned her paper over, and I saw that on it were some squiggly lines with a left chamber and a right, and ventricles leading to nowhere. She was pointing at her drawing and words were coming out of her mouth and with her pen she was sketching little holes to show how the holes let the blood go in and out in both directions between chambers when really the blood should only flow in one direction.

In that moment I understood: I couldn't protect Clementine from everything. I couldn't hold on to her for dear life.

I was shaking as the cardiologist helped me gather up my diaper bag and the stroller and Clementine and myself. She sent me home with the grim reality that we'd have to wait until her first birthday to see if the holes closed. Between now and then, there was nothing we could do. I'd have to learn to live with uncertainty.

Over the next eight months, I strapped Clementine to my chest every day and walked around our neighborhood, the same streets I meandered through five years before, wondering how I was ever going to have a baby. Now here I was a mother with a loving partner, and it dawned on me that everything I'd been worried about was noise. None of the worst-case scenarios turned out to be true.

In the months since Clementine was born, I'd reckoned with the fact that even though she and I didn't share DNA, I was her real mother. There were moments early on when I'd hold her up to our bathroom mirror and look for a trace of resemblance between us. When strangers would stop us to say, "She looks just like her dad," I would feel erased. Once, a friend sat next to me on my couch drinking bubbly and asked what Clementine's "real mom" looked like.

"I'm her real mom," I snapped back, feeling territorial. *I pushed her out of my vagina,* I thought. *My immune system protected her. My blood ran through her.* "You mean her donor?" I asked, trying to seem like this whole conversation wasn't a big deal. "Her donor is her genetic 'mother,' so to speak, but I'm her biological mother."

"Yeah, that's what I meant," my friend said, seemingly oblivious to the grenade she threw between us.

I walked to my bedroom and grabbed my laptop, clicking on a photo of the donor as I sat back down. I wasn't sure if Rob knew I still had her picture. That every once in a while, I still looked at it. I turned the screen around to show my friend. "Yeah, I can see the resemblance," my friend said.

At that moment, I grieved that Clementine and I didn't have a simpler story. I grieved that there might be even the tiniest sliver of a wedge between us. I grieved that there was a shadow mother that haunts our relationship.

But now I also know that so many of us live with a shadow mother that lurks in our minds. She's the "perfect" mother, the one who never gets upset, the one who always looks put together, whose house is always clean, who works, and makes bento box lunches, and plans enriching activities for her kids and doesn't get flustered or exhausted. I'm not special in that way. I just have a name for the shadow mother—it's Rachel.

That night after my friend left, I googled "What's a real mother?" and the search engine didn't even know what to do with my question. Everywhere I looked, Google spit back platitudes: "Mothers and their children share half their DNA."

But that's not always true. "What about when a child is adopted?" I yelled at the computer. "What about when someone uses donor eggs?" "What about when there's two moms?"

Google, I realized, needed to update its definition of "mother."

I waited so long to feel "normal," not understanding that productivity at all costs is "normal" in a capitalist-patriarchal society. Grind culture is normal. Lack of rest is normal. The belief that women have a special instinct or caretaking gene that makes them better able to parent than men is normal.

What's normal gets confused with what's natural. And we're told that "nature knows best."

"One of the most harmful myths about motherhood is that it comes naturally," said the writer Leni Zumas. From getting pregnant to giving birth to breastfeeding, the idea that there is a natural—and therefore unnatural—way to do things sets up a dichotomy between the good girls and the failures, between those who follow the "correct" mother code and those who don't.

I now know that the whole idea of motherhood as "natural" is part of the lie that keeps women believing their place is in the home. It's part of the lie of maternal instinct. Parenting doesn't come naturally to women more than men. Women aren't inherently better able to do the emotional and physical labor of motherhood. It's a skillset that can be learned. I know that from my own father who raised me from the time I was an infant. There is no mom gene. The whole idea of the primacy of the mother is a glitch in the system. Not in *my* system. But in the patriarchal system.

In the months to come I would learn to redefine what was normal. As Rob, Clementine, and I sat at our dinner table playing peekaboo, her head thrown back in laughter every time she saw my face pop out from between my hands, I would think: *this is normal.* When I watched Rob tickle her or bounce her on his knee, I would think: *this is normal.* When I sang her the lullaby my mom used to sing to me, and Clementine eventually began singing the words "You are my precious little angel, I will always love you" along with me, I would think: *this is normal.*

29

Our Own Imperfect Circle

"I'm grateful, greedy, for every kind of model," the author Belle Boggs writes.

And I, too, am grateful and greedy for every kind of motherhood story. There are as many different shapes and forms as there are genetic codes. We each draw our own. The idea that there's one set of expectations is bogus. That we all have to hew to the same path. That our identities and hopes and dreams have to be annihilated.

As Clementine continued to grow up, I began to spot outlaw mothers everywhere. Women not following the rigid set of roles and rules set out for them. Angela Garbes, Julietta Singh, Amanda Montei, Lyz Lenz—and these were just the ones who shared their stories about motherhood in books.

I was sure there were others, women living under-the-radar lives, working thankless jobs in offices or in their own homes. Just because I couldn't see the shapes that their lives made didn't mean they weren't outlaws.

I also began to see how many stories of motherhood there are in the world. As Clementine morphed from a wriggling, crawling baby into a full-fledged person of her own who wanted to adventure around our neighborhood and make new friends, I encountered women with their own unique stories. Kathy adopted her child and remained close with her son's birth mother. Allison chose to be a solo parent and then met her life partner and had another child with him. Jessica lost a baby and went on to have two others. Some identified as queer. Some lived in homes with multiple partners. The more I sought out outlaw mothers and people embracing different types of mothering—the more I actively invited and welcomed them in—the more I understood that motherhood has room for all varieties. The mother code isn't rigid, it's expansive.

And it includes women like me. Women who used a donor egg and were initially ambivalent about being "all-in" on motherhood. Women who aren't "selfless" and don't have Instagram-worthy lives. Women who long for self-actualization, who believe their desires are as vital as their partners' and children's. Women who work outside of the home and those who don't. Women married to women. Trans men. Nonbinary people.

There are parts of my experience as a heterosexual woman navigating the complex process of finding an egg donor that are similar to what people in queer relationships who want to be parents go through. And there are parts that are vastly different. In a sense, the very structure of LGBT+ families implies a mother code that goes beyond genetics and places a value on community and "chosen families," which are part of this new mother code, too.

I used to believe inheritance was a shackle, but what if, like Saidiya Hartman writes in *Lose Your Mother*, we get to choose what we want to inherit—and, in turn, what we want to pass down? I've chosen to instill in Clementine a feeling of belonging. Of safety and security. Of knowing that she is enough.

Since childhood, I've wrestled with feeling like I'm always outside the windows of the warm house, looking in. But now I've created a home where I've chosen to put myself *inside* the charmed circle with Rob, whom I can see and feel is on my team, and Clementine, whom I grow closer with every year. Rachel is inside the circle, too. Clementine wouldn't be who she is without Rachel. Or me. Or Rob. It took all of us. No one needs to be on the outside.

Once in a while my mind flashes back to Adam as a young boy, the little kid he once was, racing across the playground, hoping the other kids would want to play with him as I protectively stood watch nearby. And then suddenly, I blink and it's Clementine, three and a half now, climbing up the slide backward, pushing a friend on the swing, fearless, carefree, strong. Looking back every so often to make sure I'm still there.

Recently, Rob, Clementine, and I drove to Boston to eat lunch with Adam. At one point, he put out his hand, palm facing up, and Clementine placed her tiny fingers in his. "My niece, my beautiful niece," he said, and she smiled. It was the four of us in a booth, our own imperfect circle.

Creating a warm hearth, a thriving family, isn't a linear process. There are no clear steps, no rights and wrongs, no one-size-fits-all. But it's one that feels important for me to cultivate alongside learning to parent Clementine. When Clementine says, "Mom, do you need a hug?" or calls for me at night, it's enough. When she cries in my arms and I feel her sink into me, comforted by my body, it's enough. When she says, "You're doing a great job," it's enough.

30

Bloodlines

Now that Clementine is old enough to start to understand, Rob and I have been preparing to tell her about how she came to be. We bought a book, *Our Village: There's More Than One Way To Make A Family,* by Ann Reddy, and we've begun to read it. We talk about sperm and eggs—and how some bodies have them and some don't.

Recently Clementine drew me a picture, and when I asked her what it was she said, "That's you," pointing at the taller of two stick figures, "that's me," at the smaller one, and then she put her finger on a circle at the edge of the paper. "That's an egg."

"An egg?" I asked curiously, waiting for her to expand, but instead she just nodded. I breathed deeply trying to gauge how I felt. There was no tickle of sadness in my throat. No tug at my heart. It was just an egg—and that's all it had to be.

Rob and I talk about how our only hope is that when Clementine is a bit older, she will understand how loved she is—that it didn't just take two people to create her, but three, plus a team of doctors, nurses, and a doula. She'll understand there are all kinds of families, in all shapes and forms, and ours is just as much a part of the tapestry as any other.

I recently read an interview between author Anne Helen Petersen and Nicole Chung, whose second memoir, *A Living Remedy,* is about how her ideas on inheritance have been shaped by her experience being adopted from Korea and raised in Oregon by white Catholic parents. In the conversation, Anne and Nicole discussed how we've come to understand inheritance "as running through blood lines," but how inheritance can also mean all the things that can "be cultivated and passed down to the next generation." Debt. Decisions—both good and bad. "Warmth, grace, and understanding."

Even though Nicole won't see her dad "live on" in her own children, as she quotes a friend once saying to her, and I won't see my own parents and grandparents in Clementine, there's another legacy that I hope will be passed down. In Nicole's case, her parents "always let me know that I was enough for them—without action, without proof, without accomplishing anything in particular, I was enough."

No, she's not from my "bloodline," but it's my hope that Clementine's inheritance is that she hears her own voice, her own deepest desires, and knows that she has permission to follow her heart.

THERE ARE THOSE who say we have to love ourselves to find love. And we must learn to mother ourselves to become a mother. But what if the opposite could be true, too? What if by becoming a mother I learned to believe I was lovable? What if by becoming a mother I learned to remother myself?

I don't mean that I needed my child to love and fulfill me. But what if we heal through being in relationship with each other? What if we heal through understanding our own agency over our lives? What if by loving my daughter, and seeing the way she loved me back, I was able to embrace a different image of motherhood? What if I was able to break the cycle? Not in a perfect way. But in a this-is-something-worth-striving-for way.

"Our children," Andrew Solomon writes in *Far from the Tree: Parents, Children, and the Search for Identity,* "are the children we had to have; we could have had no others. They will never seem to us to be happenstance; we love them because they are our destiny."

I no longer wonder what a child from my DNA would be like. I no longer feel flawed or like a failure for not using my eggs. I no longer feel unloved or unlovable.

It feels like Clementine is the child I had to have. I wouldn't go so far as to say was *meant* to have, because that sounds like life is preordained and I don't believe that is true. But it feels like Clementine is my destiny, and she is because destiny is the life we create for ourselves.

Now I know I wouldn't trade the beaches in Africa and backpacking through Europe to become a mom at twenty-seven instead of forty-three. I try not to waste time wondering what a different life would have looked like. In my twenties and thirties I wish I had understood that there is no "right" way to live. Marriage is a choice. Motherhood is a choice. Life is not a labyrinth with only one path in and out.

The choice to opt out, to challenge the norms, to rewrite

the rules we are blindly expected to follow is, and has always been, in my hands. The mother I want to be is an "outlaw mother," a mother who believes her self-fulfillment enables her child's happiness. A mother who mothers in contradiction to the prescriptive ideals of the patriarchy. A mother who creates her own mother code, who carves out a space for herself, her partner, and her child on the inside next to the warm fire.

Rewriting my mother code is a daily practice. But at least I can see it now. There is a North Star. Something to aspire to. A place I can point to, to show Clementine, that I was here, that I tried.

ACKNOWLEDGMENTS

This book wouldn't have been possible without so many people.

Immense gratitude to the outlaws who didn't follow the prescribed path; who rocked the boat; who instead of seeing clocks saw compasses; and who returned from their adventures to share with the world what they discovered. I would not have written this book without your inspiration. Thank you for showing me the way.

Thank you to my agent, Jane von Mehren, who listened to countless versions of this story, prodding me to go deeper, to find the universal in the personal, and then helped me shape the muck and mess in my mind into something we could share with publishers.

The entire Random House team, for taking such amazing care of my book and nurturing it into being. My editor Jamia Wilson and the incomparable Miriam Khanukaev for their tireless work on every aspect of this project, from shepherding it into the Random House family to ensuring that I wrote the exact book I wanted to write, and, maybe most importantly, for keeping me sane along the way.

Carrie Frye. Where do I begin? This book wouldn't be the book it is today without you. Thank you for responding to my "emergency" emails telling you I was stuck, I couldn't move forward, I had no idea what this book was or what it was supposed to be. You have been the calm to my storm, the anchor that has kept me tethered, the compass that has shown me the way.

Lisa Paradis, for interrogating my ideas and my writing in all the best ways, for the brilliant feedback even if I always seemed to ask for it at the 11th hour, and for all the Sancerre and oysters over the years. Our cherished annual trips are some of my favorite memories. I can't wait until we're old enough to move into our house with the porch and the rocking chairs so we can sip our wine and reflect on the silliness of our past selves.

Ellen Fridland, for pushing me to question the systems that feed the narratives around motherhood. I've always known that the personal is political, but you also showed me that the personal is philosophical, and you helped me to understand that I didn't have to accept society's philosophies. I could make up my own.

Elisabeth Eaves, for believing this was a book before I did and for calling and checking in on my progress even when I couldn't see my way out of the dark tunnel. Thank you for New Hampshire and Oaxaca and Oregon and so many more places where the ideas in this book were born before they became stories I could share with the world.

For reading various versions (some better than others) and

for letting me talk your ear off about the ideas that were swirling in my head, whether or not they made any sense at all: Rob Heath, Lisa Paradis, Ellen Fridland, Elisabeth Eaves, Margot Khan, Nell Casey, Tessa Stuart, and Hannah Beresford. Those who perpetuate the story of writers as lone wolves haven't met my wolf pack.

For all the writers in The Ignite Writers Collective, for inspiring me with your willingness to "go there" and for sharing your hearts with me. So many of you have supported me and cheered me on throughout this book writing process, and I can't thank you enough. You'll never know how much you've inspired me in my own writing. Enormous gratitude goes to Melisse Gelula, Tiffany Dyba, Stephanie Kruse, Carla Fernandez, Sarah Gormley, and Susan Sawyers.

The fearless Megan Stielstra, thank you for all the times you said, "Why isn't that on the page?" And for leading our year-long StoryStudio class where so much of this book was workshopped.

I'm forever grateful for the conversations that changed my thinking and my writing: Joanna Hershon, Elisa Albert, Rachel Yoder, Diana Bianchi, Kathryn Paige Harden, Charles Sawyer, Dr. Isaac Sasson, and Siddhartha Mukherjee, to name just a few.

Lisa John Rogers, for digging up documents for my long-dead ancestors—marriage and divorce records, newspaper articles, medical files, and more—and helping me to understand that there's no such thing as objective truth.

Charity Hoffman, research assistant extraordinaire, for bringing your expertise, enthusiasm, and friendship to this project. Not only did you locate studies and stories I never would have found, but you pushed me to find the true heart of what I was trying to say.

Joanna Arcieri, my fact checker, for keeping me honest.

Emma Wooley, for showing me how to talk about my book in a way that didn't make me cringe or run crying.

Roxanne Edwards, who I've trusted day in and day out for four years with our most precious Clementine. There is no way I could have written a book, or anything at all for that matter, if I didn't know Clem was well cared for and in good hands.

My Joy Squad (you know who you are), you've been my lifeline through the ups and downs not only of book writing, but of life. Thank you for being just a text message away.

Dr. Isaac Sasson, thank you for the best gift—our darling Clementine—without which this book wouldn't be possible.

Alissa, Acks, and Alec, for sharing a quarter of your genes with me and for helping me to see that my version of history has value too.

Aunt Tracy, the keeper of the family tree and the one who's always up for unraveling family lore and legends.

My great-grandmother and my grandmother, two women who tried to live their lives for their own pleasure and struggled against the limits imposed on them by the time and place they were born into.

I think it's safe to say that no parent wants their child to grow up to be a memoirist. I'm grateful to my mom, for always telling me that everything I touched turned to gold. I hope I spun something beautiful from our family's story. My dad and Fran, for always asking, "How's your book coming along?" and for being proud of my writing even though you didn't know what I was writing about much of the time.

Finally, Rob and Clementine, my moon and my stars. If I hadn't wandered, gotten lost along the way, followed my own messy, mercurial heart, I would never have been able to create this beautiful life with you.

BIBLIOGRAPHY

Acker, Joan. "Hierarchies, Jobs, Bodies: A Theory of Gendered Organizations." *Gender & Society* 4, no. 2 (June 1, 1990): 139–58. https://doi.org/10.1177/089124390004002002.

Albert, Elisa. *After Birth.* Reprint edition. Mariner Books, 2016.

———, ed. *Freud's Blind Spot: 23 Original Essays on Cherished, Estranged, Lost, Hurtful, Hopeful, Complicated Siblings.* Original edition. Free Press, 2010.

———. "Long Overdue: A New Anthology of Pregnancy and Birth." *Los Angeles Review of Books,* May 22, 2014. https://lareviewofbooks.org/article/long-overdue-new-anthology-pregnancy-birth/.

"American Women Are Waiting to Begin Families." News release. Center for Disease Control and Prevention, December 11, 2002. https://www.cdc.gov/nchs/pressroom/02news/ameriwomen.htm.

Andersen, Charlotte Hilton. "The Worst (and Weirdest) Parenting Advice From Every Decade Since the 1900s." Redbook, February 2, 2017. https://www.redbookmag.com/life/mom-kids/g4109/worst-parenting-advice-through-the-decades/.

Anzaldúa, Gloria, Norma Cantú, and Aída Hurtado. *Borderlands / La Frontera: The New Mestiza.* 4th edition. Aunt Lute Books, 2012.

Armstrong, Elizabeth. "Feminist Idols and Generational Legacies." *Signs: Journal of Women in Culture and Society,* September 28, 2022. http://signsjournal.org/short-takes-bad-sex-by-nona-willis-aronowitz/.

Armstrong, Elizabeth A., Laura T. Hamilton, Spencer A. Garrison, Kelly N. Giles, Charity M. Hoffman, and Angela K. Perone. " 'It's Complicated': How Black and White Women Innovate with Situationships at Midlife." *Social Problems,* April 26, 2024. https://doi.org/10.1093/socpro/spae021.

Aronowitz, Nona Willis. "The Education of Natalie Jean." ELLE, November 5, 2019. https://www.elle.com/life-love/a29438763/natalie-lovin-mommy-blog-influencer/.

Atrium Health. "Baby, Times Have Changed: Guide for Newborn Mothers Unearthed from 1968." Accessed June 22, 2023. https://atriumhealth.org/dailydose/2019/05/16/baby-times-have-changed-guide-for-newborn-mothers-unearthed-from-1968.

Autism Speaks. "Autism Statistics and Facts: Autism Prevalence." Accessed June 10, 2024. https://www.autismspeaks.org/autism-statistics-asd.

BabyCenter. "How Big Is My Baby? Baby Fruit Size Comparisons." BabyCenter. Accessed June 22, 2023. https://www.babycenter.com/pregnancy/your-body/how-big-is-my-baby-week-by-week-fruit-and-veggie-comparisons_5223185.

Bambara, Toni Cade. *This Bridge Called My Back: Writings by Radical Women of Color.* 2nd edition. Edited by Cherríe Moraga and Gloria Anzaldúa. Kitchen Table/Women of Color Press, 1983.

Barbie. Warner Bros. Pictures, 2023.

Bayindir, Turgay. "A House of Her Own: Alice Walker's Readjustment of Virginia Woolf's A Room of One's Own in The Color Purple." In *Alice Walker's The Color Purple,* 209–23. Brill, 2009. https://doi.org/10.1163/9789042028913_012.

Beck, Martha. *Expecting Adam: A True Story of Birth, Rebirth, and Everyday Magic.* Reprint edition. Harmony, 2011.

Becker, Gay, and Robert D. Nachtigall. "Eager for Medicalisation: The Social Production of Infertility as a Disease." *Sociology of Health & Illness* 14, no. 4 (1992): 456–71. https://doi.org/10.1111/1467-9566.ep10493093.

Belgray, Laura. "Why Won't People Just Let Me Not Be a Mom?" ELLE,

May 10, 2023. https://www.elle.com/life-love/a43807245/why-wont
-people-just-let-me-not-be-a-mom/.

Berry, Cecelie, ed. *Rise Up Singing: Black Women Writers on Motherhood.*
First Edition. Doubleday, 2004.

Bilger, Audrey. "The Art of Fiction No. 150." *The Paris Review,* 1997.
https://www.theparisreview.org/interviews/1188/the-art-of-fiction-no
-150-jeanette-winterson.

BioCouriers. "Infertility in History." Accessed June 27, 2023. https://
www.biocouriers.com/en/blog/596-infertility-in-history.

Black, Emily Rapp. *The Still Point of the Turning World.* Reprint edition.
Penguin Books, 2014.

Blair-Loy, Mary. *Competing Devotions: Career and Family among Women Executives.* Harvard University Press, 2005.

Boggs, Belle. *The Art of Waiting: On Fertility, Medicine, and Motherhood.*
Graywolf Press, 2016.

Bonaparte, Alicia D. "Physicians' Discourse for Establishing Authorita-
tive Knowledge in Birthing Work and Reducing the Presence of the
Granny Midwife." *Journal of Historical Sociology* 28, no. 2 (2015):
166–94. https://doi.org/10.1111/johs.12045.

———. "The Persecution and Prosecution of Granny Midwives in South
Carolina, 1900-1940," July 30, 2007. https://ir.vanderbilt.edu/
handle/1803/13563.

Braverman, Blair. *Welcome to the Goddamn Ice Cube: Chasing Fear and Finding Home in the Great White North.* Reprint edition. Ecco, 2017.

Brodesser-Akner, Taffy. *Fleishman Is in Trouble.* Random House, 2019.

Brown, Brené. *The Gifts of Imperfection.* Tenth anniversary edition. Hazelden
Publishing, 2022.

Brown, Elizabeth Anne. "Your DNA Can Now Be Pulled From Thin Air.
Privacy Experts Are Worried." *The New York Times,* May 15, 2023,
sec. Science. https://www.nytimes.com/2023/05/15/science/
environmental-dna-ethics-privacy.html.

Brown University. "Dr. Eli Adashi on in Vitro Gametogenesis: 'It's Time
for the Public to Get a Sense of the Possible.'" April 30, 2024.
https://www.brown.edu/news/2023-10-23/adashi-ivg.

Burkeman, Oliver. *Four Thousand Weeks: Time Management for Mortals.*
Farrar, Straus and Giroux, 2021.

Butts, Samantha F. "Health Disparities of African Americans in Reproductive Medicine." *Fertility and Sterility* 116, no. 2 (August 1, 2021): 287–91. https://doi.org/10.1016/j.fertnstert.2021.06.041.

Cahen, Fabrice. "Obstacles to the Establishment of a Policy to Combat Infertility in France, c. 1920–1950." In *The Palgrave Handbook of Infertility in History: Approaches, Contexts and Perspectives.* Edited by Gayle Davis and Tracey Loughran, 199–219. Palgrave Macmillan UK, 2017. https://doi.org/10.1057/978-1-137-52080-7_11.

Campbell, S. "A Short History of Sonography in Obstetrics and Gynaecology." *Facts, Views & Vision in ObGyn* 5, no. 3 (2013): 213–29.

Campoamor, Danielle. "What Is Pregnancy Ambivalence? It's a Lot More Common than People Know." TODAY.com, May 1, 2023. https://www.today.com/parents/pregnancy/pregnancy-ambivalence-rcna81221.

Carroll, Rebecca. "Margaret Garner, a Runaway Slave Who Killed Her Own Daughter." *The New York Times,* January 31, 2019, sec. Obituaries. https://www.nytimes.com/interactive/2019/obituaries/margaret-garner-overlooked.html.

Chan, Jessamine. *The School for Good Mothers.* Reprint edition. 37 Ink, 2023.

Chang, Grace, Evelyn Nakano Glenn, and Linda Rennie Forcey, eds. *Mothering: Ideology, Experience, and Agency.* Routledge, 1994.

Cheung, Kylie. "Kourtney Kardashian, Pregnant at 44, Joins Growing List of Celebrities to Conceive Well Into Their 40s." Jezebel, October 5, 2022. https://jezebel.com/celebrities-pregnant-over-40-hilary-swank-1849619446.

Cho, Catherine. *Inferno: A Memoir of Motherhood and Madness.* Bloomsbury Publishing, 2021.

Chollet, Mona, and Carmen Maria Machado. *In Defense of Witches: The Legacy of the Witch Hunts and Why Women Are Still on Trial.* Translated by Sophie R. Lewis. St. Martin's Press, 2022.

Chuck, Elizabeth. "Freezing Your Eggs Is an 'Expensive Lottery Ticket' That Not Everyone Wins." NBC News, March 5, 2019. https://www.nbcnews.com/health/health-news/expensive-lottery-ticket-freezing-eggs-offers-women-hope-not-everyone-n975921.

Chung, Nicole. *A Living Remedy: A Memoir.* Ecco, 2023.

Cobb, M. "An Amazing 10 Years: The Discovery of Egg and Sperm in the 17th Century." *Reproduction in Domestic Animals* 47, no. s4 (2012): 2–6. https://doi.org/10.1111/j.1439-0531.2012.02105.x.

Cohen, Elizabeth, Carma Hassan, and Amanda Musa. "Because of Florida

Abortion Laws, She Carried Her Baby to Term Knowing He Would Die." CNN, May 3, 2023. https://www.cnn.com/2023/05/02/health/florida-abortion-term-pregnancy/index.html.

Cohen, Rachel M. "How Millennials Learned to Dread Motherhood." Vox, December 4, 2023. https://www.vox.com/features/23979357/millennials-motherhood-dread-parenting-birthrate-women-policy.

Collins, Patricia Hill. "Shifting the Center: Race, Class, and Feminist Theorizing About Motherhood." In *Mothering: Ideology, Experience, and Agency.* Routledge, 1994.

"Comparing the Costs of Generations (2024) | ConsumerAffairs," June 12, 2024. https://www.consumeraffairs.com/finance/comparing-the-costs-of-generations.html.

Conaboy, Chelsea. *Mother Brain: How Neuroscience Is Rewriting the Story of Parenthood.* Henry Holt and Co., 2022.

———. "The Big Idea: Why the Maternal Instinct Is a Myth." *The Guardian,* October 10, 2022, sec. Books. https://www.theguardian.com/books/2022/oct/10/the-big-idea-why-the-maternal-instinct-is-a-myth.

Coontz, Stephanie. *The Way We Never Were: American Families and the Nostalgia Trap.* Reprint edition. Basic Books, 1993.

Courtemanche, Eleanor. "The Fourth and Fifth Waves | Stanford Humanities Center." Stanford Humanities Today, January 8, 2019. https://shc.stanford.edu/arcade/interventions/fourth-and-fifth-waves.

Crowder, Stephanie Buckhanon. *When Momma Speaks: The Bible and Motherhood from a Womanist Perspective.* Westminster John Knox Press, 2016.

"DAA Awardee: Jerome K. Sherman." Accessed June 27, 2023. https://www.foriowa.org/daa/daa-profile.php?namer=true&profileid=460.

Daum, Meghan. *Selfish, Shallow, and Self-Absorbed: Sixteen Writers on the Decision Not to Have Kids.* Picador, 2015.

Davies, Dave. "How Poverty and Racism 'Weather' the Body, Accelerating Aging and Disease." NPR, March 28, 2023, sec. Public Health. https://www.npr.org/sections/health-shots/2023/03/28/1166404485/weathering-arline-geronimus-poverty-racism-stress-health.

Davis, KC. *How to Keep House While Drowning.* Simon Element, 2022.

Dear Sugars. "Looking For The One, Part 2: The Reality." January 22, 2016. https://www.wbur.org/dearsugar/2016/01/22/dear-sugar-episode-forty.

Dederer, Claire. *Monsters: A Fan's Dilemma.* Knopf, 2023.

———. "What Do We Do with the Art of Monstrous Men?" *The Paris Review,* November 20, 2017. https://www.theparisreview.org/blog/2017/11/20/art-monstrous-men/.

Dias, Brian G., and Kerry J. Ressler. "Parental Olfactory Experience Influences Behavior and Neural Structure in Subsequent Generations." *Nature Neuroscience* 17, no. 1 (January 2014): 89–96. https://doi.org/10.1038/nn.3594.

Didion, Joan. *Blue Nights: A Memoir.* Reprint edition. Vintage, 2012.

———. "Goodbye to All That." *Slouching Towards Bethlehem.* Reprint edition. Farrar, Straus and Giroux, 1968, 225–38.

D'Mello, Anila M., Isabelle R. Frosch, Cindy E. Li, Annie L. Cardinaux, and John D.E. Gabrieli. "Exclusion of Females in Autism Research: Empirical Evidence for a 'Leaky' Recruitment-to-research Pipeline." *Autism Research* 15, no. 10 (October 2022): 1929–40. https://doi.org/10.1002/aur.2795.

"Donor Egg IVF (In-Vitro Fertilization) Market." www.futuremarketinsights.com. Accessed May 2, 2024. https://www.futuremarketinsights.com/reports/donor-egg-ivf-market.

Dotti Sani, Giulia M., and Judith Treas. "Educational Gradients in Parents' Child-Care Time Across Countries, 1965–2012." *Journal of Marriage and Family* 78, no. 4 (2016): 1083–96. https://doi.org/10.1111/jomf.12305.

Dudley, Jessica, Sarah McLaughlin, and Thomas H. Lee. "Why So Many Women Physicians Are Quitting." *Harvard Business Review,* January 19, 2022. https://hbr.org/2022/01/why-so-many-women-physicians-are-quitting.

Dunn, Kate M., Lynn F. Cherkas, and Tim D. Spector. "Genetic Influences on Variation in Female Orgasmic Function: A Twin Study." *Biology Letters* 1, no. 3 (September 22, 2005): 260–63. https://doi.org/10.1098/rsbl.2005.0308.

Eardley, Siobhan. "Monstrous Motherhood in the 'Alien' Franchise." *In Their Own League,* October 3, 2019. https://intheirownleague.com/2019/10/03/monstrous-motherhood-in-the-alien-franchise/.

Ebiri, Bilge. "Behold, an Actually Good Omen Movie." Vulture, April 5, 2024. https://www.vulture.com/article/review-the-first-omen-is-actually-a-good-omen-movie.html.

Education Data Initiative. "Student Loan Debt by Graduation Year
    [2023]: Total + per Student." Accessed July 28, 2023. https://
    educationdata.org/average-student-loan-debt-by-year.

Eisenberg, Arlene, Heidi Murkoff, and Sandee Hathaway. *What to Expect
    When You're Expecting.* Revised edition. Workman Publishing Com-
    pany, 1996.

Elizalde, Molly. "How Egg Freezing Went Mainstream." *The New York
    Times,* April 17, 2020, sec. Parenting. https://www.nytimes.com/
    2020/04/17/parenting/fertility/egg-freezing.html.

Ellis, Nicquel Terry. "A Texas Family Fought for Weeks to Regain Cus-
    tody of Their Newborn. Experts Say the Case Shows How Black Par-
    ents Are Criminalized." CNN, April 24, 2023. https://www.cnn
    .com/2023/04/24/us/texas-family-newborn-removed-reaj/index.html.

Engel, Pamela. "CHARTS: Guys Like Women In Their Early 20s Regard-
    less Of How Old They Get." Business Insider. Accessed June 25,
    2023. https://www.businessinsider.com/dataclysm-shows-men-are
    -attracted-to-women-in-their-20s-2014-10.

English, Deirdre. "The Long Fight of Barbara Ehrenreich." *Mother Jones,*
    September 7, 2022. https://www.motherjones.com/media/2022/09/
    the-long-fight-of-barbara-ehrenreich/.

Erdrich, Louise. *The Blue Jay's Dance: A Memoir of Early Motherhood.* Re-
    issue edition. Harper Perennial, 2010.

Eyal, Maytal. "Self-Silencing Is Making Women Sick." *Time,* October 3,
    2023. https://time.com/6319549/silencing-women-sick-essay/.

Farr, Christina. "Apple, Facebook Will Pay for Female Employees to
    Freeze Their Eggs." *Reuters,* October 14, 2014, sec. Lifestyle. https://
    www.reuters.com/article/us-tech-fertility-idUKKCN0I32KQ
    20141014.

Feinglos, Rebecca, and Sophia Laurenzi. "'It's Hell': How Divorce Laws
    Are Designed to Create Unnecessary Financial Hardship for
    Women." *Fortune.* Accessed May 2, 2024. https://fortune.com/2023/
    08/23/divorce-laws-designed-create-unnecessary-financial-hardship
    -women-personal-finance/.

Ferguson, Amber. "America Has a Black Sperm Donor Shortage. Black
    Women Are Paying the Price." *Washington Post,* October 20, 2022.
    https://www.washingtonpost.com/business/2022/10/20/black-sperm
    -donors/.

————. "Why Gay Men and Other Groups Are Banned from Donating
Sperm." *Washington Post,* October 20, 2022. https://www
.washingtonpost.com/business/2022/10/20/sperm-donor-criteria/.

Ferguson, Stephanie, Isabella Lucy. "Data Deep Dive: A Decline of
Women in the Workforce," April 27, 2022. https://www.uschamber
.com/workforce/data-deep-dive-a-decline-of-women-in-the-workforce.

Filipovic, Jill. "The Uncertain Loneliness of Ambivalence on Motherhood." Slate, December 5, 2023. https://slate.com/human-interest/
2023/12/ambivalent-motherhood-how-to-choose.html.

Firestone, Shulamith. *The Dialectic of Sex: The Case for Feminist Revolution.*
Farrar, Straus and Giroux, 2003.

Fleshman, Lauren. *Good for a Girl: A Woman Running in a Man's World.*
Penguin Press, 2023.

Fox, Andrew S., Ronald A. Harris, Laura Del Rosso, Muthuswamy
Raveendran, Shawn Kamboj, Erin L. Kinnally, John P. Capitanio, and
Jeffrey Rogers. "Infant Inhibited Temperament in Primates Predicts
Adult Behavior, Is Heritable, and Is Associated with Anxiety-
Relevant Genetic Variation." *Molecular Psychiatry* 26, no. 11 (Novem-
ber 2021): 6609–18. https://doi.org/10.1038/s41380-021-01156-4.

Fraiberg, Selma, E. Adelson, and V. Shapiro. "Ghosts in the Nursery: A
Psychoanalytic Approach to the Problems of Impaired Infant-Mother
Relationships." *Journal of the American Academy of Child Psychiatry* 14,
no. 3 (1975): 387–421. https://doi.org/10.1016/s0002-7138(09)
61442-4.

Friedan, Betty. *The Feminine Mystique.* Dell Books, 1974.

Friedmann, Jessica. *Things That Helped: On Postpartum Depression.* FSG
Originals, 2018.

Gage, Beverly. "Nobody Has My Condition But Me." *The New Yorker,*
January 23, 2023. https://www.newyorker.com/magazine/2023/01/
30/nobody-has-my-condition-but-me.

Garber, Megan. "When *Newsweek* 'Struck Terror in the Hearts of Single
Women.'" *The Atlantic,* June 2, 2016. https://www.theatlantic.com/
entertainment/archive/2016/06/more-likely-to-be-killed-by-a
-terrorist-than-to-get-married/485171/.

Garbes, Angela. *Essential Labor: Mothering as Social Change.* Harper Wave,
2022.

————. *Like a Mother: A Feminist Journey Through the Science and Culture of
Pregnancy.* Harper Wave, 2018.

Gladwell, Malcolm. "Matters of Choice Muddled by Thought." *Washington Post,* March 4, 1991. https://www.washingtonpost.com/archive/politics/1991/03/04/matters-of-choice-muddled-by-thought/5e6f1511-0d9e-4263-bac0-9ee2fb2770ef/.

Glynn, Sarah Jane. "Breadwinning Mothers Continue To Be the U.S. Norm." Center for American Progress, May 10, 2019. https://www.americanprogress.org/article/breadwinning-mothers-continue-u-s-norm/.

Goldberg, Emma. "What Sheryl Sandberg's 'Lean In' Has Meant to Women." *The New York Times,* June 2, 2022, sec. Business. https://www.nytimes.com/2022/06/02/business/sheryl-sandberg-lean-in.html.

Golembiewski, Kate, and François Brunelle. "Your Doppelgänger Is Out There and You Probably Share DNA With Them." *The New York Times,* August 23, 2022, sec. Science. https://www.nytimes.com/2022/08/23/science/doppelgangers-twins-dna.html.

Gone Girl. Twentieth Century Studios, 2014.

Goodby, John, ed., Dylan Thomas. *The Poems of Dylan Thomas.* New Directions, 1971.

Gosse, Johanna. "The Only Position for Women in the Movement Is 'Prone'," October 27, 2011. https://flexner.blogs.brynmawr.edu/2011/10/27/the-only-place-for-women-in-the-movement-is-'prone'-2/.

Greene, Jayson. *Once More We Saw Stars: A Memoir.* Knopf, 2019.

Grose, Jessica. "Mother's Little Helper Is Back, and Daddy's Partaking Too." *The New York Times,* October 3, 2020, sec. Style. https://www.nytimes.com/2020/10/03/style/am-i-drinking-too-much.html.

———. *Screaming on the Inside: The Unsustainability of American Motherhood.* Mariner Books, 2022.

Gross, Rachel E. *Vagina Obscura: An Anatomical Voyage.* W. W. Norton & Company, 2022.

Gross, Terry. "The Sports World Is Still Built for Men. This Elite Runner Wants to Change That." NPR, January 10, 2023, sec. Your Health. https://www.npr.org/sections/health-shots/2023/01/10/1147816860/sports-world-still-built-for-men-elite-runner-wants-to-change-that.

Gu, Fang, Yaqin Wu, Meiling Tan, Rui Hu, Yao Chen, Xuemei Li, Bing Lin, et al. "Programmed Frozen Embryo Transfer Cycle Increased Risk of Hypertensive Disorders of Pregnancy: A Multicenter Cohort

Study in Ovulatory Women." *American Journal of Obstetrics & Gynecology MFM* 5, no. 1 (January 1, 2023): 100752. https://doi.org/10 .1016/j.ajogmf.2022.100752.

Hammond, Camille. "Reasons Black Patients Get Treated Later." Fertility IQ. Accessed May 2, 2024. https://www.fertilityiq.com/fertilityiq/ black-african-american-fertility/delay-treatment.

Harden, Kathryn Paige. *The Genetic Lottery: Why DNA Matters for Social Equality.* Princeton University Press, 2021.

Hartman, Saidiya V. *Lose Your Mother: A Journey Along the Atlantic Slave Route.* Farrar, Straus and Giroux, 2008.

Hartocollis, Anemona, and Wendy Ruderman. "Mother Called Her Final Act 'Evil.'" *The New York Times,* March 15, 2013, sec. New York. https://www.nytimes.com/2013/03/15/nyregion/son-survives-cynthia -wachenheims-suicide-jump-in-harlem.html.

Havrilesky, Heather. "I'm Broke and Mostly Friendless and I've Wasted My Whole Life." The Cut, November 28, 2018. https://www.thecut .com/2018/11/im-broke-and-friendless-and-ive-wasted-my-whole -life.html.

Hays, Sharon. *The Cultural Contradictions of Motherhood.* Yale University Press, 1998.

Heffington, Peggy O'Donnell. "Opinion | Why Women Not Having Kids Became a Panic." *The New York Times,* May 6, 2023, sec. Opinion. https://www.nytimes.com/2023/05/06/opinion/women-without -children-history.html.

Hershon, Joanna. "Any Day Now." In *Freud's Blind Spot: 23 Original Essays on Cherished, Estranged, Lost, Hurtful, Hopeful, Complicated Siblings.* Edited by Elisa Albert, 23. Free Press, 2010.

Heti, Sheila. *Motherhood.* Henry Holt and Co., 2018.

Hewlett, Sylvia Ann. *Creating a Life: Professional Women and the Quest for Children.* Miramax, 2002.

———. "Executive Women and the Myth of Having It All." *Harvard Business Review,* April 1, 2002. https://hbr.org/2002/04/executive -women-and-the-myth-of-having-it-all.

Hirsch, Aubrey. "It's 2022 and People Are Still Confused That My Kids Have Their Mother's Last Name." *Time,* February 4, 2022. https:// time.com/6143476/baby-with-mothers-last-name/.

Historic House Trust of New York City. "Alice Austen House." Accessed

May 2, 2024. https://historichousetrust.org/houses/alice-austen
-house/.

Hollingworth, Leta S. "Social Devices for Impelling Women to Bear and
Rear Children." *American Journal of Sociology* 22, no. 1 (1916): 19–29.
https://www.jstor.org/stable/2763926?seq=11.

Horwitz, Allan V. "How an Age of Anxiety Became an Age of Depression." *The Milbank Quarterly* 88, no. 1 (March 2010): 112–38.
https://doi.org/10.1111/j.1468-0009.2010.00591.x.

Hrdy, Sarah Blaffer. *Mothers and Others: The Evolutionary Origins of Mutual
Understanding.* Illustrated edition. The Belknap Press, 2011.

Hu, Zoe. "The Agoraphobic Fantasy of Tradlife." *Dissent Magazine*, Winter 2023. https://www.dissentmagazine.org/article/the-agoraphobic
-fantasy-of-tradlife/.

Huey-Burns, Caitlin. "Louisiana Woman Says She Was Denied an Abortion after Fetus Developed Rare Condition: 'I Was Carrying My Baby
to Bury My Baby.'" CBS News, August 26, 2022. https://www
.cbsnews.com/news/louisiana-woman-nancy-davis-denied-an-abortion
-after-fetus-develops-rare-condition/.

Humphries, Leigh A., Olivia Chang, Kathryn Humm, Denny Sakkas, and
Michele R. Hacker. "Influence of Race and Ethnicity on in Vitro Fertilization Outcomes: Systematic Review." *American Journal of Obstetrics and Gynecology* 214, no. 2 (February 1, 2016): 212.e1-212.e17.
https://doi.org/10.1016/j.ajog.2015.09.002.

Huxley, Aldous. *Brave New World.* Reprint edition. Harper Perennial,
2006.

Imrie, Susan, Vasanti Jadva, Simon Fishel, and Susan Golombok. "Families Created by Egg Donation: Parent–Child Relationship Quality in
Infancy." *Child Development* 90, no. 4 (2018): 1333–49. https://doi
.org/10.1111/cdev.13124.

Insogna, Iris G., and Elizabeth S. Ginsburg. "Infertility, Inequality, and
How Lack of Insurance Coverage Compromises Reproductive Autonomy." *AMA Journal of Ethics* 20, no. 12 (December 1, 2018): 1152–59.
https://doi.org/10.1001/amajethics.2018.1152.

Intelligent. "1970 vs. 2020: How Working through College Has
Changed," November 12, 2021. https://www.intelligent.com/1970-v
-2020-how-working-through-college-has-changed/.

Intramural Research Program. "Diana W. Bianchi, M.D. | Principal Inves-

tigators | NIH Intramural Research Program." Accessed June 10,
2024. https://irp.nih.gov/pi/diana-bianchi.

"IVF Success Estimator | Assisted Reproductive Technology (ART) | Re-
productive Health | CDC," August 4, 2021. https://www.cdc.gov/art/
ivf-success-estimator/index.html.

Jack, Dana C., and Alisha Ali, eds. *Silencing the Self Across Cultures: Depression and Gender in the Social World.* Oxford University Press, 2010.

Jackson, Naomi. "A Litany for Survival: Giving Birth as a Black Woman
in America." Harper's Magazine, August 14, 2020. https://harpers
.org/archive/2020/09/a-litany-for-survival-black-maternal-mortality/.

Jamison, Leslie. *Splinters: Another Kind of Love Story.* Little, Brown and
Company, 2024.

Joseph, Jay. "What Do Twin Studies Prove About Genetic Influences on
Psychiatric Disorders? Absolutely Nothing." Mad in America, December 18, 2018. https://www.madinamerica.com/2018/12/twin
-studies-prove-nothing-genetics-psychiatric-disorders/.

Kahn, Mattie. "The Holocaust Started with My Great-Uncle's Murder."
The Atlantic, May 5, 2022. https://www.theatlantic.com/family/
archive/2022/05/arthur-kahn-german-jewish-holocaust-history/
629762/.

Kamel, Remah Moustafa. "Assisted Reproductive Technology after the
Birth of Louise Brown." *Journal of Reproduction & Infertility* 14, no. 3
(2013): 96. https://www.jri.ir/article/535.

Kamin, Debra. " 'Mommunes': Mothers Are Living Single Together." *The
New York Times,* May 12, 2023, sec. Real Estate. https://www.nytimes
.com/2023/05/12/realestate/single-mother-households-co-living
.html.

Kaplan, Erin Aubry. "Mother, Unconceived." In *Rise Up Singing: Black
Women Writers on Motherhood.* Edited by Cecelie S. Berry, 163. Doubleday, 2004.

Kazanjian, Dodie. "Meet the Most Brilliant Couple in Town." *Vogue,*
May 11, 2016. https://www.vogue.com/article/sarah-sze-siddhartha
-mukherjee-brilliant-couple-profile-sculptor-writer-physician
-scientist-researcher.

Kesey, Ken. *One Flew Over the Cuckoo's Nest.* Berkley, 1963.

Kim, Meeri. "Study Finds That Fear Can Travel Quickly through Generations of Mice DNA." *Washington Post,* May 17, 2023. https://www
.washingtonpost.com/national/health-science/study-finds-that-fear

-can-travel-quickly-through-generations-of-mice-dna/2013/12/07/
94dc97f2-5e8e-11e3-bc56-c6ca94801fac_story.html.

Kleeman, Alexandra. "Rachel Weisz and the Glorious Horrors of Pregnancy." *The New York Times,* April 21, 2023, sec. Magazine. https://
www.nytimes.com/2023/04/21/magazine/dead-ringers-rachel-weisz
.html.

Klein, Ezra. "The Deep Conflict Between Our Work and Parenting
Ideals." *The Ezra Klein Show.* Accessed May 2, 2024. https://www
.nytimes.com/2024/03/22/opinion/ezra-klein-podcast-caitlyn-collins
.html.

Kolata, Gina. "The Disease Took Zara, Then Sara. Could Ayla Be Saved?"
The New York Times, November 9, 2022, sec. Health. https://www
.nytimes.com/2022/11/09/health/pompe-disease-treatment.html.

Kramer, Wendy. "Why Is There a Shortage of Black Egg and Sperm Donors?" Psychology Today, July 27, 2023. https://www
.psychologytoday.com/intl/blog/donor-family-matters/202307/why-is
-there-a-shortage-of-black-egg-and-sperm-donors.

Kunkel, Sue. "Average Wages, Median Wages, and Wage Dispersion." Social Security Administration. Accessed June 10, 2024. https://www
-origin.ssa.gov/oact/cola/central.html.

Lane, Erin S. *Someone Other Than a Mother: Flipping the Scripts on a Woman's
Purpose and Making Meaning beyond Motherhood.* TarcherPerigee, 2022.

Learn.Genetics Genetics Science Learning Center. "Lick Your Rats." Accessed May 2, 2024. https://learn.genetics.utah.edu/content/
epigenetics/rats.

Lee, Margaret Juhae. "'I like Seeing Motherhood as a Journey toward
Yourself': An Interview with Literary Biographer Julie Phillips." *Another Chicago Magazine,* January 19, 2023. https://anotherchicago
magazine.net/2023/01/19/i-like-seeing-motherhood-as-a-journey
-toward-yourself-an-interview-with-literary-biographer-julie
-phillips/.

Lee, Shu-Hsin, Lin-Chuan Liu, Pi-Chao Kuo, and Maw-Sheng Lee. "Postpartum Depression and Correlated Factors in Women Who Received
In Vitro Fertilization Treatment." *Journal of Midwifery & Women's
Health* 56, no. 4 (2011): 347–52. https://doi.org/10.1111/j.1542
-2011.2011.00033.x.

Lee, Susanna S., Benjamin T. Vollmer, Cen April Yue, and Benjamin K.
Johnson. "Impartial Endorsements: Influencer and Celebrity Declara-

tions of Non-Sponsorship and Honesty." *Computers in Human Behavior* 122 (September 1, 2021): 106858. https://doi.org/10.1016/j.chb .2021.106858.

Leigh, Julia. *Avalanche: A Love Story.* W. W. Norton & Company, 2016.

Lenz, Lyz. *Belabored: A Vindication of the Rights of Pregnant Women.* Bold Type Books, 2020.

Lessing, Doris. *The Fifth Child.* Reprint edition. Vintage, 1989.

————. *Under My Skin: Volume One of My Autobiography, to 1949.* Harper Perennial, 1995.

Lesté-Lasserre, Christa. "Naked Mole Rats Reveal Biological Secrets of Lifelong Fertility." *New Scientist,* February 21, 2023. https://www .newscientist.com/article/2360377-naked-mole-rats-reveal-biological -secrets-of-lifelong-fertility/.

Levy, Ariel. *The Rules Do Not Apply: A Memoir.* Random House, 2017.

Lichter, Daniel T., Joseph P. Price, and Jeffrey M. Swigert. "Mismatches in the Marriage Market." *Journal of Marriage and Family* 82, no. 2 (2020): 796–809. https://doi.org/10.1111/jomf.12603.

Lieberman, Alicia F., Elena Padrón, Patricia Van Horn, and William W. Harris. "Angels in the Nursery: The Intergenerational Transmission of Benevolent Parental Influences." *Infant Mental Health Journal* 26, no. 6 (November 2005): 504–20. https://doi.org/10.1002/imhj .20071.

Lin, Luona. "About Eight-in-Ten Women in Opposite-Sex Marriages Say They Took Their Husband's Last Name." *Pew Research Center,* September 7, 2023. https://www.pewresearch.org/short-reads/2023/09/07/ about-eight-in-ten-women-in-opposite-sex-marriages-say-they-took -their-husbands-last-name/.

Loehnen, Elise. *On Our Best Behavior: The Seven Deadly Sins and the Price Women Pay to Be Good.* The Dial Press, 2023.

————. "Opinion | The Lies Mothers Tell Themselves and Their Children." *The New York Times,* May 17, 2023, sec. Opinion. https://www .nytimes.com/2023/05/17/opinion/motherhood-lessons-children -parenting.html.

Lumey, L.H., Aryeh D. Stein, Henry S. Kahn, Karin M. van der Pal-de Bruin, G.J. Blauw, Patricia A. Zybert, and Ezra S. Susser. "Cohort Profile: The Dutch Hunger Winter Families Study." *International Journal of Epidemiology* 36, no. 6 (December 1, 2007): 1196–1204. https://doi.org/10.1093/ije/dym126.

Lushkov, Ayelet Haimson. "Elisa Albert Takes on the Mess and Anger of Our Reproductive Lives." *Lilith Magazine,* August 3, 2022. https://lilith.org/articles/elisa-albert-takes-on-the-mess-and-anger-of-our-reproductive-lives/.

MacKenzie, Macaela. "The Simple Reason Why Egg Freezing Is All Over Your Instagram." Bustle, February 20, 2024. https://www.bustle.com/wellness/influencers-egg-freezing.

Macleans.ca. "Mothers Who Regret Having Children Are Speaking up like Never Before." Accessed July 24, 2023. https://macleans.ca/regretful-mothers/.

MacNicol, Glynnis. *No One Tells You This: A Memoir.* Simon & Schuster, 2019.

Madrigal, Alexis C. "The Surprising Birthplace of the First Sperm Bank." *The Atlantic,* April 28, 2014. https://www.theatlantic.com/technology/archive/2014/04/how-the-first-sperm-bank-began/361288/.

Poppick, Laura. "The Long, Winding Tale of Sperm Science." *Smithsonian Magazine.* Accessed July 25, 2023. https://www.smithsonianmag.com/science-nature/scientists-finally-unravel-mysteries-sperm-180963578/.

Mani, Purnima. "I Finally Got My IVF Baby, So What Right Did I Have To Be Depressed?" Romper, May 8, 2023. https://www.romper.com/parenting/ppd-after-ivf-postpartum.

Manne, Kate. *Down Girl: The Logic of Misogyny.* Oxford University Press, 2017.

———. *Entitled: How Male Privilege Hurts Women.* Crown, 2020.

Marte, Jonnelle. "Are Home Prices Rising Too Quickly for Millennials?" *Washington Post,* August 18, 2015. https://www.washingtonpost.com/news/get-there/wp/2015/08/18/are-home-prices-rising-too-quickly-for-millennials/.

Martin, Emily. "The Egg and the Sperm: How Science Has Constructed a Romance Based on Stereotypical Male-Female Roles." *Signs: Journal of Women in Culture and Society* 16, no. 3 (April 1991): 485–501. https://doi.org/10.1086/494680.

Martin, Emmie. "Here's How Much Housing Prices Have Skyrocketed over the Last 50 Years." CNBC, June 23, 2017. https://www.cnbc.com/2017/06/23/how-much-housing-prices-have-risen-since-1940.html.

Mass.gov. CMR 37.00 Infertility Benefits (n.d.). https://www.mass.gov/doc/211-37-infertility-benefits/download.

Maté, Gabor, and Daniel Maté. *The Myth of Normal: Trauma, Illness, and Healing in a Toxic Culture.* Avery, 2022.

Matthews, Timothy, Avshalom Caspi, Andrea Danese, Helen L. Fisher, Terrie E. Moffitt, and Louise Arseneault. "A Longitudinal Twin Study of Victimization and Loneliness from Childhood to Young Adulthood." *Development and Psychopathology* 34, no. 1 (February 2022): 367–77. https://doi.org/10.1017/S0954579420001005.

McCarthy, Ellen. "She Famously Said That Women Can't Have It All. Now She Realizes That No One Can." *Washington Post,* April 12, 2023. https://www.washingtonpost.com/lifestyle/style/she-famously-said-that-women-cant-have-it-all-now-she-realizes-that-no-one-can/2016/08/26/889944e4-5bf3-11e6-831d-0324760ca856_story.html.

McClain, Dani. "Mom Talk: The Political Power of Black Motherhood," *Mother,* June 1, 2020. https://www.mothermag.com/we-live-for-the-we-the-political-power-of-black-motherhood/.

———. *We Live for the We: The Political Power of Black Motherhood.* Bold Type Books, 2019.

———. "We Live for the We: The Political Power of Black Motherhood," June 1, 2020. https://www.mothermag.com/we-live-for-the-we-the-political-power-of-black-motherhood/.

McClelland, W. Spencer. "Age 35 Isn't a Fertility Cliff. Why Do We Think It Is?" *Slate,* August 17, 2020. https://slate.com/technology/2020/08/fertility-cliff-advanced-maternal-age-outdated.html.

McMasters, Kelly. "The Ethics of Writing Hard Things in Family Memoir," May 31, 2023. https://lithub.com/the-ethics-of-writing-hard-things-in-family-memoir/.

McQueen, Dana B., Ann Schufreider, Sang Mee Lee, Eve C. Feinberg, and Meike L. Uhler. "Racial Disparities in in Vitro Fertilization Outcomes." *Fertility and Sterility* 104, no. 2 (August 1, 2015): 398–402. e1. https://doi.org/10.1016/j.fertnstert.2015.05.012.

Meier, Barry. "Inside a Secretive Group Where Women Are Branded." *The New York Times,* October 17, 2017, sec. New York. https://www.nytimes.com/2017/10/17/nyregion/nxivm-women-branded-albany.html.

Metzl, Jonathan. "The New Science of Blaming Moms." MSNBC.com,

July 15, 2014. https://www.msnbc.com/melissa-harris-perry/the-new
-science-blaming-moms-msna369896.

Miller, Claire Cain. "Freezing Eggs as Part of Employee Benefits: Some
Women See Darker Message." *The New York Times,* October 15,
2014, sec. The Upshot. https://www.nytimes.com/2014/10/15/
upshot/egg-freezing-as-a-work-benefit-some-women-see-darker
-message.html.

Miller, Jean Baker. *Toward a New Psychology of Women.* Beacon Press, 2012.

Montei, Amanda. "I Think, like Marriage, Home Is a Fantasy." *Mad
Woman,* May 17, 2023. https://amandamontei.substack.com/p/i-think
-like-marriage-home-is-a-fantasy?.

———. "Mother's Day Sucks." *Mad Woman,* May 12, 2023. https://
amandamontei.substack.com/p/mothers-day-sucks.

———. *Touched Out: Motherhood, Misogyny, Consent, and Control.* Beacon
Press, 2023.

Moraga, Cherríe. "Cherríe Moraga on Writing About Queer Motherhood." Literary Hub. Accessed June 6, 2024. https://lithub.com/
cherrie-moraga-on-writing-about-queer-motherhood/.

Moraga, Cherríe. *Waiting in the Wings: Portrait of a Queer Motherhood.* Firebrand Books, 1997.

Moran, Rosalind, and Jolie Zhou. "Artificial Wombs Will Change Abortion Rights Forever." *Wired,* April 3, 2023. https://www.wired.com/
story/ectogenesis-reproductive-health-abortion/.

Moyers, Bill. "Toni Morrison on Love and Writing (Part One)." Accessed
May 2, 2024. https://billmoyers.com/content/toni-morrison-part-1/.

Mukherjee, Siddhartha. *The Gene: An Intimate History.* Large Print Press,
2017.

Mull, Amanda. "The New, Invasive Ways Women Are Encouraged to
Freeze Their Eggs." *The Atlantic,* March 4, 2019. https://www
.theatlantic.com/health/archive/2019/03/egg-freezing-instagram/
584053/.

Navarro, Meagan. "Queen Mother: The Enduring Theme of Motherhood
in the 'Alien' Franchise." *Bloody Disgusting!,* May 10, 2019. https://
bloody-disgusting.com/editorials/3559576/queen-mother-enduring
-theme-motherhood-alien-franchise/.

Naylor, Brian. "Trump Backtracks on Comments about Abortion and
'Punishment' for Women." *NPR,* March 30, 2016, sec. Politics.

https://www.npr.org/2016/03/30/472444293/trump-calls-for
-punishing-women-who-have-abortions-then-backtracks.

Nelson, J. Lee. "Your Cells Are My Cells." *Scientific American,* February 1, 2008. https://www.scientificamerican.com/article/your-cells-are-my -cells/.

Newhouse, Alana. "When Motherhood Requires Lifting a Whole World Off Its Axis." *The Free Press,* May 13, 2023. https://www.thefp.com/p/ when-motherhood-requires-lifting.

Nguyen, Janet. "Money and Millennials: The Cost of Living in 2022 vs. 1972." *Marketplace,* August 17, 2022. https://www.marketplace.org/ 2022/08/17/money-and-millennials-the-cost-of-living-in-2022-vs -1972/.

Nilsson, Lennart. *A Child Is Born.* Revised edition. Delta, 2004.

North, Anna. "The 'You're Doing It Wrong'-Ification of TikTok." Vox, March 23, 2023. https://www.vox.com/culture/23648715/tiktok -instagram-advice-mistakes-howto-tutorial.

———. "The Expensive, Unrealistic, and Extremely White World of " 'Momfluencers.' "

Vox, April 25, 2023. https://www.vox.com/23690126/mothers-parenting -momfluenced-sara-petersen-tiktok-instagram?tpcc=nlbroadsheet.

O'Brien, Mary. *The Politics of Reproduction.* Routledge & Kegan Paul, 1981.

Oren-Magidor, Daphna. "From Anne to Hannah: Religious Views of In- fertility in Post-Reformation England." *Journal of Women's History* 27, no. 3 (2015): 86–108. https://doi.org/10.1353/jowh.2015.0036.

Orenstein, Peggy. "Unraveling." Accessed June 1, 2023. https://www .peggyorenstein.com/unraveling.

OUPblog. "Silencing the Self Theory." OUPblog, March 29, 2010. https://blog.oup.com/2010/03/silencing-the-self/.

Paul, L. A. *Transformative Experience.* Reprint edition. Oxford University Press, 2016.

Peikoff, Kira. "Israeli Egg Farming." *New York Magazine,* March 30, 2007. https://nymag.com/news/intelligencer/30032/.

Penaluna, Regan. "Kate Manne: The Shock Collar That Is Misogyny." *Guernica,* February 7, 2018. https://www.guernicamag.com/kate -manne-why-misogyny-isnt-really-about-hating-women/.

Perhach, Paulette. "A Story of a Fuck Off Fund." The Billfold, January 20, 2016. https://www.thebillfold.com/2016/01/a-story-of-a-fuck-off -fund/.

Petersen, Anne Helen. "Memoir of a Broken Safety Net." *Culture Study,* June 14, 2023. https://annehelen.substack.com/p/memoir-of-a -broken-safety-net.

Petersen, Sara. *Momfluenced: Inside the Maddening, Picture-Perfect World of Mommy Influencer Culture.* Beacon Press, 2023.

———. "We Don't Perform Motherhood for Our Kids." The Cut, April 20, 2023. https://www.thecut.com/2023/04/momfluenced -book-excerpt.html.

Pew Research Center. "Jews," December 18, 2012. https://www .pewresearch.org/religion/2012/12/18/global-religious-landscape -jew/.

Phillips, Julie. *The Baby on the Fire Escape: Creativity, Motherhood, and the Mind-Baby Problem.* W. W. Norton & Company, 2022.

Piazza, Jo. *How to Be Married: What I Learned from Real Women on Five Con- tinents About Surviving My First (Really Hard) Year of Marriage.* Har- mony, 2017.

Picheta, Rob. "Moms Who Use Egg Donors Lack Confidence in Parenting Ability, Study Finds." CNN, October 9, 2018. https://www.cnn.com/ 2018/10/09/health/egg-donor-mothers-babies-bond-intl/index.html.

"Pick Yourself Up", *Swing Time,* 1936. Composed by Jerome Kern; lyrics by Dorothy Fields.

Plank, Liz. *For the Love of Men: From Toxic to a More Mindful Masculinity.* Advanced Copy edition. St. Martin's Press, 2019.

———. "My Fertility and Me." *Airplane Mode with Liz Plank,* August 14, 2022. https://lizplank.substack.com/p/my-fertility-and-me.

Plath, Sylvia. *The Bell Jar.* Faber and Faber, 1963.

Quilter, Jenni. *Hatching: Experiments in Motherhood and Technology.* Riverhead Books, 2022.

———. "The Optimistic, Expansive Visions of Pregnancy and Mother- hood in the 1962 Novel *Memoirs of a Spacewoman.*" *Literary Hub,* De- cember 13, 2022. https://lithub.com/the-optimistic-expansive -visions-of-pregnancy-and-motherhood-in-the-1962-novel-memoirs -of-a-spacewoman/.

Raeburn, Paul. "Genetic Battle of the Sexes." *Discover Magazine,* May 23, 2014. https://www.discovermagazine.com/health/genetic-battle-of -the-sexes.

Regaignon, Dara Rossman. *Writing Maternity: Medicine, Anxiety, Rhetoric, and Genre.* Ohio State University Press, 2021.

Resolve: The National Infertility Association. "Insurance Coverage by
    State," August 27, 2021. https://resolve.org/learn/financial-resources
    -for-family-building/insurance-coverage/insurance-coverage-by-state/.

Reuters. "Israeli Scientists Create Model of Human Embryo without Eggs
    or Sperm." September 7, 2023. https://www.reuters.com/science/
    israeli-scientists-create-model-human-embryo-without-eggs-or
    -sperm-2023-09-07/.

Rich, Adrienne. *Of Woman Born: Motherhood as Experience and Institution.*
    Norton, 1976.

Riesman, David, Nathan Glazer, and Reuel Denney. *The Lonely Crowd, Re-
    vised Edition: A Study of the Changing American Character.* 2nd Edition.
    Yale University Press, 2001.

Risi, Alixandra, Judy A. Pickard, and Amy L. Bird. "The Implications of
    Parent Mental Health and Wellbeing for Parent-Child Attachment:
    A Systematic Review." *PLOS ONE* 16, no. 12 (December 16, 2021):
    e0260891. https://doi.org/10.1371/journal.pone.0260891.

Rivers, Caryl. "Newsweek's Apology Comes 20 Years Too Late." Women's
    eNews, June 14, 2006. https://womensenews.org/2006/06/
    newsweeks-apology-comes-20-years-too-late/.

Robertson, Lesley, Jantien Backer, Claud Biemans, Joop van Doorn, Klaas
    Krab, Willem Reijnders, Henk Smit, and Peter Willemsen. "Antoni
    van Leeuwenhoek and the Question of Generation." In *Antoni van
    Leeuwenhoek, Master of the Minuscule,* 2016. https://doi.org/10.1163/
    9789004304307_008.

Rose, Andy. "Texas Woman Forced to Carry High-Risk Pregnancy Files
    Lawsuit to Have Abortion." CNN, 12 2023. https://www.cnn.com/
    2023/12/05/us/texas-woman-high-risk-pregnancy-abortion-lawsuit/
    index.html.

Rosenblatt, J. S. "Nonhormonal Basis of Maternal Behavior in the Rat."
    Science 156, no. 3781 (June 16, 1967): 1512–14. https://doi.org/10
    .1126/science.156.3781.1512.

Ross, Janelle. "The Radical Joy of Rachel Cargle." *Time,* May 11, 2023.
    https://time.com/6278752/rachel-cargle-a-renaissance-of-our-own/.

Ross, Loretta J. *Revolutionary Mothering: Love on the Front Lines.* Edited by
    Alexis Pauline Gumbs, China Martens, and Mai'a Williams. Illus-
    trated edition. PM Press, 2016.

Rowland, Robyn. "Technology and Motherhood: Reproductive Choice

Reconsidered." *Signs: Journal of Women in Culture and Society* 12, no. 3 (April 1987): 512–28. https://doi.org/10.1086/494342.

sandiegozoo.org. "Flamingo | San Diego Zoo Animals & Plants." Accessed June 15, 2023. https://animals.sandiegozoo.org/animals/flamingo.

Sauerbrun-Cutler, May-Tal, Emma Charlotte Brown, Warren J. Huber, Phinnara Has, and Gary N. Frishman. "IVF Clinic Websites: Buyer Beware the System Is Broken." *Fertility and Sterility* 112, no. 3 (September 1, 2019): e51–52. https://doi.org/10.1016/j.fertnstert.2019 .07.261.

Scala, Francesca, and Michael Orsini. "Problematising Older Motherhood in Canada: Ageism, Ableism, and the Risky Maternal Subject." *Health, Risk & Society* 24, no. 3–4 (May 19, 2022): 149–66. https:// doi.org/10.1080/13698575.2022.2057453.

Scanlon, Suzanne. *Committed: On Meaning and Madwomen.* Vintage, 2024.

Schwartzmann, Rachel. "This New Novel Explores What It Means to Mother And to Be Mothered." April 17, 2023. https://coveteur.com/ molly-prentiss-book-interview-2023.

Shafrir, Doree. "I Was Sure Freezing My Eggs Would Solve Everything." BuzzFeed News, June 22, 2014. https://www.buzzfeednews.com/ article/doree/i-was-sure-freezing-my-eggs-would-solve-everything.

———. *Thanks for Waiting: The Joy (& Weirdness) of Being a Late Bloomer.* Ballantine Books, 2021.

Shelasky, Alyssa. *This Might Be Too Personal: And Other Intimate Stories.* St. Martin's Griffin, 2022.

Armstrong, Elizabeth A. "Nona Willis Aronowitz's Bad Sex: Reviews," *Signs: Journal of Women in Culture and Society,* September 28, 2022. http://signsjournal.org/short-takes-bad-sex-by-nona-willis -aronowitz/.

Singh, Julietta. *The Breaks.* Coffee House Press, 2021.

Slaughter, Anne-Marie. "Why Women Still Can't Have It All." *The Atlantic,* June 13, 2012. https://www.theatlantic.com/magazine/archive/ 2012/07/why-women-still-cant-have-it-all/309020/.

Solnit, Rebecca. *A Field Guide to Getting Lost.* Penguin Books, 2006.

———. "A Short History of Silence." *The Mother of All Questions,* Haymarket Books, 2017, 17–66.

———. *The Mother of All Questions. Harper's Magazine,* October 2015. https://harpers.org/archive/2015/10/the-mother-of-all-questions/.

Solomon, Andrew. *Far From the Tree: Parents, Children and the Search for Identity.* Reprint edition. New York: Scribner, 2013.

Spock, Benjamin. *Baby and Child Care.* 4th edition. hawthorn books, 1976.

Spock, Benjamin, and Steven Parker. *Dr Spocks Baby and Child Care: A Handbook for Parents of Developing Children from Birth Through Adolescence.* 7th Revised & Updated edition. Pocket, 1998.

Sternburg, Janet. *The Writer on Her Work.* W. W. Norton & Company, 2000.

Stielstra, Megan. *The Wrong Way to Save Your Life: Essays.* Harper Perennial, 2017.

Strayed, Cheryl. "DEAR SUGAR, The Rumpus Advice Column #71: The Ghost Ship That Didn't Carry Us." The Rumpus, April 21, 2011. https://therumpus.net/2011/04/21/dear-sugar-the-rumpus-advice-column-71-the-ghost-ship-that-didnt-carry-us/.

Strodel, Rachel. "Fertility Clinics Are Being Taken over by For-Profit Companies Selling False Hope." NBC News, March 1, 2020. https://www.nbcnews.com/think/opinion/fertility-clinics-are-being-taken-over-profit-companies-selling-false-ncna1145671.

Study, Culture. "Memoir of a Broken Safety Net." *Culture Study,* June 14, 2023. https://annehelen.substack.com/p/memoir-of-a-broken-safety-net-8f9?utm_medium=email.

Subbaraman, Nidhi. "Anti-Incest App Built by Iceland College Students." NBC News, April 17, 2013. http://www.nbcnews.com/tech/gadgets/anti-incest-app-built-iceland-college-students-flna1C9392483.

Sugar. "DEAR SUGAR, The Rumpus Advice Column #71: The Ghost Ship That Didn't Carry Us." The Rumpus, April 21, 2011. https://therumpus.net/2011/04/21/dear-sugar-the-rumpus-advice-column-71-the-ghost-ship-that-didnt-carry-us/.

Sullivan, Patrick F., Cecilia Magnusson, Abraham Reichenberg, Marcus Boman, Christina Dalman, Michael Davidson, Eyal Fruchter, et al. "Family History of Schizophrenia and Bipolar Disorder as Risk Factors for Autism." *Archives of General Psychiatry* 69, no. 11 (November 2012): 1099–1103. https://doi.org/10.1001/archgenpsychiatry.2012.730.

Swanson, Kara W. "The Birth of the Sperm Bank." *The Annals of Iowa* 71, no. 3 (2012). https://pubs.lib.uiowa.edu/annals-of-iowa/article/id/5964/download/pdf/.

Tate, Claudia, ed. *Black Women Writers at Work*. Haymarket Books, 2023.

Tea, Michelle. *Knocking Myself Up: A Memoir of My (In)Fertility*. Dey Street Books, 2022.

The Economist. "IVF Remains Largely a Numbers Game." Accessed June 6, 2024. https://www.economist.com/technology-quarterly/2023/07/17/ivf-remains-largely-a-numbers-game.

The Economist. "Making Babymaking Better." Accessed May 2, 2024. https://www.economist.com/leaders/2023/07/20/making-babymaking-better.

The Economist. "The Fertility Sector Is Booming." 17 2023. https://www.economist.com/technology-quarterly/2023/07/17/the-fertility-sector-is-booming.

The New York Times. "David Riesman, Sociologist Whose 'Lonely Crowd' Became a Best Seller, Dies at 92." May 11, 2002, sec. Books. https://www.nytimes.com/2002/05/11/books/david-riesman-sociologist-whose-lonely-crowd-became-a-best-seller-dies-at-92.html.

The New York Times. "Wendy Wasserstein's Women." February 5, 2006, sec. Week in Review. https://www.nytimes.com/2006/02/05/weekinreview/wendy-wassersteins-women.html.

Thompson, Gael. "Angels and Ghosts in the Nursery: Trauma-Informed Child-Parent Therapy." Wilder Foundation, December 17, 2020. https://www.wilder.org/articles/angels-and-ghosts-nursery-trauma-informed-child-parent-therapy.

Tillotson, Kenneth J., and Wolfgang Sulzbach. "A Comparative Study and Evaluation of Electric Shock Therapy in Depressive States." *American Journal of Psychiatry* 101, no. 4 (January 1945): 455–59. https://doi.org/10.1176/ajp.101.4.455.

Tolentino, Jia. *Trick Mirror: Reflections on Self-Delusion*. Random House, 2019.

Townsend, Regina. "The Lasting Trauma of Infertility." *The New York Times*, October 23, 2019, sec. Parenting. https://www.nytimes.com/2019/10/23/parenting/the-lasting-trauma-of-infertility.html.

Tramontana, Mary Katharine. "She Never Wanted to Be a Mother. Now She's Written a Book for Women Like Her." *The New York Times*, May 13, 2023, sec. Style. https://www.nytimes.com/2023/05/13/style/ruby-warrington-women-without-kids.html.

Tran, Mark. "Apple and Facebook Offer to Freeze Eggs for Female Employees." *The Guardian*, October 15, 2014, sec. Technology. https://

www.theguardian.com/technology/2014/oct/15/apple-facebook-offer
-freeze-eggs-female-employees.

Triplett, Katja. "For Mothers and Sisters: Care of the Reproductive Female Body in the Medico-Ritual World of Early and Medieval Japan." *Dynamis (Granada, Spain)* 34, no. 2 (2014): 337–56. https://doi.org/10.4321/s0211-95362014000200004.

Tucker, Abigail. "The New Science of Motherhood." *Smithsonian*, May 2021. https://www.smithsonianmag.com/science-nature/new-science -motherhood-180977456/.

U Minnesota Center for Twin and Family Research. "Twin Family Study." Accessed May 2, 2024. https://mctfr.psych.umn.edu/our-research/ twin-family-study.

Umoh, Edikan. "The Immeasurable Joy of Becoming a Black Egg Donor," April 11, 2023. https://www.refinery29.com/en-us/2023/04/ 11355383/ivf-fertility-black-egg-donors.

United States Bureau of Labor Statistics. "American Time Use Survey-2019." U.S. Department of Labor, June 25, 2020. https://www.bls .gov/news.release/archives/atus_06252020.pdf.

UT Health San Antonio| Physicians. "What Are My Chances of Success with IVF?" Accessed June 10, 2024. https://uthscsa.edu/physicians/ services/assisted-reproduction/what-are-my-chances-success-ivf.

Vance, Todd, Hermine H. Maes, and Kenneth S. Kendler. "A Multivariate Twin Study of the Dimensions of Religiosity and Common Psychiatric and Substance Use Disorders." *The Journal of Nervous and Mental Disease* 202, no. 5 (May 2014): 360–67. https://doi.org/10.1097/ NMD.0000000000000131.

Vigdal, Julia Schønning, and Kolbjørn Kallesten Brønnick. "A Systematic Review of 'Helicopter Parenting' and Its Relationship with Anxiety and Depression." *Frontiers in Psychology* 13 (2022). https://www .frontiersin.org/articles/10.3389/fpsyg.2022.872981.

Vonnegut, Kurt. *Mother Night.* Dial Press Trade Paperback, 1999.

Wade, Nicholas. "Meet Luca, the Ancestor of All Living Things." *The New York Times,* July 25, 2016, sec. Science. https://www.nytimes .com/2016/07/26/science/last-universal-ancestor.html.

Walker, Alice. "One Child of One's Own: A Meaningful Digression within the Work(s)." In *The Writer on Her Work,* 121–39. W. W. Norton & Company, 2000.

Warrington, Ruby. *Women Without Kids: The Revolutionary Rise of an Unsung Sisterhood.* Sounds True, 2023.

Wasserstein, Wendy. *The Heidi Chronicles,* 1988

Weller, Chris. "What You Need to Know about Egg-Freezing, the Hot New Perk at Google, Apple, and Facebook." Business Insider. Accessed June 26, 2023. https://www.businessinsider.com/egg-freezing -at-facebook-apple-google-hot-new-perk-2017-9.

Wheeler, Sarah. "Moms Gone Wild." The Cut, May 11, 2023. https:// www.thecut.com/2023/05/moms-gone-wild.html.

White House. "Fact Sheet: Biden-Harris Administration Announces New Actions to Support and Advance Women's Economic Security." The White House, February 2, 2023. https://www.whitehouse.gov/ briefing-room/statements-releases/2023/02/02/fact-sheet-biden-harris -administration-announces-new-actions-to-support-and-advance -womens-economic-security/.

"Why Millennials Can't Afford Homes: Housing Prices vs. Inflation." Accessed July 28, 2023. https://anytimeestimate.com/research/housing -prices-vs-inflation/.

Witt, Emily. "The Future of Fertility." *The New Yorker,* April 17, 2023. https://www.newyorker.com/magazine/2023/04/24/the-future-of -fertility.

Wu, Katherine J. "The Most Mysterious Cells in Our Bodies Don't Belong to Us." *The Atlantic,* January 3, 2024. https://www.theatlantic .com/science/archive/2024/01/fetal-maternal-cells-microchimerism/ 676996/.

Yarrow, Allison. *Birth Control: The Insidious Power of Men Over Motherhood.* Seal Press, 2023.

Yellin, Jessica. "Single, Female and Desperate No More." *The New York Times,* June 4, 2006, sec. Week in Review. https://www.nytimes.com/ 2006/06/04/weekinreview/04yellin.html.

Yoder, Rachel. *Nightbitch.* Doubleday, 2021.

Yopo Díaz, Martina. "The Biological Clock: Age, Risk, and the Biopolitics of Reproductive Time." *Sex Roles* 84, no. 11 (June 1, 2021): 765–78. https://doi.org/10.1007/s11199-020-01198-y.

Zaslow, Jeffrey. "An Iconic Report 20 Years Later: Many of Those Women Married After All." *The Wall Street Journal,* May 25, 2006, sec. Personal Journal. https://www.wsj.com/articles/SB114852403706762691.

Zhang, Sarah. "The Last Children of Down Syndrome." *The Atlantic,*
    November 18, 2020. https://www.theatlantic.com/magazine/archive/
    2020/12/the-last-children-of-down-syndrome/616928/.

Zhang, Xing, and Sharon Sassler. "Opting out of Marriage? Factors Pre-
    dicting Non-Marriage by Midlife across Race, Ethnicity, and Gen-
    der." *Social Currents* 10, no. 5 (October 1, 2023): 403–28. https://doi
    .org/10.1177/23294965221142769.

Zumas, Leni. "Maybe There's Nothing Natural About Motherhood." The
    Cut, February 7, 2018. https://www.thecut.com/2018/02/maybe
    -theres-nothing-natural-about-motherhood.html.

Zuvker, Bonnie. "From a Psychologist: No, It's Not All Mom's Fault."
    Scary Mommy, June 25, 2021. https://www.scarymommy.com/
    lifestyle/psychologist-not-moms-fault.

NOTES

Chapter 3

17 **In fact, Dr. Veerle Bergink** Danielle Campoamor, "What Is Pregnancy Ambivalence? It's a Lot More Common than People Know," TODAY.com, May 1, 2023, https://www.today.com/parents/pregnancy/pregnancy-ambivalence-rcna81221.

17 **My whole life** Maytal Eyal, "Self-Silencing Is Making Women Sick," *Time,* October 3, 2023, https://time.com/6319549/silencing-women-sick-essay/.

17 **"As if there is"** Jill Filipovic, "The Uncertain Loneliness of Ambivalence on Motherhood," *Slate,* December 5, 2023, https://slate.com/human-interest/2023/12/ambivalent-motherhood-how-to-choose.html.

20 **Every female writer** Louise Erdrich, *The Blue Jay's Dance: A Memoir of Early Motherhood* (Harper Perennial, 2010), p. 144.

Chapter 4

28 **I hadn't yet read the work** Shulamith Firestone, *The Dialectic of Sex: The Case for Feminist Revolution* (Farrar, Straus and Giroux, 2003).

30 **"I was the captain"** Jo Piazza, *How to Be Married: What I Learned from Real Women on Five Continents About Surviving My First (Really Hard) Year of Marriage* (Harmony, 2017).

32 Much later I'd read Claire Dederer, "What Do We Do with the
    Art of Monstrous Men?," *The Paris Review,* November 20, 2017,
    https://www.theparisreview.org/blog/2017/11/20/art-monstrous
    -men/.

Chapter 5

43 I didn't know that Molly Elizalde, "How Egg Freezing Went
    Mainstream," *The New York Times,* April 17, 2020, sec. Parenting,
    https://www.nytimes.com/2020/04/17/parenting/fertility/egg
    -freezing.html.

43 While sperm was first seen M Cobb, "An Amazing 10 Years: The
    Discovery of Egg and Sperm in the 17th Century," *Reproduction in
    Domestic Animals* 47, no. s4 (2012): 2–6, https://doi.org/10.1111/j
    .1439-0531.2012.02105.x.

43 the egg was not seen Jenni Quilter, *Hatching: Experiments in Mother-
    hood and Technology* (Riverhead Books, 2022).

44 Claire Cain Miller Claire Cain Miller, "Freezing Eggs as Part of Em-
    ployee Benefits: Some Women See Darker Message," *The New York
    Times,* October 15, 2014, sec. The Upshot, https://www.nytimes
    .com/2014/10/15/upshot/egg-freezing-as-a-work-benefit-some
    -women-see-darker-message.html.

45 Around the same time Doree Shafrir, "I Was Sure Freezing My
    Eggs Would Solve Everything," *BuzzFeed News,* June 22, 2014,
    https://www.buzzfeednews.com/article/doree/i-was-sure-freezing-my
    -eggs-would-solve-everything.

46 Now the trend Liz Plank, "My Fertility and Me," *Airplane Mode
    with Liz Plank,* August 14, 2022, https://lizplank.substack.com/p/
    my-fertility-and-me.

46 Decades earlier Maytal Eyal, "Self-Silencing Is Making Women
    Sick," *Time,* October 3, 2023, https://time.com/6319549/silencing
    -women-sick-essay/.

49 "To hold the word *no*" Erdrich, *The Blue Jay's Dance: A Memoir of
    Early Motherhood.*

Chapter 6

54 "Each pair of parents" Kathryn Paige Harden, *The Genetic Lottery:
    Why DNA Matters for Social Equality* (Princeton University Press,
    2021).

54 I'd recently read Doris Lessing, *The Fifth Child* (Vintage, 1989).

56 "I think of how" Joanna Hershon, "Any Day Now," in *Freud's Blind*

Spot: 23 Original Essays on Cherished, Estranged, Lost, Hurtful, Hopeful, Complicated Siblings, ed. Elisa Albert (Free Press, 2010), 23.

60 **Or like Jayson Greene's daughter** Jayson Greene, *Once More We Saw Stars: A Memoir* (Knopf, 2019).

Chapter 7

63 **But after reading about** Rebecca Carroll, "Margaret Garner, a Runaway Slave Who Killed Her Own Daughter," *The New York Times,* January 31, 2019, sec. Obituaries, https://www.nytimes.com/interactive/2019/obituaries/margaret-garner-overlooked.html.

67 **The author Suzanne Scanlon** Suzanne Scanlon, *Committed: On Meaning and Madwomen* (Vintage, 2024).

Chapter 8

72 **In fact, in 1956** Stephanie Coontz, *The Way We Never Were: American Families and the Nostalgia Trap* (Basic Books, 1993).

72 **It was the messages** Coontz, *The Way We Never Were.*

72 **Some, like Ruth, took** Jessica Grose, "Mother's Little Helper Is Back, and Daddy's Partaking Too," *The New York Times,* October 3, 2020, sec. Style, https://www.nytimes.com/2020/10/03/style/am-i-drinking-too-much.html.

73 **The idea of having my own** Paulette Perhach, "A Story of a Fuck Off Fund," *The Billfold,* January 20, 2016, https://www.thebillfold.com/2016/01/a-story-of-a-fuck-off-fund/.

74 **"The story that she walked away"** Julie Phillips, *The Baby on the Fire Escape: Creativity, Motherhood, and the Mind-Baby Problem* (W. W. Norton & Company, 2022), p. 74.

75 **But then there was** Julie Phillips, *The Baby on the Fire Escape.*

75 **"If you say"** Doris Lessing, *Under My Skin: Volume One of My Autobiography, to 1949* (Harper Perennial, 1995).

75 **Recently, I sat** Claire Dederer, *Monsters: A Fan's Dilemma* (Knopf, 2023).

76 **"But I wanted to paint"** Phillips, *The Baby on the Fire Escape.*

77 **"I can't find a model"** Audrey Bilger, "The Art of Fiction No. 150," *The Paris Review,* 1997, https://www.theparisreview.org/interviews/1188/the-art-of-fiction-no-150-jeanette-winterson.

Chapter 9

79 **In a parallel life** Alyssa Shelasky, *This Might Be Too Personal: And Other Intimate Stories* (St. Martin's Griffin, 2022).

81 **I still remember listening** "Looking for The One, Part 2: The Re-ality," *Dear Sugars,* January 22, 2016, https://www.wbur.org/dearsugar/2016/01/22/dear-sugar-episode-forty.

82 **Adrienne Rich saw this** Adrienne Rich, *Of Woman Born: Motherhood as Experience and Institution* (Norton, 1976).

82 **Yet here many of us are** Mona Chollet and Carmen Maria Machado, *In Defense of Witches: The Legacy of the Witch Hunts and Why Women Are Still on Trial,* trans. Sophie R. Lewis (St. Martin's Press, 2022).

83 **Controlling, policing, punishing** Kate Manne, *Down Girl: The Logic of Misogyny* (Oxford University Press, 2017).

84 **I remember reading** Rebecca Solnit, "The Mother of All Ques-tions," *Harper's Magazine,* October 2015, https://harpers.org/archive/2015/10/the-mother-of-all-questions/.

84 **The stories of those** Nona Willis Aronowitz, "The Education of Natalie Jean." *ELLE,* November 5, 2019, https://www.elle.com/life-love/a29438763/natalie-lovin-mommy-blog-influencer/.

85 **It took reading Solnit's words** Solnit, "The Mother of All Ques-tions."

85 **It was Taffy Brodesser-Akner's** Taffy Brodesser-Akner, *Fleishman Is in Trouble* (Random House, 2019).

Chapter 10

88 **Five years later, I'd** Loretta J. Ross, *Revolutionary Mothering: Love on the Front Lines,* edited by Alexis Pauline Gumbs, China Martens, and Mai'a Williams, Illustrated edition (PM Press, 2016), p. XV.

88 **In fact, from the 1970s** Ross, *Revolutionary Mothering;* Cherríe Mor-aga, "Cherríe Moraga on Writing About Queer Motherhood," *Liter-ary Hub,* accessed June 6, 2024, https://lithub.com/cherrie-moraga-on-writing-about-queer-motherhood/; Cherríe Moraga, *Waiting in the Wings: Portrait of a Queer Motherhood* (Firebrand Books, 1997).

89 **Toni Morrison believed** Bill Moyers, "Toni Morrison on Love and Writing (Part One)," accessed May 2, 2024, https://billmoyers.com/content/toni-morrison-part-1/.

89 **It was a "queer thing"** Alexis Pauline Gumbs in Ross, *Revolution-ary Mothering.*

89 **You could do that?** Deirdre English, "The Long Fight of Barbara Ehren-reich," *Mother Jones,* September 7, 2022, https://www.motherjones.com/media/2022/09/the-long-fight-of-barbara-ehrenreich/.

90 **And then there's** Angela Garbes, *Essential Labor: Mothering as Social Change* (HarperCollins, 2022).

90 **The poet Adrienne Rich** Adrienne Rich, *Of Woman Born: Motherhood as Experience and Institution* (Norton, 1976).

90 **Before same-sex marriage** Moraga, "Cherríe Moraga on Writing About Queer Motherhood," *Literary Hub.*

91 **What would it mean** Grumbs in Ross, *Revolutionary Mothering.*

93 **"When you are a woman"** Jia Tolentino, *Trick Mirror: Reflections on Self-Delusion* (Random House, 2019).

93 **"We don't have the luxury"** Dani McClain, "Mom Talk: The Political Power of Black Motherhood," *Mother,* June 1, 2020, https://www.mothermag.com/we-live-for-the-we-the-political-power-of-black-motherhood/.

93 **"I tell my daughter"** McClain, "Mom Talk: The Political Power of Black Motherhood," *Mother.*

94 **Or as Adrienne Rich** Rich, *Of Woman Born.*

94 **The sexist idea** Patricia Hill Collins, "Shifting the Center: Race, Class, and Feminist Theorizing About Motherhood," in *Mothering* (Routledge, 1994).

94 **often in the "mammy" role** Stephanie Buckhanon Crowder, *When Momma Speaks: The Bible and Motherhood from a Womanist Perspective* (Westminster John Knox Press, 2016).

94 **"There is no one-size-fits-all** Crowder, *When Momma Speaks.*

94 **It took Rich** Rich, *Of Woman Born,* p. 195.

Chapter 11

98 **"It is remarkable"** Emily Martin, "The Egg and the Sperm: How Science Has Constructed a Romance Based on Stereotypical Male-Female Roles," *Signs: Journal of Women in Culture and Society* 16, no. 3 (April 1991): 485–501, https://doi.org/10.1086/494680.

Chapter 13

107 **Jewish people are** "Jews," *Pew Research Center,* December 18, 2012, https://www.pewresearch.org/religion/2012/12/18/global-religious-landscape-jew/.

110 **I'd read about an experiment** Malcolm Gladwell, "Matters of Choice Muddled by Thought," *Washington Post,* March 4, 1991, https://www.washingtonpost.com/archive/politics/1991/03/04/matters-of-choice-muddled-by-thought/5e6f1511-0d9e-4263-baco-9ee2fb2770ef/.

111 **I'd tried so hard** *Gone Girl* (Twentieth Century Studios, 2014). Script by Gillian Flynn. Directed by David Fincher.

112 **Later, I'd read** Megan Stielstra, *The Wrong Way to Save Your Life: Essays* (Harper Perennial, 2017), p. 246.

113 **But I wasn't yet willing** *Barbie* (Warner Bros. Pictures, 2023). Script by Noah Baumbach and Greta Gerwig. Directed by Greta Gerwig.

113 **As philosopher Kate** Regan Penaluna, "Kate Manne: The Shock Collar That Is Misogyny," *Guernica,* February 7, 2018, https://www .guernicamag.com/kate-manne-why-misogyny-isnt-really-about -hating-women/.

113 **misogyny polices women** Penaluna, "Kate Manne: The Shock Collar That Is Misogyny."

113 **"A bit like the shock collar"** Kate Manne, *Entitled: How Male Privilege Hurts Women* (Crown, 2020).

114 **Joan Didion famously wrote** Joan Didion, "Goodbye to All That," *Slouching Towards Bethlehem* (Farrar, Straus and Giroux, 1968), 225–38.

120 **She never married** "Alice Austen House," Historic House Trust of New York City, accessed May 2, 2024, https://historichousetrust.org/ houses/alice-austen-house/.

122 **I couldn't stop myself** "Pick Yourself Up," *Swing Time.* 1936. Composed by Jerome Kern; lyrics by Dorothy Fields.

Chapter 14

124 **In fact, a cover story** Megan Garber, "The Article That 'Struck Terror in the Hearts of Single Women Everywhere,'" *The Atlantic,* June 2, 2016, https://www.theatlantic.com/entertainment/archive/ 2016/06/more-likely-to-be-killed-by-a-terrorist-than-to-get -married/485171/.

124 *"It feels true"* Megan Garber, "The Article That 'Struck Terror in the Hearts of Single Women Everywhere,'" *The Atlantic,* June 2, 2016, https://www.theatlantic.com/entertainment/archive/2016/06/ more-likely-to-be-killed-by-a-terrorist-than-to-get-married/ 485171/.

125 **Even though it was debunked** Jeffrey Zaslow, "An Iconic Report 20 Years Later: Many of Those Women Married After All," *Wall Street Journal,* May 25, 2006, sec. Personal Journal, https://www.wsj .com/articles/SB114852403706762691.

125 **In fact, the terrorist line** Caryl Rivers, "Newsweek's Apology Comes 20 Years Too Late," *Women's eNews,* June 14, 2006, https:// womensenews.org/2006/06/newsweeks-apology-comes-20-years-too -late/.

125 **In 2006, Jessica Yellin** Jessica Yellin, "Single, Female and Desperate No More," *The New York Times,* June 4, 2006, sec. Week in Review, https://www.nytimes.com/2006/06/04/weekinreview/04yellin .html.

125 **Or as Wendy Wasserstein writes** *The Heidi Chronicles,* 1988; "Wendy Wasserstein's Women," *The New York Times,* February 5, 2006, sec. Week in Review, https://www.nytimes.com/2006/02/05/ weekinreview/wendy-wassersteins-women.html.

130 **I'd read Joan Didion's** Joan Didion, *Blue Nights: A Memoir,* Reprint edition (Vintage, 2012).

133 **Rebecca Solnit calls losing oneself** Rebecca Solnit, *A Field Guide to Getting Lost,* Reprint edition (Penguin Books, 2006).

135 **It didn't matter at that moment** "IVF Remains Largely a Numbers Game," *The Economist,* accessed June 6, 2024, https://www.economist .com/technology-quarterly/2023/07/17/ivf-remains-largely-a -numbers-game.

135 **"Pregnancy is our first lesson"** Angela Garbes, *Like a Mother: A Feminist Journey Through the Science and Culture of Pregnancy* (Harper, 2018).

135 **As the psychologist Kathryn Paige Harden writes** Kathryn Paige Harden, *The Genetic Lottery: Why DNA Matters for Social Equality* (Princeton University Press, 2021), p. 31.

136 **It was Gregor Mendel** Harden, *The Genetic Lottery.*

136 **"The human characteristics"** Harden, *The Genetic Lottery,* p. 33.

136 **Mendel's ideas about inheritance** Harden, *The Genetic Lottery.*

137 **"We lived in a world"** Ariel Levy, *The Rules Do Not Apply: A Memoir* (Random House, 2017).

137 **Women over thirty-five years old** Fang Gu et al., "Programmed Frozen Embryo Transfer Cycle Increased Risk of Hypertensive Disorders of Pregnancy: A Multicenter Cohort Study in Ovulatory Women," *American Journal of Obstetrics & Gynecology MFM* 5, no. 1 (January 1, 2023): 100752, https://doi.org/10.1016/j.ajogmf.2022.100752.

139 **It's no surprise** Regina Townsend, "The Lasting Trauma of Infertility," *The New York Times,* October 23, 2019, sec. Parenting, https:// www.nytimes.com/2019/10/23/parenting/the-lasting-trauma-of -infertility.html,

140 **Eduardo Hariton, a fertility specialist** "The Fertility Sector Is Booming," *The Economist,* accessed June 6, 2024, https://www .economist.com/technology-quarterly/2023/07/17/the-fertility-sector -is-booming.

140 **These clinics, backed by private equity** Amanda Mull, "The New,

Invasive Ways Women Are Encouraged to Freeze Their Eggs," *The Atlantic,* March 4, 2019, https://www.theatlantic.com/health/ archive/2019/03/egg-freezing-instagram/584053/.

140 **Unlike the United Kingdom** Rachel Strodel, "Fertility Clinics Are Being Taken over by For-Profit Companies Selling False Hope," *NBC News,* March 1, 2020, https://www.nbcnews.com/think/ opinion/fertility-clinics-are-being-taken-over-profit-companies -selling-false-ncna1145671.

141 **Technology *does* set out guidelines** May-Tal Sauerbrun-Cutler et al., "IVF Clinic Websites: Buyer Beware the System Is Broken," *Fertility and Sterility* 112, no. 3 (September 1, 2019): e51–52, https://doi.org/10.1016/j.fertnstert.2019.07.261.

141 **Success rates** "What Are My Chances of Success with IVF?," UT Health San Antonio| Physicians, accessed June 10, 2024, https:// uthscsa.edu/physicians/services/assisted-reproduction/what-are-my -chances-success-ivf.

141 **As Dr. Emily Goulet** Elizabeth Chuck, "Freezing Your Eggs Is an 'Expensive Lottery Ticket' That Not Everyone Wins," *NBC News,* March 5, 2019, https://www.nbcnews.com/health/health-news/ expensive-lottery-ticket-freezing-eggs-offers-women-hope-not -everyone-n975921.

Chapter 15

143 **Globally, up to seven out of ten** "IVF Remains Largely a Numbers Game," *The Economist,* accessed June 6, 2024, https://www.economist .com/technology-quarterly/2023/07/17/ivf-remains-largely-a -numbers-game.

143 **That night after we got home** "IVF Success Estimator | Assisted Reproductive Technology (ART) | Reproductive Health | CDC," August 4, 2021, https://wwwdev.cdc.gov/art/ivf-success-estimator/ index.html.

146 **In *The Still Point*** Emily Rapp Black, *The Still Point of the Turning World,* Reprint edition (Penguin Books, 2014).

147 **In Martha Beck's bestseller** Martha Beck, *Expecting Adam: A True Story of Birth, Rebirth, and Everyday Magic,* Reprint edition (Harmony, 2011).

147 **I woke up early** "Twin Family Study," U Minnesota Center for Twin and Family Research, accessed May 2, 2024, https://mctfr .psych.umn.edu/our-research/twin-family-study;

148 **While psychiatric twin research** Timothy Matthews et al., "A Longitudinal Twin Study of Victimization and Loneliness from

Childhood to Young Adulthood," *Development and Psychopathology* 34, no. 1 (February 2022): 367–77.

148 **to their likelihood of believing** Todd Vance, Hermine H. Maes, and Kenneth S. Kendler, "A Multivariate Twin Study of the Dimensions of Religiosity and Common Psychiatric and Substance Use Disorders," *The Journal of Nervous and Mental Disease* 202, no. 5 (May 2014): 360–67.

148 **the frequency of female orgasm** Kate M. Dunn, Lynn F. Cherkas, and Tim D. Spector, "Genetic Influences on Variation in Female Orgasmic Function: A Twin Study," *Biology Letters* 1, no. 3 (September 22, 2005): 260–63.

148 **stumped researchers** Jay Joseph, "What Do Twin Studies Prove About Genetic Influences on Psychiatric Disorders? Absolutely Nothing," Mad in America, December 18, 2018, https://www.madinamerica.com/2018/12/twin-studies-prove-nothing-genetics-psychiatric-disorders/.

148 **Around this time** Patrick F. Sullivan et al., "Family History of Schizophrenia and Bipolar Disorder as Risk Factors for Autism," *Archives of General Psychiatry* 69, no. 11 (November 2012): 1099–1103, https://doi.org/10.1001/archgenpsychiatry.2012.730.

148 **I learned that** Nidhi Subbaraman, "Anti-Incest App Built by Iceland College Students," *NBC News,* April 17, 2013, http://www.nbcnews.com/tech/gadgets/anti-incest-app-built-iceland-college-students-flna1C9392483.

149 **I later read about Denmark** Sarah Zhang, "The Last Children of Down Syndrome," *The Atlantic,* November 18, 2020, https://www.theatlantic.com/magazine/archive/2020/12/the-last-children-of-down-syndrome/616928/.

150 **In *The Atlantic* article** Zhang, Ibid.

Chapter 16

153 **And I know how privileged** Rebecca Feinglos and Sophia Laurenzi, "'It's Hell': How Divorce Laws Are Designed to Create Unnecessary Financial Hardship for Women," *Fortune,* accessed May 2, 2024, https://fortune.com/2023/08/23/divorce-laws-designed-create-unnecessary-financial-hardship-women-personal-finance/.

153 **Meanwhile, the median annual wage** Sue Kunkel, "Average Wages, Median Wages, and Wage Dispersion," Social Security Administration, accessed June 10, 2024, https://www-origin.ssa.gov/oact/cola/central.html.

154 **Some states, like Massachusetts** Mass.gov, "CMR 37.00 Infertility

Benefits" (n.d.), chrome-extension://efaidnbmnnnibpcajpcglcle
findmkaj/https://www.mass.gov/doc/211-37-infertility-benefits/
download.

156 **It reminded me of NXIVM** Barry Meier, "Inside a Secretive Group
Where Women Are Branded," *The New York Times,* October 17,
2017, sec. New York, https://www.nytimes.com/2017/10/17/
nyregion/nxivm-women-branded-albany.html.

159 **"Yes, the genetic differences"** Kathryn Paige Harden, *The Genetic
Lottery.*

Chapter 17

161 **Before I met Rob** Siddhartha Mukherjee, *The Gene: An Intimate History* (Large Print Press, 2017).

162 **I'd read the *Vogue* profile** Dodie Kazanjian, "Meet the Most Brilliant Couple in Town," *Vogue,* May 11, 2016, https://www.vogue
.com/article/sarah-sze-siddhartha-mukherjee-brilliant-couple-profile
-sculptor-writer-physician-scientist-researcher.

164 **Siddhartha also mentioned** L.H. Lumey et al., "Cohort Profile:
The Dutch Hunger Winter Families Study," *International Journal of
Epidemiology* 36, no. 6 (December 1, 2007): 1196–1204, https://doi
.org/10.1093/ije/dym126.

164 **One of the most fascinating** Brian G. Dias and Kerry J. Ressler, "Parental Olfactory Experience Influences Behavior and
Neural Structure in Subsequent Generations," *Nature Neuroscience* 17,
no. 1 (January 2014): 89–96, https://doi.org/10.1038/nn.3594.

170 **As women continue to start** "Donor Egg IVF (In-Vitro Fertilization) Market," *Future Market Insights Inc.,* accessed May 2, 2024,
https://www.futuremarketinsights.com/reports/donor-egg-ivf
-market.

170 **In those weeks** Elizabeth Anne Brown, "Your DNA Can Now Be
Pulled From Thin Air. Privacy Experts Are Worried.," *The New York
Times,* May 15, 2023, sec. Science, https://www.nytimes.com/2023/
05/15/science/environmental-dna-ethics-privacy.html.

170 **A few days later** "Lick Your Rats," Learn.Genetics Genetics Science
Learning Center, accessed May 2, 2024, https://learn.genetics.utah
.edu/content/epigenetics/rats.

171 **"New research shows"** Belle Boggs, *The Art of Waiting: On Fertility, Medicine, and Motherhood* (Graywolf Press, 2016).

Chapter 19

187 **The problem** Kira Peikoff, "Israeli Egg Farming," *New York Magazine*, March 30, 2007, https://nymag.com/news/intelligencer/30032/.

187 **The situation is even worse** Wendy Kramer, "Why Is There a Shortage of Black Egg and Sperm Donors?," *Psychology Today*, July 27, 2023, https://www.psychologytoday.com/intl/blog/donor-family-matters/202307/why-is-there-a-shortage-of-black-egg-and-sperm-donors.

188 **While Black men and women** Samantha F. Butts, "Health Disparities of African Americans in Reproductive Medicine," *Fertility and Sterility* 116, no. 2 (August 1, 2021): 287–91, https://doi.org/10.1016/j.fertnstert.2021.06.041.

188 **And the situation** Amber Ferguson, "America Has a Black Sperm Donor Shortage. Black Women Are Paying the Price.," *Washington Post*, October 20, 2022, https://www.washingtonpost.com/business/2022/10/20/black-sperm-donors/.

188 **This might have to do** Amber Ferguson, "Why Gay Men and Other Groups Are Banned from Donating Sperm," *Washington Post*, October 20, 2022, https://www.washingtonpost.com/business/2022/10/20/sperm-donor-criteria/.

188 **Religion may keep people** Camille Hammond, "Reasons Black Patients Get Treated Later," FertilityIQ, accessed May 2, 2024, https://www.fertilityiq.com/fertilityiq/black-african-american-fertility/delay-treatment.

194 **I wanted to feel** Erdrich, *The Blue Jay's Dance: A Memoir of Early Motherhood*.

194 **Sitting in the living room** Susan Imrie et al., "Families Created by Egg Donation: Parent–Child Relationship Quality in Infancy," *Child Development* 90, no. 4 (2019): 1333–49, https://doi.org/10.1111/cdev.13124.

Chapter 21

206 **The data showed** Anila M. D'Mello et al., "Exclusion of Females in Autism Research: Empirical Evidence for a 'Leaky' Recruitment-to-research Pipeline," *Autism Research* 15, no. 10 (October 2022): 1929–40, https://www.ncbi.nlm.nih.gov/pmc/articles/PMC9804357/.

207 **Oliver Burkeman points out** Oliver Burkeman, *Four Thousand Weeks: Time Management for Mortals* (Farrar, Straus and Giroux, 2021).

209 **Despite the fact that** Lesley Robertson et al., "Antoni van Leeu-

wenhoek and the Question of Generation," in *Antoni van Leeuwenhoek, Master of the Minuscule,* 2016, https://doi.org/10.1163/9789004304307_008.

Chapter 22

217 **"While commercials for home pregnancy tests"** Garbes, *Like a Mother.*

220 ***Rosemary's Baby* is** Lyz Lenz, *Belabored: A Vindication of the Rights of Pregnant Women* (Bold Type Books, 2020).

220 **In the *Alien* movie** Siobhan Eardley, "Monstrous Motherhood in the 'Alien' Franchise," *In Their Own League,* October 3, 2019, https://intheirownleague.com/2019/10/03/monstrous-motherhood-in-the-alien-franchise/.

221 **"The placenta does not"** Garbes, *Like a Mother,* p. 62.

221 **There have been many recent cases** Rachel M. Cohen, "How Millennials Learned to Dread Motherhood," *Vox,* December 4, 2023, https://www.vox.com/features/23979357/millennials-motherhood-dread-parenting-birthrate-women-policy.

221 **David Haig's research** Paul Raeburn, "Genetic Battle of the Sexes," *Discover Magazine,* May 23, 2014, https://www.discovermagazine.com/health/genetic-battle-of-the-sexes.

221 **"medically necessary" termination** Caitlin Huey-Burns, "Louisiana Woman Says She Was Denied an Abortion after Fetus Developed Rare Condition: 'I Was Carrying My Baby to Bury My Baby,'" *CBS News,* 26 2022, https://www.cbsnews.com/news/louisiana-woman-nancy-davis-denied-an-abortion-after-fetus-develops-rare-condition/.

222 **In 2024, as more states** Bilge Ebiri, "Behold, an Actually Good Omen Movie," *Vulture,* April 5, 2024, https://www.vulture.com/article/review-the-first-omen-is-actually-a-good-omen-movie.html.

222 **During this time** Paul Raeburn, "Genetic Battle of the Sexes," *Discover Magazine,* May 23, 2014, https://www.discovermagazine.com/health/genetic-battle-of-the-sexes.

Chapter 23

226 **I may have been** Andy Rose, "Texas Woman Forced to Carry High-Risk Pregnancy Files Lawsuit to Have Abortion," *CNN,* December 12, 2023, https://www.cnn.com/2023/12/05/us/texas-woman-high-risk-pregnancy-abortion-lawsuit/index.html.

227 **But it's her research on microchimerism** "Diana W. Bianchi, M.D. | Principal Investigators | NIH Intramural Research Program,"

Intramural Research Program, accessed June 10, 2024, https://irp
.nih.gov/pi/diana-bianchi.

227 **When Bianchi was at Tufts** J. Lee Nelson, "Your Cells Are My
Cells," *Scientific American,* February 1, 2008, https://www
.scientificamerican.com/article/your-cells-are-my-cells/.

228 **At the Mount Sinai Hospital lab** Abigail Tucker, "The New Science of Motherhood," *Smithsonian Magazine,* May 2021, https://www
.smithsonianmag.com/science-nature/new-science-motherhood
-180977456/.

229 **"It's like you carry"** Katherine J. Wu, "The Most Mysterious Cells
in Our Bodies Don't Belong to Us," *The Atlantic,* January 3, 2024,
https://www.theatlantic.com/science/archive/2024/01/fetal-maternal
-cells-microchimerism/676996/.

Chapter 25

249 **"We assume the person telling us"** Allison Yarrow, *Birth Control:
The Insidious Power of Men Over Motherhood* (Seal Press, 2023).

240 **It seemed like a fitting act** Aubrey Hirsch, "It's 2022 and People
Are Still Confused That My Kids Have Their Mother's Last Name,"
Time, February 4, 2022, https://time.com/6143476/baby-with
-mothers-last-name/.

Chapter 26

243 **"We choose powerlessness"** Yarrow, *Birth Control: The Insidious
Power of Men Over Motherhood.*

Chapter 27

256 **What I didn't know** "Flamingo | San Diego Zoo Animals &
Plants," sandiegozoo.org, accessed June 15, 2023, https://animals
.sandiegozoo.org/animals/flamingo.

Chapter 28

261 **But I wanted to stand up** S. Fraiberg, E. Adelson, and V. Shapiro,
"Ghosts in the Nursery: A Psychoanalytic Approach to the Problems
of Impaired Infant-Mother Relationships," *Journal of the American
Academy of Child Psychiatry* 14, no. 3 (1975): 387–421, https://doi
.org/10.1016/s0002-7138(09)61442-4.

267 **"One of the most harmful myths"** Leni Zumas, "Maybe There's
Nothing Natural About Motherhood," *The Cut,* February 7, 2018,
https://www.thecut.com/2018/02/maybe-theres-nothing-natural
-about-motherhood.html.

267 **Parenting doesn't come naturally** Chelsea Conaboy, *Mother Brain: How Neuroscience Is Rewriting the Story of Parenthood* (Henry Holt and Co., 2022).

Chapter 29

268 **"I'm grateful, greedy"** Boggs, *The Art of Waiting: On Fertility, Medicine, and Motherhood.*
269 **I used to believe** Saidiya V. Hartman, *Lose Your Mother: A Journey Along the Atlantic Slave Route* (Farrar, Straus and Giroux, 2008).

Chapter 30

272 **I recently read** Nicole Chung, *A Living Remedy: A Memoir* (Ecco, 2023).
272 **In the conversation** Sara Petersen, "We Don't Perform Motherhood for Our Kids," *The Cut,* April 20, 2023, https://www.thecut.com/2023/04/momfluenced-book-excerpt.html.
273 **"Our children"** Andrew Solomon, *Far from the Tree: Parents, Children and the Search for Identity,* Reprint edition (Scribner, 2013), p. 100.

ABOUT THE AUTHOR

RUTHIE ACKERMAN's writing has been published in *Vogue, Glamour, O Magazine, The New York Times, The Atlantic, The Wall Street Journal, Forbes, Salon, Slate,* and *Newsweek.* Her Modern Love essay for the *New York Times* became the launching point for *The Mother Code.* Ruthie launched the Ignite Writers Collective in 2019 and since then has become an in-demand book coach and developmental editor. Her client wins include a *USA Today* bestseller, book deals with Big 5 publishers, representation by buzzy book agents, and essays in prestigious outlets. She has a master's degree in journalism from New York University and lives in Brooklyn, New York, with her family.